Harold Laws
2041 Adams
Quincy Ill,

THE MINISTER'S MISSION

THE MINISTER'S MISSION

A Survey of Ministerial Responsibilities and Relationships

by

C. E. COLTON

Author of

The Sermon on the Mount, etc.

ZONDERVAN PUBLISHING HOUSE

GRAND RAPIDS, MICHIGAN

To my wife
Lois
for her interest and encouragement
without which this work
could not have
been realized

INTRODUCTION

The suggestions made in this study of ministerial ethics were born and nurtured during thirty years of pastoral and teaching ministry. Many books have been published on the various areas of ministerial ethics. I have found helpful suggestions in all that I have read. Some of the suggestions offered in this work will be repetitious of that which has been offered by other authors in this field, but in the practical application of some of the principles there will be some degree of distinctiveness.

The reader will soon discover that this treatment of ministerial ethics has a pronounced southern flavor. It is also written from the Baptist point of view. This is to be expected, coming from a Southern Baptist pastor. And yet we feel that most of the material found in this study can be easily adapted to ministerial life in any denomination or section of the country.

During recent years some excellent books have come from the press dealing with ministerial life, but none of them seems to deal with some of the more practical situations as those discussed in this work. A helpful bibliography is given at the close of the book.

I have tried, as far as possible, to avoid being too technical, limiting the discussions to a common sense, down-to-earth, practical application of the fundamental principles of ministerial ethics. I have not tried to be exhaustive in discussing the various fields of ministerial activity, but I have sought to be comprehensive in the scope of this study, covering every phase of ministerial life. There remains much left to be said in these various areas, but we do trust that this study will give a survey of the general field of ministerial life and a basis for more advanced study in the particular fields.

Quotations from other works have been used rather freely. In every case the footnote will indicate the source. These are used not only to identify the source, but also to introduce the reader to other books in this field from which he will find profit in study.

For several years now, in between the many duties and responsibilities of a busy pastorate, I have been trying to put into writing the results of my study and experience in this field with the hope that it might be of some help and benefit to other preachers along the way, especially to the young ministers in our colleges and seminaries. While I trust that this study will be a help to all ministers, my first concern is for the young minister who is in the process of orientation as a minister of the Gospel. This work was first published some ten years ago and has been used as a text book in many colleges and seminaries. I am deeply grateful for the encouraging response which has been given to it. In this second and revised edition I have made some corrections in the text and have tried to bring the information up to date.

I am indebted to many for inspiration and help in making possible this work. Besides the authors whose names appear in the bibliography, I am indebted to the following fellow ministers who read the manuscript and made valuable suggestions: Arthur B. Rutledge, Jeff D. Ray, Clyde J. Childers, George Humphrey, and Ralph Phelps. I am also grateful for the efficient work of Mrs. Tom Mc-Brayer in copying the original manuscript for publication. Time and space do not permit the listing of many others who have helped in one way or another.

God has called and is calling a great army of young ministers who are destined to play an increasingly important role in the religious life of our generation and the next. If any thing has been said in this book which will contribute to the happiness and usefulness of some other minister's life, I will feel that my efforts have not been in vain and will thank God for the privilege of having some little part beyond my own personal ministry in the lives of others who have been called into this high and holy calling as ministers of the glorious Gospel of our crucified and risen Saviour.

CONTENTS

Part I
The Minister and His Lord

1 | THE DIVINE CALL

The most vital relationship any Christian has is his relationship with the Lord. A genuine experience of regeneration through faith in the living Christ is absolutely indispensable for any degree of effectiveness in Christian service. But apart from this, the minister has a peculiar relationship with the Lord. It is with this in mind that we give this first section of our study to the minister's relation to the Lord. This peculiar relationship involves a distinct call or commission from the Lord. In a sense, every person ought to feel that the Lord has led and is leading in the profession in which he is engaged; but the minister must feel more than this. He must be conscious of a definite and distinct call from the Lord. Dr. J. H. Jowett, in his lectures to Yale students, expressed it like this: "Now I hold with profound conviction that before a man selects the Christian ministry as his vocation he must have the assurance that the selection has been imperatively constrained by the eternal God. The call of the Eternal must ring through the rooms of his soul as clearly as the sound of the morning bell rings through the valleys of Switzerland, calling the peasants to early prayer and praise."[1]

The Question of a Divine Call

The idea of a God-called ministry has been placed in disrepute by some modern-day religious leaders who look upon the ministry as they do upon all other vocations, simply a choice of what might seem to fit in best with the talents and disposition of the individual. These make no distinction in the choice of the ministry and the choice of any other vocation in life. In general the religious bodies which have advocated such an attitude toward the ministry have developed a ministry which has departed from the proclamation of the simple Gospel of salvation in a crucified and risen Christ and has substituted high-sounding, weak-spirited, philosophical lectures on insignificant and intangible themes. This is no surprise to us when we understand their attitude toward the ministry.

[1] *The Preacher: His Life and Work,* p. 12.

13

In this study we are thinking only of the man who is called of God to preach, with the understanding that such a call of God is peculiar to a preacher. If the Gospel of redemption through the atoning blood of Christ is to be proclaimed to the world, it will be done by the men who have experienced a definite call from God to this ministry. Men who feel called of God will also seek to know and proclaim the true message of God to the world, for the call of God is not only a call to preach but also a call to preach a certain God-given message. We agree with Dr. Jeff D. Ray that "if a man feels that he has been directly called or summoned by the Holy Ghost to preach the Gospel, it will give a romantic dignity, a knightly chivalry and sacrificial devotion otherwise impossible."[2] Every genuine preacher must feel the hand of God laid upon him for this specific task; otherwise his ministry will be unhappy and unproductive. "Only the consciousness of a divine call to do a great and awful work can give that confidence and feeling of authority necessary to make one's ministry successful."[3]

THE NECESSITY OF A DIVINE CALL

As stated in the foregoing paragraphs, our premise is that a Divine Call is absolutely imperative for any degree of effectiveness in the Christian ministry. It is not our purpose here to attempt a detailed description of the technical elements involved in a Divine Call. It simply means "that one comes to have a conviction that preaching the gospel is God's will for his life. It is not experienced as something that one takes on himself of his own initiative. It is experienced as something required by the will of God. It is felt as something imposed."[4] However, we do want to give some consideration to the basic principles which will prove our thesis: that a Divine Call is imperative in the Christian ministry.

The certainty of this conclusion becomes even more emphatic in the light of one's own experience. Those who have been "called" are conscious of such a call. This consciousness which grows out of experience is a convincing voice. Dr. W. T. Conner explains this plainly and forcibly in an article which occurred in the *Baptist Standard:* "The assurance of a call lies in the experience itself. Like all other experience, it is self-validating. Like the new birth one cannot tell how it comes. It can be known only in the experience itself. Somehow one comes to the fixed conviction that preaching is God's will for his life. As we believe, it is put there by the creative and redemptive Spirit of God. We can no more tell how he does this than

2 *The Highest Office,* p. 82.
3 Barrett, R. N., *Ethics of the Ministry,* p. 99.
4 Conner, W. T., "A Call to Preach" in *Baptist Standard* issue of March 3, 1949.

we can explain any other activity of the Almighty."[5] I am preaching today because of a conviction that God definitely laid His hand upon me for this ministry. Why, I do not know. But the call to preach is as definite in my own heart as my own conversion experience. It was not a case of my seeking out the ministry as a noble and serviceable vocation to which I could give my life. Rather, it was a case of God's seeking me out and laying His hand upon me with the commission to be a minister of His blessed Gospel. I have never lost, through the years, the assurance of this call. Thousands of other ministers could give testimony to a similar conviction. This voice of experience testifies to the necessity of the Divine Call.

A second proof for the imperativeness of the Divine Call is found in the teachings of the New Testament on this subject. One cannot read the New Testament without being impressed with the fact that the preachers mentioned therein were divinely called to the task in which they were engaged. Paul was convinced that it was God's call and not his own choice that put him into the ministry. This is clear from his words in I Corinthians 9:16, 17 — "For though I preach the gospel, I have nothing to glory of for necessity it laid upon me; yea, woe is unto me, if I preach not the gospel! For if I do this thing willingly, I have a reward; but if against my will, a dispensation of the Gospel is committed unto me." In nearly all of his epistles Paul emphasizes at the very beginning the fact of his divine call into the ministry. Neither can we suppose that such a feeling of divine call was peculiar to Paul. Other preachers, such as Peter and John, indicate a similar call in their own lives. Furthermore, Paul himself intimates in the expressions concerning his own call that all preachers have the same experience. A careful study of Paul's first letter to the Corinthians will make all of this clear and convincing.

There is still a third reason for believing in the necessity of a divine call for the Christian minister. It is found in the very nature of God. There are two aspects of the character of God which imply the idea of a divine call for the minister. One is the personal nature of God. Since God is a personal God, He deals with men in a personal way, which would involve a personal call to those whom He has chosen to preach. Dr. Conner is right in saying that "aside from the idea of a personal God, of course, the idea of a call to preach is without meaning."[6] The other is the sovereignty of God. If God is sovereign in all things, it is only natural and logical that He appoint, choose, and call whom He will into this ministry. As God moves by His

---

[5] "A Call to Preach" in issue of March 3, 1949.
[6] "Principles Underlying a Call to Preach" in May 5, 1949, issue of *Baptist Standard*.

sovereign grace to save men, even so by that same sovereign grace does He Himself call men into the ministry. It is the sovereign God who always takes the initiative. "Reason itself would teach us that God being sovereign, would reserve to himself the right to choose those whom he would send out to represent him in the world."[7] Other observations might be given,[8] but these will suffice to justify sufficiently our thesis concerning the imperativeness of a divine call in the Christian ministry.

Two Common Mistakes with Reference to the Divine Call

In regard to this call two fatal mistakes can be made. The first mistake is that of refusing to answer the call of God to the ministry. There are men who realize that God has called them to preach, but they have not responded to this call. Perhaps the most unhappy Christian living is the man who is living in the consciousness of a call of God from which he has fled. I have met such men and they give every evidence of such infelicity. It never pays to disobey the known call of God to the work of the ministry. Happiness, usefulness, and contentment are impossible in the realm of such rebellion.

On the other hand it is just as serious a mistake to take up the ministry as a vocation without the consciousness of a divine call. Some have made this fatal mistake. The ministry of such a man can never be truly effective however great may be his ability. Neither can it give satisfaction and contentment however unselfish may be the service. God wants *all* of those who have been called to give themselves to the ministry, but He also wants *only* those who have been called to give themselves to the ministry.

The Means Used in Making Known the Divine Call

Even though the reader may agree with all the foregoing, there is one pertinent question still unanswered. How may one know that he is called of God? Or in what way does God call and how may we recognize that call if and when it comes? These are serious questions and need to be given careful consideration. Perhaps we cannot answer these questions decisively for each individual, but we can offer some suggestions that may be of help in seeking for an answer to these questions.

From the negative standpoint, let us remind all that the apparent qualifications for leadership, such as: oratorical ability, love for people, and intellectual ability, do not necessarily indicate a call to the

---

[7] Roberts, Morris A., "The Pastor's Place of Leadership" in April 21, 1949, issue of *Baptist Standard*.

[8] See Dobbins, G. S., *Building Better Churches*, p. 296.

ministry. In fact, many times God deliberately calls those who do not have the evidence of these abilities in order that He might show forth His power through them. Paul tells us this very plainly in I Corinthians 1:26-28 — "For ye see your calling, brethren, how that not many wise men after the flesh, not many mighty, not many noble, are called; but God hath chosen the foolish things of the world to confound the things which are mighty; and base things of the world, and things which are despised, hath God chosen, yea, and things which are not, to bring to naught things that are; that no flesh should glory in his presence." There is a developing philosophy among some present day ecclesiastical leaders that candidates for the ministry should be chosen exclusively from the ranks of those who have natural leadership qualities and social standing.[9] But this method does not fit into the principles as set out in the New Testament. On the other hand, we are not to despair should some of these qualities be found in those whom God has called. We simply want to emphasize the fact that native abilities do not necessarily give evidence of a divine call.

The call of God may come through one or more of several different channels. There is no cut-and-dried method which God uses in calling men. He may call one man in one way and the next man He may call in an entirely different way. The call is the same in either case, but the method of making known that call will vary and change.

Some men receive the call through a sudden and phenomenal experience. This was true in Paul's case, but God does not approach all men in this manner. Perhaps very few men receive the call of God through such a sudden and phenomenal revelation. I have known men who had such experiences and I have no reason to doubt the genuineness of their experience. The danger is that some people may think they are not called unless God miraculously and literally writes it across the sky. But again we say, not all men are called in this manner.

Some men receive the call through the impressions of others. Sometimes God may call through the voice of another man. This does not mean that one should feel called of God every time someone else expresses his desire that he enter the ministry. God may call through the voice of another, but when He does so call He will make that call impressive to the one called. This method God used in His call to George W. Truett. The whole church at Whitewright was impressed of God that Truett should preach, and so expressed it, be-

---

[9] See Tucker, W. J., "The Making and Unmaking of the Preacher," p. 31ff and Hutton, John, *That the Ministry Be Not Blamed.*

fore he himself felt and answered the call. And who will doubt that George W. Truett was called of God to His glorious and fruitful ministry? Many other preachers have heard the voice of God calling into the ministry through the expressed impressions of others.

Others receive the call of God through a series of impressionable experiences. In this case the call does not come like a flash of lightning, but little by little the impression is deepened until it becomes a conviction of God's call. Perhaps this is the most common method of God's approach to those whom He has chosen for the ministry. It is just as definite and just as distinct as in the case of the man who receives some sudden and phenomenal revelation. Many Christians have momentary impressions which cause them to feel that they might be called to the ministry. But when this impression keeps coming back repeatedly and with increasing clarity, we may interpret it to be a call from the Lord. This is the admonition I would give to all young men who may be struggling with this question. If there is a genuine call, it will not be a momentary feeling that is gone when the pressure of some high emotional hour has passed. It will linger on and it will come back repeatedly. And when it does, the call should be recognized and accepted.

Now let us add a word just here concerning the attitude of the one who is experiencing the divine impressions. It is a word of warning. There are those who seem to have the idea that every one who is called of God must go through a period of "fighting against the call." This is not necessarily so. Some men do resist the call for a time after it is made known, but others respond to the call as soon as they are sure of it. There is no advantage in resisting the call even for a time. And there are others who feel that a man should have a definite personal dislike for the ministry as a vocation before God will call him to it. Such an idea is erroneous and misleading. Some men who are called did have a personal dislike for it before they were called, but this is not always the case. Whether one has a natural like or dislike for the ministry, God does call some to be ministers and those who respond to this call will find life's greatest joy in a life of service through the ministry of the Word.

EVIDENCES OF THE GENUINENESS OF THE DIVINE CALL

Let us suppose now that one has entered the ministry as the result of an urge which he has interpreted to be the call of God. Are there any confirming and corroborative evidences which will convince him that he has been genuinely called into this ministry? The answer is in the affirmative. There are some tests which we may apply to our ministry. These tests, when applied, will prove the genuineness of the call, especially when all of them are considered together.

The first test concerns one's own feeling in the matter. If he has been genuinely called of God, he will find in the ministry a source of deep inner satisfaction. Contrariwise, he who enters the ministry, not having been genuinely called, will feel a sense of keen discontent and dissatisfaction. This does not mean that a dissatisfaction with everything else is necessarily an indication of a call to the ministry. Some men are misfits in everything. But for those who are called of God into the ministry there will be no feeling of contentment and satisfaction except in the ministry.

Another evidence of the genuineness of a call to the ministry is the conviction on the part of others with reference to this call. Dr. Conner has very aptly said, "If one is called to preach, the Lord will usually make known a knowledge of this fact to others. The one called will arrive at this conviction, but so will others."[10] This does not mean that everybody will think that the one called should preach, but if no one seems to feel that the one in question has been called, then there may be reason to doubt the genuineness of the call.

A third evidence of the authenticity of the call is the fact that some people will be blessed and helped by the ministry. "If God calls a man to preach He will call somebody to hear him, and somebody who will want to hear him and somebody who will be helped when he hears him."[11] God does not call men for nought: neither does He call men to waste their breath on the desert air. This does not mean, however, that, if he is called to preach, multitudes will always flock to hear him. In fact, even for the genuinely called minister there are seasons of barrenness. But over a period of time people will be blessed by his ministry and some will be saved. The number of those so blessed and saved will vary with different ministers. For some this number will be large; for others it will be small. But in every case there will be some. Nor does this mean that one will be immediately called to a church the moment he surrenders to preach. However, a degree of success over a period of time is evidence of a genuine call. Again may we quote from Dr. Conner, whose statement is concise and conclusive: "Not every God-called man will have crowds flock to hear him when he preaches. And some men who are about as much God-called as Balaam's ass may have thousands to go to hear them. But when a God-called and Spirit-directed man preaches somebody will get a blessing from his message."[12]

[10] "Evidence of a Call to Preach" in March 10, 1949, issue of *Baptist Standard*.
[11] Ray, Jeff D., *The Highest Office*, p. 78.
[12] "Evidence of a Call to Preach" in March 10, 1949, issue of *Baptist Standard*.

There are other evidences which might be mentioned,[13] but these we have mentioned are sufficient to prove the integrity of the call.

In this chapter we have seen something of the nature of the divine call, the imperativeness of it, the means God uses to make it known, and the evidences which prove the genuineness of it. In it all we have sought to impress the reader with the sacredness and significance of God's call and the practical application of it to the human life, to the end that young men may recognize and follow this call when it comes and that those who have already responded to the call may find greater inspiration and effectiveness in the execution of the responsibilities of the ministry.

[13] Ray, Jeff D., *The Highest Office*, pp. 73-78.

2 | DIVINE LEADERSHIP: GENERAL

The experience of a Divine call is only the beginning of a unique fellowship and alliance with God. It is a relationship which must remain increasingly real and intimate. Let us look at this affinity, first in a general sense as we look at the ministerial life in its entirety; then in a more particular sense as we look at the minister's life in relation to a particular field of labor, the latter to be discussed in the next chapter.

THE LORD POSSESSES THE MINISTER

Not only is the minister called of the Lord, but he is also in a peculiar sense completely led and directed by the Lord. In a sense, every Christian is, or should be, led of the Lord in all of life's endeavors, but in a special sense the minister is owned and controlled by the Lord. The minister is God's special possession by creation, providence, redemption, and commission. In discussing ministers with the Corinthian Church Paul describes ministers as "God's fellow-laborers" (I Corinthians 3:9). The King James version reads: "laborers together with God"; but the revised version seems to be a better rendering of the meaning of the original language. Every preacher ought to feel as Paul felt, that in a very intimate way he is God's possession. He created us; He protects us; He redeemed us; He called us into this glorious ministry. It is not our own work that we are doing; it is the work of Him who called us and owns us.

THE LORD GIVES THE MINISTER HIS MESSAGE

This relation of the minister to his Lord is enhanced by the fact that God Himself gives to the preacher his message. The minister does not go out to proclaim an idea or a philosophy that he himself has worked out; rather, he goes out to proclaim a message which is given to him by the Lord. It is not our message; it is God's message. In his great message on the resurrection Paul makes it clear that this is not a product of his own mind but that it is a message which he received from the Lord: "For I delivered unto you first of all that

21

which I also received, how that Christ died for our sins according to the scriptures" (I Corinthians 15:3). For his message the minister is dependent upon the Lord. The preacher is not called to manufacture a message or to invent a new philosophy; he is called to give to the people that which God has given to him.

THE LORD GIVES EFFICIENCY FOR THE MINISTRY

We may go a step further and say that God not only gives the message but also the power and unction with which to proclaim it. Whatever power and effectiveness is experienced in any ministerial function is that which God gives. The first century preachers were conscious of the fact that whatever power was manifested in the work of the ministry was given of God. Paul expressed this very vividly when he said, "I have planted, Apollos watered, but God gave the increase" (I Corinthians 3:6). God does not always call to the ministry men that are naturally qualified for such work, but God always gives to all whom He has called the power and efficiency to accomplish that for which they have been called. God does not depend upon the native qualities of His ministers to accomplish His purpose through them, but with the call God gives the strength, power, and efficiency. This efficiency is given through the agency of the Holy Spirit working in and through His ministers. The following quotation from T. H. Lewis in "The Minister and His Own Soul" vividly expresses what we are trying to say here: "The preacher of the cross is not to be limited to the resources of his own natural qualities even when these are refined and heightened by divine grace. He is to be re-enforced by direct communication of spiritual power from on high, to be made the instrument of supernatural activities. In this process his own spirit is to be made holy, his love purged of all hypocrisy, his word to be informed with absolute truth, and his power to be merged into the power of God. What a barren, hopeless ministry would be ours if the supernatural were eliminated, if we did not believe in a Holy Spirit, in a Divine love, in a Word of truth, in a Power of God!"[1]

THE LORD IS THE FINAL JUDGE OF THE MINISTER

As we delve still deeper into this relationship we observe that the Lord is also the only and final judge of the minister's work. There are people in the congregations who pass judgment constantly on the minister and his ministry, and such judgments should be carefully weighed by the preacher, but in the final analysis there is only one judge whose judgment really counts. Again, let us use Paul for

[1] *Ibid.*, p. 125.

an illustration. Paul tells the Corinthians in no uncertain terms that he is not concerned about their judgment. "But with me it is a very small thing that I should be judged of you, or of man's judgment; yet, I judge not mine own self. For I know nothing by myself; yet am I not hereby justified; but he that judgeth me is the Lord" (I Corinthians 4:3, 4). If God only is the judge of the preacher's ministry, why should we be always passing judgment on the minister's message or ministry? Such judgments are usually given without full knowledge and are often prejudiced. Only God has the ability and the right to judge the minister.

Furthermore, if God only is the judge of the preacher, why should we as preachers become so affected, influenced, and governed in our ministry by the judgment of those to whom we preach? Should we not preach that which God has inspired regardless of the judgment or opinions of the congregation? Too many preachers allow their preaching to be conformed to the whims and fancies of the people because they are afraid of the judgment of the people. But if we recognize only the judgment of God we will seek to proclaim the message as God gives it regardless of the opinions and judgments of the people. The prophet Isaiah condemned the preachers who preached for the favor of the people rather than the favor of God (Isaiah 5:20-24). After all, what shall we profit if we gain the favor of all the people and become the most popular man among men, if we have not been faithful to the commission which we received of God. It is God who shall pronounce the final evaluation of our ministry. We must be faithful to our trust. "Preach the Word, in season, out of season," if we would receive the final "well done" of our Lord and judge.

THE LORD IS THE FINAL REWARDER OF THE MINISTER

There is one last thought in regard to this phase of the minister's relation to the Lord. It is the Lord who rewards the minister for his labors. There are many joys and blessings which come to the minister along the way from those with whom he works, but we must remember that the final reward for a faithful ministry is bestowed by the Lord Himself. This thought gives inspiration and stimulation to the faithful minister in his hours of trial, opposition, and hardship. We may expect experiences of compensation from time to time, but our greatest and ultimate hope is to be found in the anticipation of God's "well done." Paul was talking about preachers when he said, "If any man's work abide which he hath built thereupon, he shall receive a reward. If any man's work shall be burned, he shall suffer loss, but he himself shall be saved; yet so as by fire"

(I Corinthians 3:14, 15). This reward is not on the basis of the amount of accomplishments as compared to others but on the basis of faithfulness. "Moreover it is required in stewards, that a man be found faithful" (I Corinthians 4:2). When the minister's path leads him through barren fields and troublesome tribulations, he can find comfort and inspiration in the fact that God, in due time, will reward his ministers for faithful service in the execution of a divine call.

In all of these things we have seen the inseparable link between the minister and His Lord. With this in mind the minister must seek always to keep himself conscious of his utter dependence upon God and of his peculiar relation to God. In the light of this relationship it is not presumptuous to expect efficiency in the ministry to which we have been called, keeping always in mind that it is not the ability of the preacher, but the ability of God through an intimate and continuous relationship with His ministers.

3 | DIVINE LEADERSHIP: PARTICULAR

THE PROBLEM OF A FIELD OF LABOR

Recognizing the necessity and importance of divine leadership in every aspect of his life and work, the minister is brought face to face with the more particular and definite phases of the work, not the least of which is the leadership of God in the choice of a particular field of labor. After the minister surrenders to the ministerial call, one of the first questions to face him is this: Where shall I preach or in what particular field shall I bestow my labors in the ministry? Then, all through life the minister is faced repeatedly with the question of a change in his field of labor. These are tremendously serious questions for the minister and it is our purpose in this chapter to study these questions in the light of divine leadership as applied to practical experience.

THE HUMAN SIDE OF GOD'S LEADERSHIP

In solving the problem of his field of labor the minister must rely upon the leadership of God. Indeed, this is the key which unlocks the door into a happy and useful ministry in any particular field of labor. Grave mistakes are made and serious injuries are inflicted upon the preacher as well as the people when the leadership of God is not sought and followed in the choice of a field of labor. We cannot put too much emphasis upon this basic principle in effective ministerial living.

Practically all preachers will readily concur with the writer in this emphasis upon the exigency of divine leadership. But the question which disturbs us is this: How can we intelligently recognize and interpret divine leadership in the choice of a field of labor? There are times when the minister earnestly seeks to follow the leadership of the Lord but finds it extremely difficult to ascertain the will of God in making a decision concerning his field of labor. But may we say with all assurance that God does make known his will for those who earnestly seek it. In making known His will to man God has always used human instrumentality. In the act of some decision the preacher need not expect God to make known His will by writing it across the sky or by giving some fantastic and phenomenal vision. In exceptional cases He has and He may make known His will in some phenomenal way, but usually God makes known His will through the normal experiences of life and many times through the expressions of others. The preacher must learn to ask God for a revelation of His will; then he must look for that revelation in the experiences and movements of men. God will give it to him in one way or another, and not always in the same identical way.

THE PROBLEM OF THE YOUNG PREACHER

In our search for the proper interpretation of the will of God with reference to our fields of labor, let us study a little more closely the human side of this experience, suggesting some practical hints which, we trust, will prove helpful to the minister in his desire to follow the leadership of God in his life. Let us take the case of a young man who has just surrendered to the ministerial call. Of course, he will begin immediately to prepare himself in every possible way, but even in this preparation period there will be many thoughts crowding in concerning his place of service in the ministry. To what particular phase of ministerial life shall he give himself? The first question, then, to be settled is the question of type of ministerial work. Ministerial activity may take any one of several different channels or forms, such as: pastoral work, mission work, evangelism, or Bible teaching, etc. The young minister will first want to determine which of these various forms of ministerial activity he should follow. It is possible that one may feel led to follow a certain general course, only to discover later that another course should be followed in keeping with God's will. Usually, however, the general course of one's ministerial life is determined early in his ministry, and ought to be so determined if possible. Then there are cases in which the minister feels led of God to change the general course of his ministry after years of service. In either of these cases there should be no embarrassment. But what we are saying is that, in the main, the general course of one's ministerial life should be determined early. In determining the form of one's ministerial labors the leadership of God may be made known through some climactic experience or it may be made known through an ever deepening impression. In any case, the general direction of one's ministry must be determined. If the will of God can be learned early, it will make possible a more thorough preparation for the particular type of work to which we feel led of God to give our lives.

Having settled the question of the general course of one's ministry, the next problem is that of finding a location in some particular field. In this, too, the minister must seek the leadership of God's Spirit, remembering that God usually works through human agency and human experience. Since most preachers enter the pastoral field and since many of the same principles will be applicable to other forms of ministerial labor, in discussing the problem of finding a particular field of labor we are thinking in terms of the pastor. Just how should a man go about the task of finding a pastorate? We are thinking now of the young man who is seeking his first pastorate or the man who is without pastoral work. Of course, he will pray and wait for God to lead the way. While he is doing this there are certain things which he can and should do, and through which God will reveal His will and lead the way. This is the human side of the picture at which we are now looking. And from this human side of the picture let us point out several pertinent suggestions for the minister.

THE DILEMMA OF THE YOUNG PREACHER

Our first suggestion is on the negative side. The preacher should never be the aggressor in his desire to become pastor. Aggression on the part of the preacher in this matter is neither ethically proper nor theologically sound. Unlike other professional work, in the ministry the preacher must not seek the place; rather the place must seek the preacher. And this is the dilemma of the young preacher whose heart is burning to get into a pastorate. If he is not to take the initiative, how can he ever expect to become a pastor? Let us assure the young preacher that if God has called him, God will also open some field of labor to him in due time. And, furthermore, though he must not take the initiative, there are things which he can do from the human standpoint and which God will use in opening the field to him.

This brings us to our second suggestion: namely, that the preacher should take advantage of every preaching opportunity, whether it be in a large church, small church, jail, or on the street. There are some young preachers who refuse to preach until some desirable church invites. The author knew a young ministerial student in school who refused to preach at the jail or in some remote church. He was waiting for "The First Brick Church" in a county seat town to call him; then he would begin to preach. That was twenty years ago. He is still waiting for the call from that "First Brick Church." The man who thinks he is too good to preach in the jail or at the forks of the creek is not worthy to be pastor of the largest church in the land. By this we do not mean that the young preacher should neglect his studies and give all of his time to preaching here, there, and yonder. It does mean that when opportunity presents itself he should be willing to preach whenever and wherever the occasion arises. He can take advantage of occasions for preaching without doing any injustice to his scholastic training. In fact, he will be enhancing the value of his training by such experience. And furthermore, he will be enhancing his prospects of becoming pastor. The men who are first considered by the churches are the men who love to preach and who give evidence of their desire to preach by taking advantage of every opportunity.

THE YOUNG PREACHER AND HIS FELLOW PREACHERS

Another suggestion for the young preacher seeking a pastorate is that he cultivate friendship among fellow preachers. Of course, this must not be done from the mere selfish standpoint of seeking a recommendation to a church. Apart from this, there are distinct advantages in every way for the preacher who cultivates friendship among his fellow preachers. The young preacher should cultivate such friendships with the older ministers as well as with those of his own age group. We have no patience whatsoever with political wire pulling on the part of preachers in order to get before churches, but it is only natural and right that God should work through preachers in order to get together the proper preacher and the proper church. This is a natural and ordinary channel through which God works. While the preacher is enriching his own life by his fellowship with other preachers, he is incidentally placing himself in a position which may lead to the pastorate. When a preacher is in position to make a recommendation to a church, he will naturally and wisely recommend someone whom he knows and understands.

This leads us to the question of whether the preacher should ask a recommendation to a church from another preacher. We agree with R. N. Barrett that "it is not improper to ask some influential brother to propose your name, that the church may know who is available, though after a man has some experience, and has acquired some degree of reputation, this should not be necessary, as his work will speak for itself."[1] However, this ought to be done only on rare occasions and then with great care and tact. Such recommendation should not be requested of some one who is not familiar with the life and character of the one making the request. No preacher is justified in asking a recommendation from another preacher who knows little or nothing about him. Promiscuous requests for recommendation to churches are neither becoming nor wise, and often become embarrassing and detrimental to the cause of Christ. Let

[1] *Ethics of the Ministry.* pp. 104, 105.

the young minister use with caution this privilege of requesting recommendation from a fellow minister, lest by its abuse he do injury to himself and the cause. And, as Dr. Barrett has said, when one has established himself in the ministry there is very little occasion for requesting recommendations, though they may be and will be voluntarily given by others.

The requesting of the recommendation should always be for the sole purpose of getting the individual before the church. When once he is before the church, the rest should be left entirely up to the church and the Lord. Any move on the part of the preacher to precipitate the call is entirely out of order and inexcusable. The minister may be excused for using some human agency in getting his name before the church, but the preacher is not worthy of the name who continues pulling wires in order to assure the call.

For the young minister there is one more suggestion: Be patient! He must learn to wait. Too many young preachers become overanxious and impatient if some church does not call soon after they have surrendered to the ministry. God will lead every one of those whom He has called to some field of labor in His own due time. It may be several years, but He will open the way. The matter of being called to a particular field of labor is only the first in a series of life-long experiences in which the preacher will be called upon to exercise that priceless Christian virtue of patience, and of which the preacher needs a double share.

THE PROBLEM OF CHANGING FIELDS OF LABOR

Now let us consider the problem of a change in the minister's particular field of labor. All through the minister's life there will be the problem of making a choice between two fields of labor. This involves the changing of pastorate. There are times when the church will initiate the question of a change in field of labor and there are other times when the preacher himself will initiate the question of a change. There are times when the static condition of the church will suggest to the minister that he ought to change his field of labor. Or it may be the case of the church giving expression of its feeling that the pastor should leave for another field of labor. Then, the question of change may be suggested by the invitation of another church to become its pastor. In either of these cases the decisions must be made on the basis of divine leadership. As in the case of the young minister, so also now, the will of God is usually revealed through human agency and human experience. Because of this we dare to make several practical suggestions for ministers facing such decisions.

In the first place, may we suggest that the presence of problems in the life of the church is not always an indication that the preacher should move to a new field. There is a natural human temptation on the part of the average preacher to feel that when some serious problem arises it is time for him to move on to another field. Usually this impression is wrong. However, this does not mean that the preacher is doomed to stay because of the difficulty. In fact, it is possible that such a condition could be the means of God's leadership to another field. But, we hasten to say that usually this is not true. The grass always looks greener in the next field until we get into the field to discover that there are just as many weeds as in the previous field. Problems are seldom solved by running away from them. As preachers we need to warn ourselves against the temptation of feeling an urge to change fields every time we encounter a difficulty. The church is not in existence that does not have a problem. As long as churches are made up of human beings, even though redeemed, there will be problems arising from such imperfect human nature. There are no ideal churches. Preachers who are looking for such are wandering about aimlessly for a Utopia that never was in existence in this world and never shall be.

Our second suggestion has to do with the preacher's attitude toward personal opposition within the church. There is a difference between church problems as such and personal opposition to the pastor. It is regrettable but true that there are times when serious opposition is raised on the part of some within the church to the pastor. Many times this opposition is unjust and unfounded. At other times the opposition may be justified. To delve into the causes of such opposition we would have to take up each individual case separately. Whether the opposition is just or unjust, the preacher's work is seriously handicapped in the church. Some preachers simply ignore such opposition and others seek to stamp it out by some means of force. A conference of the church may be called for the purpose of testing the feeling of the congregation toward the pastor. And even though the pastor may receive a majority vote of confidence, if there are as many as a half dozen or dozen influential people on the opposition side, whether right or wrong, the pastor's effectiveness as a leader, if not completely destroyed, is so greatly handicapped that his work can never be what it ought to be in that place. Such opposition usually should be overlooked, but when the opposition becomes so strong and serious that a conference of the church is contemplated for a vote, the pastor would be wise indeed who sought another field of labor before such conference could ever be called. It is true that the majority rules, but a mere majority following is not sufficient for any pastor to put over an adequate church program.

Now let us take the case of the man who is invited by another church to change his field of labor. We are taking for granted that the invitation has come without solicitation on the part of the preacher. Before the invitation comes there is usually the feeler which comes in the form of a visit from the pulpit committee. Before any decision is made, careful and prayerful consideration should be given by the preacher. First of all, the preacher should never allow a committee to continue its investigation or to present his name to the church if he is absolutely sure that he would not consider moving to this new field of labor. Few things are more disgusting on the part of ministers than "church flirting," that is, leading churches to call in order to prize a raise in salary out of the present pastorate or to increase popularity among the brethren. And yet this is sometimes done. In the second place, if the preacher feels that there is a possibility of his moving to this new field of labor, he should make thorough investigation of this new field before making any decision. He should not make any decision blindly. He should have accurate knowledge as to the conditions prevailing on this new field, and especially as to the church's attitude toward the pastor. Many times a knowledge of these conditions will throw light upon the preacher's search for the revelation of God's will in the matter. And in the third place, much time should be given to agonizing prayer. Few things are more trying on a preacher than the making of decisions with reference to a field of labor. Such times of decision are times of great anxiety, and rightly so. God forbid that any preacher should make such decisions with flippancy and lightness. They must come out of hours of agonizing and travail, and then when the decision is made great joy and efficacy will be given the preacher in his new field of labor.

THE PROBLEM OF THE CHURCH IN SEEKING LEADERSHIP

From the human side, this choice of a field of labor involves primarily the preacher and the church which constitutes his field of labor. We have been thinking of it from the view point of the preacher. Now let us turn the picture around and look at the problem from the view point of the church. The church must seek and follow the leadership of God in calling a pastor just as the preacher must seek God's guidance in his decision concerning his field of labor. In this case also there are some practical principles which, if followed, will greatly aid the church in its desire to follow God's will.

Taking for granted that the whole church is praying earnestly for divine leadership, let the church first elect a pulpit committee, whose duty it shall be to bring recommendation to the church concerning a prospective pastor. There would be nothing but confusion and turmoil if every member is encouraged to bring whomsoever he wanted before the church. Happily, our churches are learning to apply some decency and system to the calling of their pastors. This committee should be made up of a representative group of from five to nine members. Let us remember that it is not the responsibility of this committee to name a pastor for the church. It is for the purpose of recommending a pastor. The church, in the final analysis, may either accept or reject the recommendation. The committee simply makes possible a more orderly and efficient method of getting the church and the prospective pastor together. Paul said, "Let all things be done decently and in order" (I Corinthians 14:40).

As soon as this committee is named it should begin immediately to consider prayerfully and carefully the task which is before it. Every suggestion, especially by members of the church, should be given some consideration by the committee. In the case of a larger church there may be hundreds of names recommended. From a study of the list, the most likely names in the mind of the committee should be set aside and properly investigated. There is no set order in which an investigation ought to be made, but it certainly ought to include the following steps:

An inquiry ought to be made among other preachers, pastors, and denominational leaders who might be acquainted with the prospective pastor. Many times these men can give insight into the character of the man and his work which cannot be found in any other way. This inquiry does not need to be extended. Contact with a few representative men will suffice to give the information which the committee seeks to know.

The investigation should by all means include a hearing by the committee of the prospective preacher in his own pulpit. Never is it wise to have the prospective pastor come to the vacant pulpit to deliver a "sample sermon," especially before the committee has heard the man in his own pulpit. Such a procedure would only add confusion in the minds of the people. Furthermore, a natural picture of the preacher's type and calibre of preaching can be more accurately seen in his own pulpit, where he is free from the scrutinizing and critical eye of a new congregation. And if possible, the committee should come into the service unnoticed. In order to do this it is usually best to come into the service separately rather than in a group. It is also wise, if possible, to give the prospective pastor two hearings. One particular sermon may not always give a true picture of the preacher. Preachers are never at their best or at their worst all of the time. May we drop this further word of advice for pulpit committees: Remember that you are not looking for a mere oratorical genius, but a capable preacher of the Word.

There is the danger that a committee will make its recommendation on the basis of the impression of the sermon heard and only that, but this is perilous. There are other things to be considered, such as: his habit of study, his diligence in the work, his ability to get along with people, his honesty and integrity in the community, his attitude toward himself, his people, and his work. We will not go into these things, but let us simply emphasize in passing that a good pastor must have more than pulpit ability, though he must have that too. But how is the committee to know these things? These things can be learned in various ways. An examination of the church records in the association minutes will reveal some of these things. Other things can be learned by observation and interviews with others who know the preacher and his work. A casual conversation with the merchant will often reveal some interesting things. In every possible way a thorough investigation should be made of the prospective preacher.

When the committee has agreed upon the man to be recommended a conference should be arranged with the prospective preacher. At this time the committee and the prospective pastor should talk plainly and frankly. The committee should give an accurate and complete picture of the church situation especially as it relates to the pastor. Either at this time or when the call is extended the following facts should be made clear: "Whether the call is for a specific period or for an indefinite time; amount of salary, when and how paid, and prospects of increase with the growth and prosperity of the church; living quarters if furnished by the church, and if the pastor's home is owned by the church how its upkeep is to be maintained; provision, if any, for vacations, attendance on conventions, absences in meetings, supply of pulpit in absences; provision of suitable office, office supplies, secretarial help, transportation expenses, and similar items; participation in the minister's retirement plan; and assurance of loyal support of the pastor's leadership as he follows Christ."[2]

In such a preliminary conference the prospective pastor should not be asked or expected to give a definite answer. He should give,

[2] Dobbins, G. S., *Building Better Churches*, p. 315.

however, some indication of his disposition to give consideration to such a call if made. If he gives a definite indication that he is not interested, then the matter ought to be dropped and another man sought. If he seems to be interested and the committee still feels impressed, he should be invited to the vacant pulpit that the people may hear him and know him. Then his name should be presented to the church in conference with the recommendation that he be called as pastor. Let this one man and only this man come up for consideration by the church at this time. If the church does not feel led to call this man it may reject the recommendation of the committee. In that case the committee will continue its search for a man. Many churches have been seriously injured by the practice of having two or more preachers before the church at one time. Always some will prefer one preacher and others another. It is safe and sensible to have only one preacher before the church at one time. It is certainly possible for any member of the church to make a recommendation directly to the church concerning the calling of a pastor and it is possible for a church to disregard any recommendation of its pulpit committee, and in a few rare cases this may be wise, but ordinarily a church will want to follow the recommendation of its pulpit committee, and wisely so. In it all and through it all we are remembering that the Holy Spirit must lead the way. These things we have mentioned are simply instruments which are often used of the Lord in leading churches to pastors and pastors to churches.

4 | MINISTERIAL TERMINOLOGY

Under the general head of "The Minister and His Lord" it seems proper that we should add this chapter on "Ministerial Terminology," a study of the terms found in God's Word relating to ministerial functions. Such a study of the terminology of the Scriptures will give to us a clearer insight into the meaning and function of the ministerial office. It is not a matter of splitting hairs in the use of certain Scriptural titles for the minister. Rather, it is a matter of seeking through the study of the Scripture terms the meaning and function of the ministerial office.

THE SIGNIFICANCE OF MINISTERIAL TITLES

Many titles have been used in referring to the minister. Some dozen or more will be found in the New Testament and other terms have come into common usufruct in the ecclesiastical terminology of this modern era. There is no advantage in contentiously demanding that a certain title be used when addressing a minister. Any of these titles when used with respect ought to be acceptable to the preacher, even though some of them seem to be more appropriate than others. Then there are some that may seem awkward and out of place to us because they may not be used frequently in the particular section of the country in which we live. It is not our purpose, therefore, to quibble over the proper title to be used in addressing the minister. Our interest in titles is only that of seeking a better understanding of the preacher and his work by the connotations involved in the terms used.

While our primary purpose here is to study the terminology of the New Testament, let us first take a brief glance at some of the extra-Biblical titles which have come into existence over the years. There are in vogue five ministerial titles which are not found in the New Testament. Let us look at them briefly from the standpoint of etymology and practice. The word, *clergyman*, came originally from the Latin word, *clericus*, which meant priest, and in the early days was used to distinguish the minister from the laity. This term today is most commonly employed as an official term in documents of law and industry. It is not often used in direct address to ministers.

Another extra-Biblical title is that of *Rector*, which came from the Latin word, *regere*, meaning to lead straight or to rule. This title fits in appropriately with the ecclesiastical ideas of Episcopal heirarchy, but it would not be an appropriate title for the pastor of a congregational type church. The use of this term, therefore, has been limited generally to episcopal forms of church life.

The term, *parson*, comes from the Old French word, *persone*. It was originally employed to single out the minister as the outstanding person of the community. The average minister does not want to be so singled out and separated from the lives of others in the community. Consequently this term has lost its popularity and now it is seldom used except in derision.

Perhaps the most universally used word in referring to the minister is *Reverend*, at least in the realm of writing. In the south this term is seldom used in addressing a minister to his face, and yet it is consistently used in writing as a title for the minister. This word was originally used as a title of respect and carries the idea of giving reverence to the minister. Its use has now become so common that we seldom think of the original idea. It is now usually employed as a title to distinguish the minister from the laity. Though it is commonly used, no title is more inappropriate than this one.

In recent years, the term, *doctor*, has become a popular title in addressing the preacher. This, of course, is an academic term, referring to one who is learned and qualified to teach in a certain field. And, academically, it is proper to speak of some preachers as doctors since they are specialists in their field. This title was at first reserved for those who had reached certain academic requirements, but in more recent years it has been bestowed upon certain men for outstanding achievements in life; however, this practice has been sadly abused by some religious politicians who have pulled political wires in order to have some college bestow the degree of *Doctor of Divinity*. In fact, the term, *doctor*, has become so common that many times it is used indiscriminately with no thought of any academic recognition. Many a preacher has succumbed to the inordinate desire for self glory which finds some degree of satisfaction in being addressed as *Doctor*. We have no objection to the use of this title when referring to one who has earned the right to such a title, but the promiscuous use of it should be avoided. And for any preacher to demand or encourage the use of this title for himself is an abomination in the sight of both man and God.

We can see that these extra-Biblical titles have some elements of propriety in them, and yet it is also evident that they do not convey the original ideas of the ministry as revealed in the New Testament. These titles reveal the natural course of human nature in drifting, even though unconsciously, from the basic ideas of the New Testament. There would be no advantage in raising vociferous objection to the use of any of the common titles. So far as the title itself is concerned the preacher will be wise simply to recognize any title by which others wish to address him. But because of the connotations involved there is an inward rebellion on the part of the genuine preacher when such titles as these are used. There may be other extra-Biblical titles for the minister, but these will suffice to show the general ideas involved in the use of modern day ministerial terminology. Titles such as father, monsignor, etc., we have not included in this discussion since they are seldom, if ever, employed with reference to evangelical ministers.

NEW TESTAMENT MINISTERIAL TITLES

Let us turn now to the New Testament to study the ministerial titles which are found there. Generally, there are about twelve distinct titles which were used at one time or another with reference to preachers in the New Testament. Some of them are used with reference to all Christians, and yet they seem to have a special connotation when used on occasions to refer to preachers, such as: servant, steward, and brother. Others are used exclusively of preachers, such as: apostle, bishop, minister, elder, and pastor. Then there are still other terms which are used with reference to certain aspects of the ministerial office and give only a partial but accurate view of the ministerial life, such as prophet, evangelist, teacher, and preacher. In some cases two or three Greek words may be translated by the same English word, such as in the case of the term, minister. In all of these terms there is a common general idea expressed. For that reason there will be seen an overlapping of ideas, but each term seems to give a little different emphasis or point of view. Let us study these terms briefly, looking for the implications which give to us deeper insight into the nature of the minister's life and work.

On several occasions Paul refers to preachers as *servants*. There are really six Greek words which are sometimes translated in our English versions by the word, *servant*. Only two of these concern us just here, *doulos* and *diakonos*. The word *doulos*, has reference to a bond slave and emphasizes the submission of the servant to the Lord. These two words are closely related, but the distinction lies in the fact that *diakonos* represents the servant in his activity for the work and *doulos* represents the servant in his relation to his master.[1] *Doulos* is the more humble word and suggests a binding of one to the lordship of another. In the New Testament this word, *doulos*, is not imposed upon others. Paul used this word in describing himself as a minister, but never does he use it as a designation for preachers in general. This also corresponds with what Jesus said to the apostles: "Henceforth I call you not servants (*doulos*) . . . but I have called you friends" (John 15:15). *Diakonos* is more expressive of the true ministerial state and is more commonly used in the New Testament in reference to preachers. It emphasizes more of the voluntary spirit and magnifies the activity involved in the service rendered. Paul calls himself *diakonos* in view of specific service rendered, but *doulos* in his personal relation to Christ. The nature of the minister's task, as such, involves more than slavery, for slavery makes a man the mere will-less organ of the master. This accounts for the fact that Paul omits this word in discussing the minister though he uses it in reference to himself. The word, *diakonos*, does not always have reference to preachers. There are times when it refers to all Christians; then there are times when it refers to deacons. In fact, the English word, *deacon*, is a transliteration of the Greek word, *diakonos*. But there are other occasions when this word unmistakably refers to preachers, as in I Corinthians 3:5; II Corinthians 3:6; and Ephesians 3:7. In all such cases we see the preacher as a ministering servant.

The term, *steward*, gives to us a little different point of view. The Greek word is *oikonomos*, which means to dispense or manage. It is applied to the manager of a household or of household affairs; especially, a steward, manager, or superintendent. While this term is also used in some cases in referring to all Christians, it is especially applied in some cases to preachers. Paul refers to ministers as the stewards of the mysteries of God (I Corinthians 4:1), as those to whom the counsels of God have been committed to be made known to men. With Paul the church is the house (I Timothy 3:15); God the house-ruler or owner; its members the house-inhabiters (Galatians 6:10); and its ministers the house-keepers or overseers. In this we see the large ministry of the minister as an overseer of the work, which entails unusual significance and solemn responsibility.

The term, *brother*, is more commonly and appropriately applied to any Christian and is so applied throughout the New Testament. And yet by popular use in our day it usually has reference to a preacher, though the preacher has no more right to this title than any other Christian. It is true that Ananias addressed Paul as "Brother Saul," but he was looking upon him as a fellow Christian

[1] Trench, R. C., *Synonyms of the New Testament*, p. 32.

rather than a minister. So far as we can tell this term is never used in the New Testament in any particular sense with reference to preachers. We mention it here because in our day many people have come to think of a preacher as "Bro. So and So" and other Christians as "Mr. So and So." This distinction is not made in the New Testament and yet when used of a preacher it does suggest an idea of humility and equality, which is far more appropriate than Reverend, Rector, or Parson.

Among the terms used exclusively of ministers is the term, *apostle*, which is a transliteration of the Greek word, *apostolos*. As we begin to study this word in the New Testament a question presents itself: Was this term limited to the original twelve and Paul or is it a designation of all ministers? We must grant that in some cases the word is used in a very restricted sense, but this does not prove that it is always so used. If we take the word in its etymological sense as a commissioned agent of Jesus Christ, it would be synonymous with our modern term, Christian minister, for our modern interpretation of a Christian minister places him as a commissioned agent of Jesus Christ. It has been suggested that if the sense of *apostolos* be restricted to the twelve, there could not have been false apostles as described in II Corinthians 11:13.[2] We can justifiably say, then, that the minister is an apostle in the larger and wider sense of that term, and as such he is both called and sent of the Lord on a divine mission.

Another thought is suggested by several words which are translated variously as *overseer, master-builder,* or *bishop.* Only once does Paul use the term *architekton* (I Corinthians 3:10), from which we get our word, *architect.* It involves the idea of supervision or general direction for the whole building. As a minister Paul looked upon himself as a supervisor in the work of *building upon* Christ. This same idea is suggested by the more familiar term, *bishop.* The Greek word is *episkopos*, which is used four times by the Apostle Paul, and in each case it has reference to the preacher. It is used once by Peter, but then it refers to the Lord. The word itself carries the idea of an "overseer, a man charged with the duty of seeing that things to be done by others are done rightly, any curator, guardian, or superintendent."[3] There is absolutely no indication or intimation in the New Testament that bishops were ecclesiastical authorities with jurisdiction over a group of churches or ministers. They were overseers of local congregations. Sometimes there were more than one bishop for a church (Philippians 1:1), never one bishop for a group of churches. Ecclesiastical polity which places

---

[2] International Critical Commentary on I Corinthians 12:28.
[3] Thayer's Greek Lexicon on episkopos.

bishops as ecclesiastical overlords is far from the simple pattern of the New Testament. Every pastor is a bishop and, as such, is the general supervisor of every phase of the program of the particular church of which he is pastor.

The English word, *minister*, is very closely related to the word, *servant*. In fact, in some cases the Greek word, diakonos, is translated, *minister*, and in some other cases, *servant*. Perhaps the most common word for minister is *huperetes*. This word carries the idea of an *under rower;* it suggests subordination. Zenophon used this word as the herald who carries a solemn message. In this sense, as a minister to perform certain defined functions for Paul and Barnabas, Mark was their *huperetes*. The *minister*, according to the etymology of this word, is one who carries out an official function, or runs an errand for the purpose of conveying a message. What a vivid picture of the minister's life and work! Our use of the English word, *minister*, usually carries a different connotation from that which is suggested in the original Greek word of the New Testament. This title is seldom used with reference to preachers among the conservative groups of the south and, even when it is used, there is somewhat of a resentment on the part of the preacher. But this is no fault of the title. The title itself is an appropriate one and, if it seems somewhat awkward and out of place, it is only because we are not accustomed to using it. Whether we use this word in addressing or referring to our preachers is of little importance, but the word itself in its New Testament setting gives to us a fresh vision of the ministerial task.

Quite common among first century Christians in referring to ministers was the term, *elder*, or literally, *presbuteros*. This term was not limited to Christians nor did it originate with Christians. Even before the Christian era older men were looked up to as having wisdom and ability of leadership. Practically all leadership fell into the hands of the older men, and naturally leaders in any realm came to be known as elders. It was easy and natural, therefore, for Christians to look upon their church leaders as elders. "In its primary sense it referred to a person of advanced age but because filling a high office carried with it, like old age, the idea of honor and dignity the word came to apply to persons in high official position. It implies the dignity of this office and gravity on the part of the man who fills it."[4] By frequent use of this title there is suggested dignity, gravity, and wisdom which are necessary for the proper execution of the minister's responsibility.

The word, *Pastor*, is a most tender and affectionate word. The

[4] Ray, Jeff D., *The Highest Office*, p. 39.

original word, *poimen*, means shepherd. It is an analogous word
taken from the shepherd life of the first century. Jesus speaks of
Himself as the Good Shepherd (pastor). Only once in the New
Testament is it used with reference to the preacher. In listing the
various types of church leadership Paul mentions the pastor along
with apostles, prophets, evangelists, and teachers (Ephesians 4:11).
The word picture is an impressive one. As the under-shepherd or
pastor, the minister is to supply the needs of his flock. He should
know them, love them, lead them, feed them, and protect them.
Herein is a comprehensive picture of the ministerial function.

Prophet is a title used far more frequently in the Old Testament than in the New, and yet its occurrence in the New Testament
is common. The popular idea is that a prophet is one who fore-
tells future events, but this is not what the word directly implies.
The Greek word, *Prophetes*, literally means to speak forth. The
idea then is that of announcing, making known, or interpreting. In
the course of making known the message of God there would naturally be some foretelling, but this was simply incidental to the
larger responsibility of speaking forth the message of God to man.
It implies the inspiration of God's Spirit for such announcing. In
this sense the preacher is a prophet, sent of God to make known
the message of God to man. Paul lists the prophet among those
who are to lead in the Christian church (I Corinthians 12:28). In
this picture we see the minister as an interpreter of God and of
God's Word to man.

In our day the term, *evangelist*, has been limited to a certain
group of preachers who give their full time to the holding of revival meetings. Such a distinction does not seem to be evident in
the New Testament use of the term. The Greek word is *euangelistes*,
which simply means to bear or bring good news. The story of redemption was to the first century Christians "Good News" and those
who went out telling it were given the title of "bearers of good
news." This word is more inclusive than the term, *preacher*, which
simply means to speak out, for it indicates the message which he is
to speak out. In a word, this title puts emphasis upon the proclamation of the Good News of the Gospel of Christ which is certainly
the primary function of the minister. We agree with Dr. Jeff D. Ray
that "The New Testament evangelist was a man upon whom special
gifts were bestowed as it pleased the Spirit but that the exercise
of these gifts did not imply a distinct office. Evangelism was and
is a glorious gift to be used and not a separate office to be filled."[5]
It might appear from what Paul says in Ephesians 4:11, "And he

[5] *Ibid.*, p. 36.

gave some, apostles; and some, prophets; and some, evangelists; and some, pastors and teachers," that the work of an evangelist was a separate office in the economy of the church. But a thorough study of this passage in the light of its context and of other related passages will reveal that the primary thing is the person, not the office. God's gift to the churches was in the form of men who were known to the people as apostles, prophets, evangelists, etc. Timothy was not an evangelist in the modern day professional sense, and yet Paul urged him to do the work of an evangelist. In our complex, modern-day church life it is necessary that we have certain men giving their full time to the work of evangelism, but in the real sense of the word every preacher is, or ought to be, an evangelist, one who is constantly carrying the Good News of Christ's saving grace to men. No preacher has a monopoly on this. It ought to be the major emphasis of all preachers, though it is a fact that some give more emphasis to it than others.

Another designation for the preacher is *Teacher*. While this term has a much wider range of use, it is used on various occasions with reference to preachers. The preacher is not the only teacher, but he is a teacher, that is, one who conveys truth to another. Jesus is more often called teacher than preacher. It is almost impossible to draw a distinct line between teaching and preaching. We must not put one over against the other. All good preaching must involve an element of the teaching idea. Thus we see the minister in the role of one who helps and guides others in the knowledge and application of truth.

Perhaps the most common term (at least in the south) by which we designate the minister is *preacher*, and yet it is found only four times in the New Testament. This word describes only one aspect of the minister's life and work. It is very limited in its scope. The Greek word is *kerux*, which means one who cries out or proclaims. It has reference to the public proclamation of the Gospel. Indeed, this is a vital and fundamental responsibility of the minister. It is his primary work.

MEANING AND SIGNIFICANCE OF MINISTERIAL ORDINATION

In this study of New Testament ministerial terminology we have seen various aspects and functions of the ministerial office. These ideas we shall seek to develop in orderly arrangement as they apply to modern ministerial life in the following chapters of our study. But while we are thinking of New Testament terminology let us spend a few minutes in a brief study of the New Testament practice of ordination for the minister. There is ample reason to believe that the churches of the New Testament held ordination services for the minister at the beginning of his ministerial life. We do not have any detailed record of the order of this service or the ceremony used. There are several references in the New Testament to such an ordination, but no account of the details of the service or ceremony. The ordination of Paul and Barnabas by the church at Antioch is the nearest thing we have to a record of the order and arrangement of the service. As we study these brief accounts there are three things which impress us with reference to ordination.

First, the ordination service or ceremony was held in the local church and by the local church. There is no intimation of an ordination service conducted by an ecclesiastical organization made up of churches or by an ecclesiastical heirarch. The local church is always the ordaining agent. Second, the ordaining ceremony was a simple one. Evidently, there was nothing elaborate about the service. There was no pomp or ostentation, and there need not be in our modern day ordination service. The best and most impressive ordination service is the simple one. Dr. G. S. Dobbins gives an accurate description when he says, "Ordination is a simple and impressive ceremony by which men called of God to be ministers of Jesus Christ are set apart for a specific work, after examination and on the authorization of a local body, being thus approved to the brotherhood."[6] Third, the ordination ceremony bestowed no new authority upon the one ordained. Again let us quote from Dr. Dobbins: "This act of ordination added nothing to the man's character, it conferred upon him no priestly authority, it gave him no right or privileges superior to other members, it conferred upon him no power beyond that vested in him by the local congregation."[7] There is the idea on the part of some modern day churchmen that ordination entitles the preacher to certain new privileges and authority. But there is no basis for this idea in New Testament practice and teaching. What, then, is the purpose of ordination? It is simply a service in which both preacher and church are impressed and charged with the solemn responsibility of the ministerial office.

In the light of these observations may we mention a few of the elements which are commonly included in an ordination service and which, in keeping with the principles and practices of the New Testament, ought to be included. First, there ought to be an examination of the candidate concerning his conversion experience, call to preach, and conceptions of the fundamental tenets of the faith. This examination is usually made by preachers who are in-

6 *Building Better Churches*, p. 304.
7 *Ibid.*, p. 303.

vited by the local church, composing what we call a presbytery or council. For the benefit of the church and all concerned it seems better to have this examination before the whole church. And yet there are some definite advantages in having a private examination before the presbytery alone. After the examination comes the ordaining prayer and the laying on of hands by the presbytery, a solemn ceremony of dedication. This constitutes the ordination proper, but usually it is profitable and proper to have one or more messages following the prayer, giving emphasis to the ministerial responsibility, which may include the presentation of the Bible, a charge to the preacher, a charge to the church, and an ordination sermon. Many times for the conservation of time these ideas could be incorporated into one message. There is no set order or plan, but in it all there ought to be the idea of seeking to impress upon both preacher and church the solemnity of the responsibilities involved in executing the office of Christian minister. With these fundamental principles of New Testament *ministerialology* in mind we are ready to look at the more practical side of the minister's life as we seek to make application of these principles to modern day conditions of ministerial living.

Part II
The Minister and His Work

5 | A GENERAL VIEW OF THE MINISTER'S WORK

In coming to the more practical side of ministerial life, let us first take a panoramic view of the minister's task. When the minister's work comes into full view, the magnitude of it is staggering. The average layman is not in a position to see and to realize the enormity of the minister's task. His point of view does not permit a full scale picture. Because of this many people think that the preacher has nothing to do but spend about two hours a week in the pulpit. The rest of the time he is free to fish, rest, or play. Such a view of the preacher's life is the result of a failure to understand the nature of the preacher's work. It is tragically distorted, growing out of ignorance and misconception.

The Magnitude of the Ministerial Task

It is our purpose here to look at the picture as a whole. As we look at it we see many sides and many angles. The closer we get to it and the more we put ourselves into it the more challenging and enormous it becomes. It is no child's play. It challenges every ounce of manhood, and its demands upon the minister are stupendous. We agree with the observation of Dr. Charles Jefferson that "a Minister of the Gospel is expected to do a wider variety of things than any other man in the community. The division of labor has been carried farther in every other profession than in the ministry. His work is multiform."[1] Even in our large, super-organized churches with their plurality of paid workers, the scope of the pastor's work is narrowed very little if any. He must still give some thought to every phase of the work. "The minister is chosen head of the corporation. He is expected to be the shepherd of souls, the arbiter in disputes, the proposer of plans, the general superintendent of the various organizations, the promoter of spiritual life amongst the members, the master of assemblies."[2] The complexity and complications of modern day life only add to the scope of the minister's work. The preacher must be a specialist in a number of different

[1] *The Minister As Prophet*, p. 1.
[2] DeBlois, A. K., *Some Problems of the Modern Minister*, p. 145.

47

things. And this is the dilemma which the modern preacher faces. No man can be a specialist in everything, and yet this is what the churches demand. Dr. G. S. Dobbins points out the following interesting facts:

He must not only be a leader but also a leader of leaders. He must not only be a teacher but also a teacher of teachers. He must not only preach inspiring and helpful sermons, he must also build an organization through which the truths he preaches may be channeled into human life. He must not only conserve his own time and strength, he must also conserve the time and energies of his people who are hard pressed with manifold duties. He must be not only a student of books, but also a student of human nature and conduct. He must be able to read the signs of the times and interpret God in Christ to his disturbed and distressed generation. He must visit incessantly, keeping in vital contact with the problems of real people; yet he must somehow keep himself unspotted from the world. He must not become so consumed with serving tables that he neglects prayer and the ministry of the Word.[3]

How one man can do all of this is the problem of the modern day minister. It is the purpose of these general and preliminary observations to impress upon the reader at the outset the enormous responsibility and the wide range of duties involved in the ministerial task.

THE GENERAL DIVISIONS OF THE MINISTERIAL TASK

In order to arrive at a clearer and more comprehensive picture of the minister's work, let us classify the various aspects and divisions of ministerial labor. There are many ways to classify the various types of ministerial work, and many different arrangements have been made. It is possible, as some have done,[4] to make only two general divisions in the minister's task: his work as preacher and his work as pastor. Such a division covers the field, but the work of pastor is so inclusive that a breakdown of this phase of the work is necessary for a proper understanding of the preacher's work. Dr. Washington Gladden has broken down the minister's work so as to include seven phases or aspects: Church polity; Theory of Worship (Liturgics); Theory of preaching (Homiletics); Theory of teaching the young (Catechetics); Theory of the Care of Souls (Poimenics); Theory of pastoral training(Padagogics); Theory of missions (Halieutics).[5] All of these items are included in the minister's labor, and yet in his classification there seems to be some over-

3 *Building Better Churches*, p. 16.
4 DeBlois, A. K., *Some Problems of the Modern Minister*, p. 4; Brooks, Phillips, *Lectures on Preaching*, p. 77; Sockman, R. W., *The Highway of God*, p. 113.
5 *The Christian Pastor and the Working Church*, p. 1.

lapping and some ambiguousness in the terms used. Dr. G. S. Dobbins seems to have a clearer arrangement of the elements involved in the ministerial task. His breakdown is as follows: The Ministry of Prayer and Worship; the Ministry of Preaching and Teaching; the Ministry of Care and Comfort; the Ministry of Evangelism and Missions; the Ministry of Organization and Administration; the Ministry of Stewardship and Finance; the Ministry of Fellowship and Service; the Ministry of Publicity and Promotion; the Ministry of Public Relations; and the Ministry of Personal Counseling.[6] All ten of the particulars mentioned in this classification are apropos, but it seems that the same territory could be covered under fewer heads.

There are many other ways to classify the field of ministerial labor all of which have some merit. But for our purpose here and from our point of view we are looking at the minister's task as a four fold one. We realize that this classification is very general. It will be broken down still further in the following chapters, but for our panoramic view of the work this general classification will give to us an over-all picture. The four aspects of the minister's work which we have in mind are as follows: Preaching, Presiding, Organizing, and Personal Counseling. Practically all of the minister's duties could be classified under one of these four heads; however, a further clarification of these terms is necessary.

The foremost and primary task of the minister is that of preaching. Our next chapter will be given to a discussion of the primacy of preaching. Suffice it to say here that a major division in ministerial activity is preaching. In this general classification we have in mind any public proclamation of the Gospel, which would also include Bible teaching, and all the preparation necessary for such. We do not attempt to draw a distinct line of demarcation between preaching and teaching. The two are very closely related and often one involves the other. The general idea is simply this: that the minister is charged with the responsibility of publicly proclaiming through teaching and preaching the Gospel of God's grace. This constitutes a major interest in true ministerial conduct.

The term, *presiding*, covers a wide field of activity. We have reference to all forms of leadership in public meetings, which would include conducting public worship; moderating conferences; performing ceremonies, such as baptism and the Lord's Supper; conducting funerals; and officiating at weddings, etc. Such activities as these call for a considerable portion of the minister's time, energy,

[6] Dobbins, G. S., *Building Better Churches.* pp. 18-27.

and thought. A consideration of these various activities will come up for a more detailed discussion in following chapters.

The work of organizing or administering is making ever increasing demands on the modern day minister. The modern day church has become a great business enterprise. The pastor has become the executive of this institution, and as such he is charged with the responsibility of directing the vast and varying activities of the organization. The demands of the organization are making such inroads into the time and energy of the preacher that there is grave danger of losing the "preaching" emphasis which must always characterize the Christian ministry, else our churches are doomed. Nevertheless, the organizational work to which the pastor must give at least some attention, must be done and as the leader or overseer, the pastor must take a vital interest in every phase of the organization. There is the financial side of the organization which makes a drain on the pastor's energy. There are also the teaching and training agencies of the church to which he must give considerable time. Besides this there is the general church organization, including its policies and polity, not to mention the missionary and benevolent movements and denominational responsibilities. These, too, will be given further consideration in a later chapter.

A fourth main division and vital phase of the minister's task is that of personal counseling. The minister's work is by no means limited to the public meeting. Much of the effectiveness of his ministry is based upon his dealings with the individuals. Much of his time, therefore, must and should be spent in making personal contacts with individuals. This may take the form of pastoral visitation in the home, incidental contacts on the street, or personal conference in the study. The term *pastor*, as we have seen in a previous chapter, suggests the idea of personal guidance and personal interest. The office of pastor, therefore, cannot be properly fulfilled without personal contact with the people. For this reason it is all but impossible for any man to serve effective as *pastor* of a church of 2,000 or more people. Dr. Ray was about right in saying that "a man can preach to a thousand people, but no man can be pastor of a thousand people."[7] The successful pastor will spend many hours in personal conference and counsel. This vital and all-important phase of the minister's work will also be studied in a later chapter.

ATTITUDES TOWARD THE MINISTERIAL TASK

Having seen something of the general nature of the minister's work, let us in closing this chapter give some consideration to the

[7] Ray, Jeff D., *The Highest Office*, p. 60.

attitude of both people and preacher toward the minister as related to his work. While it is true that the average layman has little occasion to know and understand the responsibilities of the preacher, it would greatly enhance the effectiveness of the preacher's work if the laity could be led to a better understanding of the minister and his work. Just as the preacher can do a more effective work when he knows and understands the problems of his people, so also can the people do a more effective work in the church when they know something of the problems and responsibilities of the preacher. In ministerial conferences and meetings where the congregation is wholly ministerial, the problems and work of the ministry are often discussed with great profit. But seldom, if ever, do we discuss from the pulpit to the laity the nature and work of the ministry. And because this is true many of the good people of our churches have accumulated some very strange and peculiar conceptions of the minister's life and work. It would be amusing and yet almost exasperating if we had a written account of the conceptions held by the average lay-member of the Christian minister. An occasional sermon on the nature and work of the ministry as revealed in the New Testament will give this better understanding and will greatly increase the efficiency of the church. Of course, this should never be done with the idea of inspiring pity or commiseration on the part of the laity for the minister. The genuine preacher doesn't need pity, and he doesn't want it. He simply wants an understanding which will be conducive to the highest type of co-operation and efficiency. There are a few lazy preachers who shirk duty and do little or nothing, just as there are a few like this in every profession. There are a few others (very few) who go to the other extreme and wear themselves out doing more than they ought to do. The average preacher does not work any harder than the average man in business, but he does work as hard as any other average man and his responsibilities are just as strenuous, if not more so. The layman needs to know and recognize this if the preacher is to do his best.

Whether or not the layman ever recognizes the tremendous responsibilities in the minister's task, it is absolutely imperative that the minister himself comprehend the seriousness and significance of his task. Since the preacher does not have to punch a time clock, there is the temptation to become careless and indifferent to the destiny-determining responsibilities which are his. But if he succumbs to this temptation, the effectiveness and success of his ministry will be jeopardized. Indolence is deplorable anywhere, but few things are less excusable than lethargy and torpidity on the part of

a preacher. The first and basic need for any preacher is a vision
of the magnitude and far-reaching responsibility of his call to the
ministry. In the light of this vision let him solemnly dedicate himself to the faithful, enthusiastic, and diligent execution of this ministerial responsibility. The work to which God has called us demands
every ounce of our energy and ability, and only as we are willing
to give ourselves completely to it can we expect the fruits which
God has promised to those who are "faithful unto death."

6 | THE PLACE OF PREACHING

In the foregoing chapter we tried to set out the major divisions or aspects of the ministerial task, seeking to give a panoramic view of the whole. In the remaining chapters of this division of our study we shall break down these major divisions and look at the particular types of work involved in the minister's task. Since the matter of preaching is so tremendously important and involved we are giving one whole division to a study of the various aspects of preaching. In this chapter, however, it is our purpose to emphasize its place and importance in the minister's life and work. In part III we will take up other phases of the preaching ministry.

A Definition of Preaching

As we observed in a previous chapter, the verb, *preach*, literally means to cry out or proclaim aloud. It is a very general term and does not specify or imply what shall be proclaimed. However, from its use in the New Testament we know that it has reference to the public proclamation of the Gospel of Christ. The word, *evangelize*, is more specific. It carries the idea of publishing or reporting good news. This, perhaps, is a more common New Testament word for what we usually mean by *preaching*. But since *preaching* is the more common word for it in our day, we will use this term throughout our discussion. Immediately there appear many adumbrations. If preaching is the public proclamation of the Gospel, consideration must be given to the person proclaiming, the people hearing, the truth proclaimed, and the method of presentation. Phillips Brooks in his masterful "Lectures on Preaching" appropriately points out that there are fundamentally two elements in preaching: truth and personality. He builds his whole series of lectures around these two ideas. Even these two fundamental ideas involve many other things. The scope is extremely wide and we will not attempt to go into it here. We simply want to see something of the nature and general scope of this phase of the minister's task. There can be no effective preaching without a preacher, without a grasp of the truth to be preached, without an audience to hear, or without an attractive method of presentation. We agree with Dr. Charles Jefferson, who said that

> . . . the work of preaching is the most difficult of all the things which a minister is called to do. Indeed, it is the most difficult task to which any mortal can set himself. It is at once the most strenuous and the most exacting of all forms of labor. It requires a fuller combination of faculties and a finer balance of powers than are required in any other department of human effort.[1]

THE PRIMACY OF PREACHING

Having seen something of the general nature of preaching, let us hasten to come to the point for which this chapter is primarily written: that preaching is, or should be, the first and major concern of every minister. It is for the purpose of preaching primarily that the minister is called and he must never lose sight of the primacy of this phase of his labor. He may do other things, and indeed he must, but when he loses sight of preaching as the major function of his ministry he loses the effectiveness of his ministry. God calls men to preach and He expects those who are called to give their major emphasis to the proclamation of the Gospel. This is God's plan and nothing will ever take the place of it. Other things may seem to us to be more attractive, but God has seen fit to carry on the program of His kingdom through the preaching of His Word by men whom He has called for such work. Paul, the inspired apostle, made this clear when he said, "For after that in the wisdom of God the world by wisdom knew not God, it pleased God by the foolishness of preaching to save them that believe" (I Corinthians 1:21). It is not even remotely suggested in the Word of God that the minister or any minister is called to give his life to anything except that which magnifies the pulpit. To be sure, there are other duties to be performed, but every minister is called to make preaching the main issue of his life. There can be no question about this in the light of New Testament practice and teaching, and this must always be our guide in all ministerial conduct.

Not only does the New Testament emphasize the primacy of preaching, but history itself reveals and proves the necessity of the centrality of preaching. When preachers degenerated into priests, then came the dark ages. The moral and spiritual degradation of the dark ages, from about 300 to 1300 A.D., no student of history can ignore. It was during this period that Roman superstition and supremacy came into being. The moral and ecclesiastical corruptions

---

[1] *The Minister As Prophet*, p. 6.

of this period are a disgrace and shame upon civilization. But these conditions are not surprising when we consider that few, if any, preachers arose during this period to lift their voices publicly in proclamation of the Gospel of the Son of God. Preachers became priests and ecclesiastical heirarchs. The churches of Christ always suffer when preaching is relegated to a back seat or pushed behind a curtain. It was not until a great preacher began to raise his voice in the face of Roman opposition and persecution that the people were revived and the ignominy of spiritual and moral decadence was lifted. This preacher was Martin Luther. But he was not alone. Even before he raised his voice, others, less heralded, were paving the way through the public proclamation of the Gospel in spite of persecution. And still others joined with Luther in preaching the Gospel of justification by faith, such as Calvin, Zwingli, and Knox. Every great revival in history has been accompanied by great preaching. The great English revival of the seventeenth century was born in the blaze of the preaching of Baxter, Bunyan, and John Livingston. The Great Awakening (1725-1750) which shook two continents toward God was brought about by the dynamic preaching of men like the Wesleys, Jonathan Edwards, and George Whitefield. Perhaps the greatest revival of religion ever experienced in America was that of the early part of the nineteenth century. In this revival preaching of the Gospel was prominent everywhere. Never has America seen such a crusade of preaching. Preaching was the order of the day; it was not the case of two or three outstanding pulpiteers. Preachers were everywhere. They were too numerous to mention, but the list would include such men as Backus, Nettleton, Lyman Beecher, Chas. G. Finney, Kirk, Baker, Asbury, Peter Cartwright, Otterbein, Albright, Knapp, and Swan. In every generation the spiritual and moral health of the people has been in proportion to the prominence of Gospel preaching. When Gospel preaching is predominant, then spiritual and moral standards are raised. When preaching is superseded with other things, spiritual decadence always results. Every era of history is an attestation of this fact. And this fact in history gives credence to the New Testament emphasis upon preaching. The preaching may be ever so flaccid in form, but it has been and is the most vital human factor in the onward movements of the kingdom of God on earth.

PRESENT DAY TRENDS IN PREACHING

The gravest danger facing Christianity today is the danger of pushing the pulpit to the side and letting other things take precedence in our religious activities. There are perilous propensities in this direction. There is some indication that Christianity is on the wane in its influence and impact upon the world and the movements of the world. Many attempts have been made at an explanation of this, but it is our firm conviction that this condition exists because of the decadence of the pulpit. Preaching has become a minor "side line" for too many ministers. Many things are being substituted for the pulpit. The secret of the marvelous growth of some evangelical groups has been the centrality of the pulpit. But now there are tremendous influences being brought to bear upon our modern day church life which tend to move the pulpit from the center of church life and replace it with educational programs and sacramental ceremonies. The minister's study has been transformed into an executive office, and this is regrettable.

We are not suggesting that the minister must never do anything but preach. Of course, he must do other things and these things will come up for consideration in other chapters, but we are saying that the effective minister must always major on preaching.

> The preacher is called to preach. He may do many other things, but none of them will take the place of preaching. The minister is done for when he begins to take lightly his responsibility as a preacher, slighting his sermon preparation and substituting wordy extemporizing for discourses that should have cost him sweat of brain. Beset by multitudinous claims upon his time, and finding it easier to be a busy church manager than a prophet of God, the minister is in constant danger of failing at this high point of ministry — preaching.[2]

Go where you will and find the successful church — the church that is reaching the people, enriching the lives of the people, and making a contribution to the formal and spiritual welfare of the whole community — and you will find a church developed around a great pulpit ministry. People will come and people will be blessed where the preaching of the Gospel is magnified. We agree with Dr. W. B. Riley that "It is not the multiplication of priests, magnificence of rituals, attractions of music, semi-political or professedly scientific disquisitions that call men and women in crowds! It is, as always, by great preaching, and there is no indication of an approaching change."[3] Nothing can ever take the place of preaching and there is no power on earth equal to the power of a God-inspired pulpit.

The problem of a declining emphasis upon the pulpit is made all the more serious by the fact that our young preachers are getting less help in our schools in the art of preaching. While we still have

[2] Dobbins, G. S., *Building Better Churches*, p. 19.
[3] *The Preacher and His Preaching*, p. 12.

courses in most of our Seminaries on Homiletics, the major emphasis seems to be placed upon administration. It is our fear that we are putting more emphasis upon training organizers and administrators than we are upon training preachers for preaching. Fifty-five years ago Dr. Charles Jefferson made this observation: "Even in our Seminaries, which are in theory schools in which men are trained to preach, the multiplication of new and fascinating studies has had a tendency to throw homiletics into the shade."[4] If we would have great preachers, we must put a greater emphasis upon the art of preaching in our training schools.

SOME SIDE-TRACKS IN PREACHING

The young preacher who goes out to make preaching the major concern of his ministry will find himself face to face with many cross currents and counter influences. There is not much in our modern day church life to encourage and inspire the minister to preach. On the contrary, there are many influences which, if followed, will lead the preacher away from the pulpit into other lines of endeavor, most of which are good but none of which have the right to take precedence over the pulpit ministry. There are at least four major influences which tend to side-track the preacher from his preaching. One of these is the growing sacramental proclivities of modern religious activity. More and more, though it may be unconsciously, we are coming to a sacramental view of religion. There are ample evidences of this influence of Romanism in our evangelical churches. With such a view there comes the feeling on the part of the minister that he is primarily an administrator of rites. Again may we quote from Dr. Jefferson, who said, "The Prophet has always had a tendency to degenerate into the priest. The man who speaks for God is always prone to slip down into the man who performs ceremonies for God."[5]

Another influence leading the preacher away from the pulpit is the growing demand of our modern day church organizations. Today the preacher finds himself the executive of a vast and complicated organization. The requirements for administrative and organizational ability were never more exacting upon the preacher than now. If he is not extremely careful, the preacher will find himself utilizing all of his time and energy on the administration of the organization and leaving little or none for the major responsibility — preaching. This, perhaps, is the strongest temptation of the present-day preacher.

4 *The Minister As Prophet,* p. 10.
5 *Ibid.,* p. 14.

The educational program of the modern day church is another
thing that calls the preacher away from his pulpit ministry. A program of Christian education is necessary in the well-rounded church
life. We are not suggesting that it be left out. And the preacher
must give a reasonable proportion of his attention to this phase of
the work. But, here again, the preacher is tempted to give all of his
time to an educational program to the neglect of his pulpit ministry.
Let the preacher remember that the pulpit itself ought to be
a center and source of Christian education. Good preaching involves teaching. The Church program of Christian education ought
to be a supplement to the teaching ministry of the pulpit. But let
us also remember that an educational program as such can never
take the place of preaching in the pulpit. It is reported that many
churches are now showing pictures for the Sunday evening worship
services. No matter how good and wholesome and religious the
picture, it can never take the place in God's plan of the public proclamation of the Gospel through the voice of the preacher. Pictures can
be used profitably in various group meetings, but for the regular
church services the pulpit must be pre-eminent. Christianity will
suffer if and when we replace the pulpit with the screen.

Moral reform activities often tempt the preacher to turn aside
from the pulpit. Lest some one misunderstand, may we hasten to
say that the preacher must have a definite interest in moral reform
for his community and his nation. But whenever the preacher neglects the pulpit ministry to give his major attention to the working
out of moral reforms he is departing from his God-given calling.
I believe that it was Dr. W. T. Conner who said that a preacher
is the world's greatest reformer until he degenerates into a reformer.
The greatest contribution any preacher can make to the moral
reformation of any community is through the preaching of the Gospel of the crucified and risen Christ. All of these things we have
mentioned make strong bids for the preacher's time, energy, and
talent, but happy is the preacher who lets nothing keep him from
giving first place in his ministry to the preaching of the Gospel.
And blessed are the people whose pastor makes the pulpit his throne.
Give us more preachers who will give themselves to the preaching
of Christ crucified and we will have a better world.

THE PURPOSE OF PREACHING

In order to avoid any misunderstanding, we must take a moment in closing this chapter to point out the fact that preaching
is not an end within itself. When we say that preaching must be
the major emphasis in ministerial labor, we are not saying that this

is the end. If preaching is the end, then we are of all men most miserable. It is only a means to an end, but it is the means which God has chosen through which to bring men to redemption and life in Christ. All genuine preaching must have one purpose, to lead men to the living Christ and through Him to a life of usefulness and service in this life, in that which is to come. There is the danger that the preacher may make his preaching the end instead of the means to an end. Through all of his preparation and proclamation the preacher must have in mind the moving of men toward God. In order to do this they must be taught, their emotions must be stirred, and their wills must be moved. As preachers let us magnify preaching, but in our preaching let us magnify the God-ordained purpose in preaching — the winning of souls to Christ and the consequent transforming of life. The preacher who loses sight of this will become an impotent and ineffective preacher though he be a master orator.

7 | CONDUCTING THE PUBLIC MEETING

The Nature of the Responsibility

As we noted in a previous chapter, one general phase of the minister's work is that of presiding, which includes conducting the worship service, moderating the business session, administering baptism and the Lord's Supper, officiating at weddings, and conducting funerals. In this particular chapter we will consider the minister's responsibility in conducting or presiding over the various public meetings, such as the worship service, the prayer service, and the church conference or business meeting. Usually little thought is given to the conduct of these meetings, but this is to our shame. The minister who does his work well must give considerable attention to, and make adequate plans for, the conduct of these public meetings. Ordinarily the pastor presides at all of these meetings we have mentioned. The responsibility, therefore, for the conduct of the meeting lies upon his shoulders. The minister who gives no thought to, or makes no plans for, these meetings will find himself embarrassed on many occasions and will be robbing the people of the blessings and benefits which they ought to receive from such meetings.

The Worship Service

Let us consider the worship service. In his concern for the sermon and its delivery many times the minister overlooks the fact that he is responsible for the conduct of the whole worship service. This does not mean that he must do everything that is done. It simply means that he must give general direction to the plan and order of the service and preside over the service. Since many good books have been written on worship activities and suggestions for worship services, it is not our purpose here to discuss the elements which go into worship programs. These will vary and ought to vary with times, conditions, and seasons. We simply want to make some general observations on the conduct of the worship service and the responsibility of the minister in it. And our first observation is that the minister does have a responsibility in the conduct of the worship service. Too many preachers leave the conduct of the service to chance or to someone else. If the preacher is responsible for the sermon delivered, he is also responsible for the whole worship service which ought to be a unit, every phase of which ought to be correlated and co-ordinated. This cannot be done unless the minister gives general direction to the whole service.

Our second observation is that the worship service ought to be conducted in such a manner that it will create a spirit of worship and be an aid and inspiration to worship. There are two extreme tendencies seeking expression in the worship services of our day. Both of these should be avoided. One is the tendency toward extreme formalism and ritualism. It is possible to make the worship service so stiff and formal that it becomes an empty, meaningless, and spiritless form. There can be genuine worship without ritualism; in fact, true worship cannot find expression in extreme liturgical formality. The other extreme tendency in worship is that which makes the worship service a disorganized confusion of tongues. Order and decency is conducive to worship. Some worship services are little short of chaotic. Such services do not contribute to worship; they take from it. In between these two extremes is the happy medium which we ought to seek in our worship services. And it is the preacher's duty to see that such a service is maintained, enough plan and order to create reverence and enough freedom to make it warm and spirit filled. The effectiveness of the whole worship service is determined largely by the attitude of the minister and his work in planning for and presiding over this service.

A vital point in the proper conduct of the worship service is the minster's relation to those who help in the leadership of the service. Music, of course, is a vital part of the worship service. The minister is not expected to have charge of the music, but he is expected to take the initiative in securing the right kind of music leaders. Then it is also his responsibility to co-operate with the music leader in the conduct of the service. Many times serious difficulties arise at this point. The whole program should be worked out under the supervision of the pastor with the co-operation of the music leader. The minister should allow a great deal of liberty to the music director. At the same time the music director should look to the pastor for general direction in working the whole service into a unit. This cannot be done without full co-operation. Here again there is a happy medium: he must not dictate every detail; neither must he be indifferent to the musical phase of the worship program. All of this requires a spirit of love, intimacy, understanding, and mutual confidence between the minister and those who help him in the leadership of the worship service.

THE PRAYER MEETING

Conducting the prayer service is another phase of the minister's work. The prayer meeting is the service usually held on Wednesday evenings. Many churches have disbanded the mid-week service. This is regrettable. However, most of the conservative and evangelical churches of the south still maintain the mid-week service. This mid-week service has been and continues to be a vital factor in the life of the progressive church. Long may it live and thrive! Just how this service should be carried on for the utmost good of the people is a serious problem for the minister, since he is responsible for the conduct of this service. Originally this mid-week service was a prayer meeting, and thus it has come to be known as the prayer service of the church. In recent years in many churches the conduct of this service has made this title for the service a misnomer. This does not mean that it is all bad. There are many things that can be done in this service which would serve to edify the church. But just how this service should be conducted constitutes a major problem for the pastor.

We do not have any sure-fire program to suggest, but we would like to make a few general suggestions in regard to the pastor's leadership in this service. Let us first suggest that this service should not be minimized by the pastor or pushed off into a forgotten corner in his plans and work. This service can be a dynamic service and a very useful asset in the work of the church. Since the attendance is usually small, too many preachers think of it as being insignificant and give little attention to its program and conduct. Perhaps this is one reason for the unusually poor attendance at the prayer meeting service. If the prayer service is to be made a dynamic force and influence in the life of the church, it must be given a prominent place in the plans and preparations of the pastor. As pastors, we need to see the potential value of the mid-week service and seek deliberately to realize these potential values. Perhaps the greatest problem with the prayer-meeting is the indifference of the minister as well as the people. Let the minister put more time and thought into the prayer service, and he will find that the people will give more attention to it.

Another suggestion for the pastor in regard to the prayer service is in the form of a plea for variety. Too many times the prayer service becomes monotonous and therefore loses the interest of the people. We do not have any concrete program to offer, but we do know that a variation will increase the effectiveness of this service. It is not necessary that every minute of the service be given to public prayer, but certainly some time should be given to prayer at this service. Even in the seasons of prayer there can be a variety. One time there can be voluntary prayers; at another time certain ones could be designated for prayer. Then there can be variety in bodily position, sometimes standing, sometimes kneeling, sometimes sitting. There are times when definite objects can be presented for prayer. Appropriate Scriptures before each prayer will sometimes add inspiration, or a prayer chorus at the close of a season of prayer. There are many other ways of breaking the monotony.

Variety may also be realized in the type of service held. There are times when the service ought to be given wholly to prayer, but there are other times when other things can be done with great profit to the people. A series of mid-week Bible studies often proves helpful and inspiring. This idea has become very popular in some churches, and usually attendance has increased in such cases. No time is wasted in the teaching and study of God's Word. This service offers the pastor a wonderful opportunity to teach the Bible to his people. An occasional testimonial service will prove a blessing and joy to the people. Such a service encourages informality which ought to be maintained in all of the mid-week services in order to realize the greatest good from them. A devotional message or a sermon is also good for a change. Some have made the mid-week service another preaching service and this is not amiss. We have known of souls being saved on Wednesday evening, and why not? What we are trying to say is that the preacher who is "on his toes," giving sufficient attention to the service and employing the principle of diversity, will find the mid-week service an effective means of promoting every aspect of the church program and a wholesome influence upon the people, inspiring them to greater spiritual achievements.

THE BUSINESS MEETING

A third phase of the *public meeting* ministry of the pastor is his responsibility as moderator at the business meeting of the church. This sometimes is a most trying experience for the minister. There are occasions when this will demand every ounce of wisdom and grace that he can command. We are thinking, of course, in terms of the congregational type of church government. Many times embarrassing situations can be avoided by the discerning and wise moderator. If the business affairs of the church are to be properly executed in the business meeting much depends upon the ability and wisdom of the moderator. We shall not attempt to solve all the problems which come before a church in conference, but we do dare to offer some practical suggestions to the pastor for guidance in moderating the business sessions of the church.

First, let the pastor acquaint himself with the fundamental principles of parliamentary law. There is no excuse for ignorance at this point. A few hours of study in a standard book of parliamentary law, such as Kerfoot's, Trow's, Roberts, or McConnell's, will give to the pastor the necessary information for the proper conduct of the business meeting. Our Seminaries ought to require a course of study in parliamentary law for every minister, and some of them do. No pastor can afford to be without this information. It will save him many occasions of embarrassment and will save the church many hours of grief.

Second, the moderator should not allow the conference to become dull and dragging. A business session can become very dry and dull, but a wise moderator can keep things moving so as to maintain interest and enthusiasm. A change in method of voting may often give a little spice which will remove some of the dullness. Business meetings can be and should be made attractive, depending upon the alertness of the moderator. Happy is the pastor who can conduct the business session of the church so as to maintain the interest of all. It can be done if the pastor will give some thought and time to it.

Third, let the moderator always be fair and respectful. Many preachers are tempted to let their own prejudices find expression in the business meeting. But the pastor who expects to live and do well with his people, must learn to be absolutely fair and considerate to all in the business meeting of the church. The attitude of the moderator will go a long way toward keeping peace and harmony among his people in the heat of some controversial issue. Many church scissures could have been avoided by the application of wisdom and discretion on the part of the moderator. Efficient moderating is an art within itself and the successful minister must cultivate this art along with the other necessary abilities for effective ministerial living.

Besides the performing of ceremonies, there are other occasional public meetings over which the minister must preside, but these we have mentioned are the regular and oft repeated public meetings in which the minister acts as moderator and director. The performing of ceremonies will come up for separate consideration in the following chapters.

8 | THE ADMINISTRATION OF BAPTISM

Administering the ordinance of baptism is a happy responsibility for the minister. Most preachers take great delight in this privilege and feel a sense of peculiar and special interest in the lives of those whom they have baptized. It is with great delight and joy that the minister says, "I baptized that man!" Even though it is a happy privilege, it is also a solemn and significant responsibility. Too little consideration has been given to the proper observance of this ordinance by the minister.

THE MEANING AND PURPOSE OF BAPTISM

While we are not concerned in this particular study with the theological implications of the question of baptism, we cannot arrive at any proper understanding of the administration of baptism apart from a consideration of the theological implications. The two are bound up together. We will not go into detail, but we do want to set out briefly the meaning and purpose of baptism in order that we may be able to administer it more impressively. Baptism is a symbolic picture and this is all the more reason for its proper administration. The picture must be made as impressive as possible. It is not a sacrament but a symbol, and this makes a difference in the method of administration and observance.

There are two things symbolized in the picture of baptism. It is a symbol, first of all, of the death, burial, and resurrection of Jesus, the foundation fact of the Christian religion. In baptism, therefore, our minds are refreshed with these cardinal tenets of our faith. Baptism is also a picture of the death and burial of the sinner to his sins and of his resurrection to a new life in Christ. How beautiful and impressive is this picture! This is the believer's testimony to the church and to the world. What clearer testimony could he give? For this reason and others the ordinance of baptism should never be administered privately. What good is a picture if no one is present to see the picture? Furthermore, there is no other way to portray this picture than by immersion. Many people seem to think that baptism is a meaningless initiation. If so, then the method or mode would be of little consequence. But these people have overlooked the scriptural significance of this ordinance. We will not take the space here to give scriptural references in proof of what we have said, but there are many.

In all his preparation and throughout the administration, the minister should keep ever in his mind the idea of seeking to portray the symbolic picture we have just described. If this is done, great care and concern must be exercised. But this is not always true. The way some preachers baptize is a disgrace to the sacred significance of the ordinance. This condition is true mainly because too many preachers have never taken the time to learn how to baptize. This carelessness is encouraged by the fact that, so far as this author knows, until recently little or no consideration has been given in our schools and seminaries to the training of young preachers in the art of baptizing. In my own case, through ten years of college and seminary no instruction was ever given on the proper methods of administering baptism. What I learned about it was only that which I could observe in the few baptisms I was privileged to witness. Fortunately, my first pastor, S. H. Frazier, was an expert in the art of administering baptism. Through the years I have sought to follow his example as nearly as I could, realizing that there is room for much improvement yet. It seems to me that there is a great need for more specific training in our schools in this particular field of the administration of the ordinances. A demonstration class period for young ministerial students would prove of inestimable value in the proper observance of baptism.

SOME ABUSES IN THE ADMINISTRATION OF BAPTISM

Because of this lack of training and carelessness on the part of the minister, the beautiful ordinance of baptism has often been sadly abused. We have seen preachers slap people into the water, sloshing the water over the sides of the baptistry. There is no excuse for this and it detracts noticeably from the beauty and solemnity of the picture. Other preachers have been known to be so awkward that they cause the candidate to strangle or at least excite a cough. This certainly does not help to make the service what it ought to be. Other unbecoming methods have been used, such as causing the candidate to cling to the administrator. It is really not surprising that some people look with disdain upon immersion as a form of baptism if all they have seen is an unholy splashing of the water by some careless preacher. These things ought not so to be.

SOME SUGGESTIONS FOR THE ADMINISTRATION OF BAPTISM

Let us turn now to the positive side and consider some helpful suggestions in the proper administration of baptism. By all means, the pastor should have a personal conference with the candidate before the baptismal service. If there are several candidates, one conference will do for all. Many blunders can be avoided by a proper instruction of the candidate. Some pastors have this instruction period just prior to the ceremony in the entrance of the baptistry as the candidates approach.[1] This is far better than no instruction at all, but we feel that a more lengthy conference in the quiet of the pastor's study is much better and far more effective. But whether it is in the pastor's study or behind the scene in the baptistry, some conference of instruction must be held for the proper administration of baptism. It has always been my custom to have such a conference with the candidates before the service; but on one occasion the candidate was late in arriving for the service and the conference was omitted. Since she had been immersed in a church of another faith, I felt that she knew something about the method of immersion. At any rate, much to my embarrassment and hers, before I could lay her back into the water she had taken the initiative to go into the water face forward. This is an extreme case of what can happen when there is no understanding between the minister and the candidate. It may not always be this bad, but much harm can be done to the significance of the ceremony where there is not perfect understanding. The pastor must not take the knowledge of his candidate for granted.

The question now arises as to what the pastor should do in this instruction conference. First of all, the significance of baptism ought to be made clear. Even though a person is genuinely saved, he may not have the proper understanding of the meaning and significance of baptism. The ordinance cannot be properly observed unless both the administrator and the candidate understand fully the purpose and significance of it. A brief explanation will suffice to make clear this understanding. This having been done, the minister is ready to give detailed instructions, which should include such items as locality of the dressing rooms, information concerning robes or appropriate dress, entrance into the baptistry, and conduct in the baptistry. The candidate should be told where to stand in the baptistry, how he should hold his hands, and other matters relating to body movements and breathing. This information may vary with the particular style or method of the administrator.

[1] Riley, W. B., *Pastoral Problems*, pp. 73, 74.

There is no set and authoritative method when it comes to the details of the ceremony. These will vary with different preachers. Each will have his own peculiar method, but as a basis of study in the art of impressive baptizing may we offer several suggestions which have proved helpful to us in the administration of baptism. First, the minister urges the candidate to move slowly and easily without undue excitement and emotion. Then, according to previous instruction the candidate stands with his left shoulder to the congregation and about one foot to the minister's right. (This position will be reversed if the minister uses his right hand in letting the candidate down into the water.) If the candidate is unusually tall he should be placed two or three feet to the right of the minister so that his head will not be too far to the left when he is let down into the water. Some preachers have found it very helpful to have a small iron bar installed in the bottom of the baptistry, leaving three or four inches between the iron arm and the floor of the baptistry. The bar may be covered with cloth or something else which will eliminate any roughness. The candidate is instructed to stand with his toes under this iron arm. This prevents the feet from coming to the top of the water as they some times have a tendency to do. One preacher uses a concrete block with an opening on one side and a piece of quarter-round wood on the roof of the opening. The candidate stands with his toes in this opening.

The candidate's arms are folded in front of him and his eyes closed. Before the first candidate is baptized a few remarks are made to the congregation concerning the significance of the ordinance. Then with left hand lifted and eyes closed he pronounces the baptismal formula which goes something like this: "In obedience to the command of our Lord and Saviour Jesus Christ and upon your profession of faith in Him as Saviour and Lord, I baptize you, my brother, *John Smith*, in the name of the Father, the Son, and the Holy Spirit." Sometimes this formula is varied by saying, "Because of your profession of faith in Jesus Christ as your personal Saviour and upon the authority of the church, I baptize you, etc." Some preachers do not repeat the name of the candidate in the formula, but we have observed that the repeating of the name makes the ceremony more personal and makes a more indelible impression upon the candidate. If the minister is not acquainted with the names of the candidates, he may have them written on a small slip of paper and handed to him as the candidate comes into the baptistry. This takes very little effort and pays great dividends.

After the pronouncing of the formula the minister places his hand on the back of the neck of the candidate and lets him down slowly into the water. When the back of the candidate's head touches the water the minister may pause and quote an appropriate verse of Scripture (Romans 6:4, 5; Colossians 2:12; I Peter 3:21; Matthew 28:19, 20; 3:15; 3:16, etc.). At the close of the quotation or just before the close, the minister takes a fresh handkerchief from a little shelf built just inside the baptistry out of sight of the congregation and places it over the nose and mouth of the candidate as he takes the head under the water and then slowly lifts the whole body to an erect position as he makes some remark with reference to the new life which we have in Christ Jesus. According to previous instruction, the candidate holds his body rigid during all of this process and breathes normally. The candidate is also told not to help. His efforts to help only add to the confusion. In some cases, where the candidate is extremely tall, a bending of the knees may be of help to the administrator. We realize that some improvements could be made in this procedure, but we trust that some of these things will prove helpful to some of the readers.

So much for the act itself. Now let us consider the equipment. Adequate equipment can add much to the beauty and significance of the baptismal service. One necessary piece of equipment is a pool of water. Most modern day churches are equipped with built-in baptistries. Other churches have easy access to nearby churches with baptistries. Some churches in the open country still use the open pool or creek. Usually the church baptistry is more convenient and is more conducive to an impressive ceremony. However, an "old fashion" outside baptizing in a beautiful creek or lake can be most beautiful and inspiring. Even for churches with beautiful baptistries an occasional outside baptismal service (if there is an appropriate place available) would be both interesting and impressive. For those who find it necessary to have all baptismal services out doors, great care should be exercised in finding the best possible place. A muddy tank should be avoided if possible.

In the erecting of a church building the pastor should see to it that an adequate baptistry is installed, with convenient dressing rooms adjacent. Oftimes through ignorance or indifference, baptistries are built which are neither useful nor beautiful. It is just as easy and economical in the long run to build an adequate baptistry. Here are some things to be considered: It should be built high enough so that pulpit furniture will not have to be moved when the baptistry is used. It should be large enough not to cramp the minister or the candidate in the process of baptizing. It should even be large enough to accommodate two or three candidates in the pool at once if desired. It should be at least four feet wide and seven and a half feet long not counting the steps into the baptistry. Steps should be set back far enough so that the candidate is completely in the pool before he is seen by the congregation, thus avoiding undue exposure of the wet body to the congregation. Average depth for an adult is thirty-two inches. Provision should be made for a moveable step on one side that might be used in the baptizing of children. Much attractiveness can be added to the baptismal service by the installation of a plate glass at the water line. This glass should be about eight or ten inches in depth, allowing the water level to come up about two or three inches from the bottom of the glass. In this way the congregation can see the candidate as he goes under the water. It also adds beauty to have an appropriate painting as a background for the baptistry.

Other equipment for the baptismal service would include adequate dress for both minister and candidate. Until recently preachers have known very little about baptismal trousers. Usually the preacher would wear some washable clothing and change after the baptismal service. This is certainly in order and many preachers still do this. But since these water-proof trousers are accessible it is the point of wisdom, convenience and efficiency for the minister to use them. In fact, many churches furnish these for their pastor and all of them ought to do so. Some ministers wear a robe, either black or white, over the trousers; others wear an ordinary dark dress coat. Some outer cloak or coat should be worn, the kind depending upon the particular taste of the pastor. These things add to the dignity of the service, but we have no objection to any kind of dress so long as it is decent.

It is becoming more and more popular for the candidates to wear uniform robes, and where this is possible it is commendable. However, any type of decent washable clothing is certainly permissible and appropriate. In the case of robes, usually the church furnishes these. Some of the smaller churches are not able to do this, but if at all possible the church would be wise in furnishing robes for the candidates. It would not only lend dignity to the service, but it would make the problem of clothing much more simple for the candidate. We are not in favor of convenience at the expense of virtue or truth, but when convenience can be added without violence to either, then it ought to be done.

Many other suggestions might be made which would be of help to the minister in the administration of baptism, but these will serve, we trust, to stimulate the thinking of the minister and inspire him to seek the most effective methods in the administration of this most beautiful and impressive ordinance which Christ gave to His churches.

9 | THE ADMINISTRATION OF THE LORD'S SUPPER

As in baptism so also in the observance of the Lord's Supper, there can be no fitting observance apart from a consideration of the fundamental aspects of theology which are involved. Theology and practice are always linked closely together. Therefore, it will be necessary for us to give first consideration in this chapter to the theological significance of the Lord's Supper. We are tempted to plunge into a technical discussion of the theology of the Lord's Supper, but we must not do this since it is not in the range of our study here. We must limit ourselves to the bare necessities, an understanding of the general and fundamental principles involved. Like baptism, the Lord's Supper is a symbolic picture, and should be observed as such. It is a picture of the broken body of Christ and His shed blood as a reminder to those who partake of the tremendous price Jesus paid for our redemption. This ordinance was given by Christ to His Church and should be administered by the church and observed by the church. We will not go into the controversial question of who should partake, except to say that since it is a church ordinance, like baptism, it should be administered and observed by the church. Usually the pastor is the administrator for the church.

The doctrinal conception of this ordinance determines largely the method and manner of its observance. In the evangelical churches of our day there are two extreme tendencies in the observance of this ordinance. One is that which tends toward sacerdotalism. Technically, most evangelical churches deny the Roman Catholic doctrine of transubstantiation, but in practice many churches are implying it. There is a strong tendency among the ministers as well as the laity toward the idea that the very act of partaking of the Supper is a means of grace and bestows some magic charm upon the life. Even our terminology is tainted with sacerdotalism. The terms, *sacrament* and *communion,* are very inappropriate words for this ordinance if we understand it as a symbolic picture. The minister should avoid the use of such terms and should discourage the use of them by

71

others. Perhaps the best term is *The Memorial Supper*. *The Lord's Supper* is also an appropriate title. These things may seem insignificant but over a period of time they have a tremendous influence upon the attitude of the people. The growing tendencies toward sacramentalism in our evangelical churches are alarming.[1] It is the minister's responsibility to create and encourage the proper attitude on the part of those who observe this Memorial Supper.

There are others (but not many) who go to the other extreme and observe the Supper in irreverence and revelry. This is the problem Paul had with the Corinthian church. The observance of the Lord's Supper was made a hilarious occasion. By such conduct they were bringing shame and reproach upon the name of Christ and His Church. While the Supper is not a sacrament, it is sacred in significance and ought to be observed in all reverence and respect. It is to be observed solemnly and yet joyfully. The symbolism of the picture ought to stir the hearts of those who partake to new resolves of loyalty and fidelity to Him who gave so much for us. The minister's responsibility, therefore, is more than that of going through the motions of presiding; it is in the cultivating of proper attitudes and feelings in the observance of it.

THE CONSIDERATION OF TIME IN THE OBSERVANCE OF THE LORD'S SUPPER

The question of time must come in for some consideration. How often should this ordinance be observed and on what occasion? The will of the church is the authority in this matter since it is an ordinance of the church, but in most cases the pastor is looked to for guidance and leadership in this matter. We have no Scriptural commands concerning the frequency or the time of the observance of the Lord's Supper. We have only this for our guide: "This do ye, as oft as ye drink it, in remembrance of me. For as often as ye eat this bread and drink this cup, ye do shew the Lord's death till he come" (I Corinthians 11:25, 26). It should not be observed so frequently that it becomes a mere routine which loses its significance; neither should it be observed so infrequently that it becomes a novelty. Somewhere in between these two extremes is the happy medium which we ought to strike. Some churches insist on observing it each Sunday. We have no objection to this except that with this frequency there is a tendency to lose the true significance of it. Other churches observe it once a month. Perhaps most churches observe the Memorial Supper once each quarter, four times a year; others

[1] For an example of this trend see A. K. DeBlois, *Some Problems of the Modern Minister*, p. 39.

once a year; and some almost never. The quarterly basis seems to be most satisfactory, though some churches may find other plans more expedient. The point is that all churches should observe the ordinance and often enough to serve the purpose for which Christ gave it.

Not only "How often," but also "when" should this ordinance be observed? At the Sunday morning worship hour? At the evening service? At the mid-week service? Or at some special occasion? We answer by saying that at any meeting of the church it is appropriate to observe the Lord's Supper. Most churches, I suppose, have the habit of observing it at the Sunday morning worship service. We would like to suggest that a change now and then in time of observance would be helpful and stimulating. We know of one church which follows this schedule: One quarter it is observed at the Sunday morning hour; the following quarterly observance is at the Sunday evening service; once during the year it is observed at the prayer meeting hour; the fourth quarterly observance takes place at a special Sunday afternoon meeting. This at least gives variety and diversity and perhaps aids in giving emphasis to the observance. It is easy for churches and people to reduce their religious activities to mere rote. Anything reasonable to stimulate interest and life is commendable.

The Ceremonial Procedure in the Observance of the Lord's Supper

Let us come now to the observance itself. The methods of administration will vary with different preachers. We do not claim efficiency in this realm. As other preachers, we are constantly looking for ways to improve our administration of this beautiful ordinance. We are giving suggestions from our own experience merely as a stimulation of thought on the part of the reader. Of course, appropriate preliminary remarks should be made with reference to the observation of the Supper. This does not mean that the preacher should always preach a sermon directly on the Lord's Supper at each occasion of its observance. An occasional sermon on the Lord's Supper certainly ought to be preached, but many times a few preliminary remarks of some three or four minutes preceding the observance will be sufficient. We do not feel that it is wise or expedient to preach a special "Lord's Supper" sermon at every occasion of observance, just as we do not feel it necessary to preach a sermon on baptism every time we baptize. But, by all means, some appropriate introductory remarks ought to be made on each occasion.

Usually the Supper is observed after the sermon has been

preached and the invitation given. Sometimes, when the sermon is based directly on the meaning and observance of the Supper, the ceremony comes immediately following the sermon without a break for invitation. In this case the invitation may come after the observance or be omitted entirely. We know of one preacher who gave the invitation to church membership before the sermon which proved to be very effective for a change.

After the preliminary remarks, the deacons should be called to the front for the purpose of serving the people. It is much better to have these deacons already seated on the front row than to have them coming from all over the congregation which would detract from the service. There should be a previous understanding between the deacons and the pastor concerning the serving. This would avoid any confusion or bungling. Perfect order adds much to the significance of the ceremony. Someone should be designated to remove the cloth covering the vessels in which are the elements. Usually two of the deacons can best serve this purpose. Much of the bread will be already broken, but at least one large portion should be left on the top plate for the pastor to break before the congregation. The pastor may give this plate to one of the deacons for holding as he breaks the bread. A quotation from the Gospel account of the breaking of the bread would be very appropriate as he breaks the bread. The plates are then passed to the deacons for serving according to a previously understood order. While this is being done appropriate quiet music is being played on the organ. Some prefer to have no music of any kind at this time. I suppose that it is a matter of taste or custom. When all have been served the deacons return to the front and the pastor replaces the plates on the table. With the last plate he serves the deacons and the last deacon served then holds the plate for the pastor. At this juncture I usually quote from Paul's account of the supper in the eleventh chapter of I Corinthians and then lead the congregation in eating the bread. Before the fruit of the vine is served I quote the Gospel account concerning the cup and pause for a season of prayer. The fruit of the vine is distributed in the same manner as the bread. After all have been served I quote again from Paul's account and lead the congregation in the drinking from the cup. It is my custom to have the congregation stand and sing one stanza of "At The Cross" or "Jesus Paid It All" without any instrumental accompaniment and without any dismissal prayer. The Scripture says that "when they had sung an hymn, they went out." This is not the only order of the ceremony, nor is it necessarily the best, but it will perhaps give some idea of the order of the ceremony and inspire others to seek the most impressive method for the administration of the Memorial Supper.

NECESSARY EQUIPMENT IN THE OBSERVANCE OF THE LORD'S SUPPER

Before we close this discussion a word should be said about the equipment. Beautiful trays, plates, and individual glasses are now available at reasonable prices. While the ceremony can be observed without these, it is both wise and expedient for any church to secure this equipment. It lends beauty and dignity to the observance of this ordinance. These things can be purchased at almost any religious book store. The unleavened bread may also be obtained in like manner. The grape juice is available at most grocery stores. Other equipment can be obtained for the convenience of those who fill the cups. Another valuable asset is the installation of cup racks on the backs of the pews, in which the people may place their cups after they have drunk. However, if the holes are not lined with rubber, there will be a terrible and disturbing clatter when the cups are placed in the racks. Such a clatter all but ruins the impressiveness of the service. Everything that can be done to enhance the sacredness and significance of this ordinance ought to be done. In this day and time there is little excuse for ignorance in these things. Whatever may be the particular method or the type of equipment used, a serious effort ought to be made by the minister to maintain the scriptural significance of this ordinance which is ordained of God to keep our minds refreshed with the reality of the sacrifice of Jesus for our redemption.

10 | THE WEDDING

When the minister says, "I do here and now pronounce you lawfully married, husband and wife," he is performing a thrilling and yet significantly solemn duty. But there is far more to it than just this. There is far more involved in the wedding responsibility for the minister than the average layman sees, and, we are afraid, far more than the average minister feels. Many attractive and helpful books have been written by various and competent men for the purpose of helping the bride and groom to adjust themselves to a happy married life. It is not in the realm of our purpose here to discuss this aspect of the marriage relationship, except to say that the minister will do well to acquaint himself with some of these books that he might be in position to suggest such to young couples who come to him. Very little has been written, so far as we know, on the minister's responsibility in the wedding and activities related to it. The best and most complete treatment of this phase of it we have found is that of Dr. Arthur B. Rutledge, in a booklet published by the Executive Board of the Baptist General Convention of Texas for free distribution among ministers. It is titled *The Minister and Weddings*. Every minister would do well to obtain a copy and study it. A free copy may be had by writing for it. In our discussion of this phase of the minister's work we want to look at it from three angles: before the wedding, at the wedding, and after the wedding.

BEFORE THE WEDDING

The minister's responsibility in the wedding begins long before the ceremony is ever planned. It must begin with the teaching and training of young people in the principles of life, love, and ideals of marriage even before they begin to think seriously about coming to the marriage altar. Too many of us have failed just at this point. What little effort we have put forth to make marriage happy and succesful for our young people has been belated in most cases. When two young people come to the minister with a date already set for the wedding it may be too late then for the minister to do much contributing toward the happiness of matrimonial life for the two who are involved: however, we can be of some help even then, but there are fundamental principles which need to be inculcated into the thinking of our young people before they reach this stage. And this is what we have in mind. This background work is an ever present responsibility for the conscientious minister.

Just what can the minister do in laying a foundation for the matrimonial bliss of his young people? In answering this question let us make three suggestions. First, the minister can, and must if he fulfills his responsibility to his young people, keep the ideals of Christian love, courtship, and marriage before his young people through sermon and special youth conferences. This teaching and training should begin, not with those who are about to get married, but with the Intermediates, and some of it even with Juniors. The minister ought to preach an occasional sermon on some aspect of this realistic and vital concern of our young people. He should also take advantage of special youth gatherings to give consideration to these things in a heart-to-heart talk, a series of studies, or a discussion period. We will not go into the question of what he shall say or how he shall say it. This will depend upon the personality of the minister and the nature of the particular group to whom he is speaking. The minister will find much help for such discussions by a study of some of the many fine books on the subject. A list of books is given at the close of this chapter. The thing we are emphasizing is that the minister's responsibility in helping prepare his young people for happy and successful marriage is a continual process of training and teaching and must not be limited to a few remarks at the ceremony or just before.

In the second place, the minister should so manifest his love for and interest in the young people that they will feel free to come to him with their love and courtship problems. When the young person takes the initiative to come to the pastor with such a problem, the pastor is in much better position to help than he could ever be in a formal address or sermon. But these young people will not come to their pastor with such problems unless they are sure that he loves them and is vitally interested in them. It is up to the pastor to make them feel this. It is possible for a pastor to be vitally interested in his young people and their problems without giving to them any manifestation of this interest. In such a case many opportunities for lasting service are made impossible. Let the minister prove his love for his young people and invite their confidence in all problems pertaining to their welfare and the door will be open for a most effective and lasting ministry in the realm of which we are now thinking.

In the third place, the minister can and should encourage the proper acquaintances and companionships by seeking to bring his young people in contact with other noble-minded Christian young people. This he can do by encouraging more fellowship among the young people of his own congregation. He can also lead his young people to attend youth gatherings and youth camps where they will be most likely to come in contact with the right kind of young people from whom some of them may choose a life partner. This does not mean that the minister is to be a sort of matrimonial bureau, but it does mean that he can do much toward happy married life by seeking to place his young people in the company of the right kind of young people of the opposite sex. Of course, every young person must choose his life's companion for himself, but if the choice is made from contacts with other young people of the highest order he is more likely to make a good choice.

What we have said concerns the long range program of the minister in his ministry to all young people. Let us come now to the more immediate aspects of the wedding. If at all possible, the pastor should have a pre-nuptial conference with the prospective bride and groom. This should be done several days or weeks in advance of the wedding if possible. There are times, of course, when the couple comes unannounced to the minister for the ceremony. In this case a brief word with the couple just before the ceremony is better than none at all. Such unannounced weddings should be discouraged. This pre-nuptial conference should be held if possible in the pastor's study where the environment is usually more conducive to helpful counsel. It could very appropriately begin with a discussion of plans for the ceremony. There are many details to be worked out, such as the time and place of the wedding, the decorations, the attendants, the ring or rings, the type of ceremony, etc. We will discuss these in this chapter a little later. After a discussion of the plans, the pastor could very easily direct the discussion to a consideration of the sanctity and significance of marriage. Dr. Rutledge correctly observes that "it is appalling how little thought the average young couple have given to marriage. Often they seem to have the idea that the minister's final 'amen' will serve as a magic wand that will somehow insure that they will live happily ever after."[1]

In a conference such as this the couple may resent a lengthy

[1] Booklet on *The Minister and Weddings*, p. 3.

discourse involving a lot of direct "fatherly" advice. The minister will need to be cautious and tactful. His remarks must be suggestive, leaving the couple to work out the details for themselves. Timely hints should be given concerning personal, physical, economic, social, and spiritual relations. On counseling young people concerning marriage the minister will find some helpful suggestions in a little booklet by Warren D. Bowman called *Counseling with Couples Before Marriage.*[2] Many young people come to the marriage altar with little or no understanding of sex relationships and because of this marital happiness is impaired. The minister may not feel it best to go into detail in these matters, but he can recommend or make available some good book dealing with these questions. Some pastors have the custom of offering to the couple at this time a copy of *Harmony in Marriage* by Leland Foster Wood as a gift.[3] There are other good books that could be given or recommended. This practice has proved to be a blessing to many young people who stand on the threshold of matrimony.

The pastor can also be of service to the couple at this conference by recommending a good doctor to whom they should both go for physical examination and for information which he can give on matrimonial relationships. In and through it all the minister should seek to impress the sacred significance of this relationship and seek to instill proper ideas and attitudes which will make for happy and useful married life, including such virtues as common sense, co-operation, forgiveness, patience, and prayer. Certainly the minister ought to pray with the couple before they leave the conference room.

Before the wedding there are still other matters to be considered — the problems which so often arise pertaining to the wedding or the wedding party. The first problem concerns the question of marrying those who may have been married before. When it is learned by the minister that the bride or groom has been previously married and divorced, what should be the minister's attitude? The answer to this question will vary with different ministers. Some preachers absolutely refuse to marry any one who has been divorced. Others will marry only those who give Biblical reasons for the divorce. (It is seldom if ever that one will give any other reason when asked by the minister.) There are still other ministers who will perform the ceremony without question concerning a previous marriage. There are problems involved in each of these attitudes. For those who follow the first plan there is the problem of forbidding a Christian ceremony for some devoted Christian who may have been the vic-

[2] Published by Brethren Publishing House, Elgin, Illinois.
[3] Can be purchased for $1.00 each from Round Table Press, New York City.

tim of some unfaithful wife or husband who is guilty of adultery,
thus giving Biblical grounds for divorce. A refusal to perform such
a ceremony may discourage and dishearten the religious fervor and
enthusiasm of the one in question. For those who follow the second
plan there is always the question of whether the reason given is according to fact. It is quite easy for one to become prejudiced and
feel that he has Biblical grounds for divorce when in reality he has
not. Who is to be the judge in this matter? Of course, most of those
who follow this plan feel that even though the truth has not been
told the responsibility rests upon the couple rather than the minister. For those who follow the third plan there is the question of
putting endorsement on divorce by marrying those who have been
divorced. Each minister will have to follow his own conscience in
this matter. Frankly, we have never become dogmatically certain
as to which attitude should be followed. In any case the minister
ought to be consistent, and in no case should he give any kind of
an expression which would be interpreted as an endorsement of
divorce or the careless breaking down of the holy bonds of matrimony.

Another problem facing the minister immediately before the
wedding is his knowledge of the law with reference to marriage.
While marriage is a divine institution, it is administered by the state.
Each state has its own marriage laws, and these will vary in the
different states. The minister will need to inform himself concerning the particular laws of his state. Some states require a period
of time between the issuing of the license and the performing of
the ceremony. Some states require a witness and others do not.
The legal procedure for filling out the license should be known.
What to do with the license and where to send it are also questions
with which the minister should be familiar. Those who have been
in the ministry for a long period will have no difficulty here. We are
thinking now of the young minister who may be facing his first
ceremony. At any rate the laws of the state should be known.

A third problem facing the minister immediately before the
wedding is the problem of ethics. If both bride and groom are
members of the church of which he is pastor, there is no problem
here. But many times we are faced with the question of performing a ceremony for someone who may be a member of a neighboring
church. Usually if the bride and groom are members of different
churches it is proper for the bride's pastor to perform the ceremony.
Of course, this will be finally determined by the couple. If the groom
is active in his church, it would be the point of wisdom and good
ethics for the pastor to suggest that the groom's pastor be invited
to have some part in the ceremony too, perhaps to lead in prayer.

Great care and caution should be used by the minister when asked to perform the ceremony for a couple from another church, especially a neighboring church. If it can be done gracefully, the couple should be urged to go to their own pastor. If they insist on having the ceremony performed by the minister in question, he should as soon as possible contact the couple's pastor and explain. Many times grave injustices can be done to the fellowship of ministers by the unscrupulous practice of performing wedding ceremonies which rightly belong to another minister. And never should a minister go to the field of another minister and perform a ceremony unless invited by that minister. This would be the unpardonable sin. On the other hand, the wise minister will not become jealous or puffed up because one of his own flock may go to another minister for the wedding ceremony. Any jealous expression on his part would only add to his downfall. The big-hearted spirit always pays in the long run.

AT THE WEDDING

So much for the "before the wedding" activities. Let us now consider the wedding proper. In this realm there are four things to be considered. First is the place of the ceremony. Where shall the ceremony be performed? In the final analysis this will be left up to the bride and groom, but the minister may often exert some influence on the answering of this question. We feel that the wedding can be much more impressive and have a more wholesome atmosphere in the church than anywhere else. Whenever possible the minister should use his influence to lead the young people to choose the church as the place for the wedding ceremony. However, according to experience and observation few weddings, comparatively, are held in the church. Weddings are sometimes held in the home of the bride or a friend of the bride, in the pastor's home or study, or some public meeting place. Those held in the pastor's home or study are usually impromptu weddings which are held with little or no formality. In such cases the minister must make the best of it.

Weddings may range from the informal private wedding in the pastor's study or home to a pompous formal wedding in the church sanctuary. The minister, of course, must learn what kind of ceremony the couple want and fit his own plans into theirs. In the informal ceremony the bride and groom usually appear before the minister unattended and the service usually consists of a few brief remarks by the minister, followed by the exchange of vows, the giving of rings (if used), and a benediction. The formal ceremony is far more complicated and demands more preparation and rehearsal. It is also more expensive; however, a very effective formal wedding can be had at a very conservative cost. The bride may direct the order of the service in any way she sees fit, but usually the pastor is asked for suggestions on the prevailing customs for such order. He should, therefore, keep himself up to date on these matters. The usual and customary procedure is as follows: Organ prelude; seating of the groom's mother and then the bride's mother; lighting of the candles by the ushers or others who might be designated; appropriate wedding music, either vocal or instrumental number; beginning of the wedding march; entrance of minister from back or side stage door; entrance of groom from side door with best man on his right (Groom and best man wait just to the left and in front of minister or at head of steps leading to platform, looking expectantly toward the aisle down which the bride is expected to come); entrance of bridesmaids, one at a time, down center aisle or aisle to right of minister and groomsmen down aisle to left of minister (These may be positioned according to any previously arranged pattern on either side facing the minister); entrance of maid or matron of honor from center aisle; entrance of flower girl or girls and ring bearer (If any); entrance of bride with father or other relative or friend who is to give the bride away (Bride walks on the right of her father). Quiet music may be played throughout the ceremony if desired. When the bride and her father arrive before the minister he asks "Who giveth this woman to this man?", to which the father will answer "I do." This done, the bride removes her left arm from her father's right arm, transfers her flowers from her right hand to her left, and then with her right arm she takes the left arm of the groom as he puts his right hand in her right hand. As this is being done one more step is taken by both, placing them immediately in front of the minister. The father takes his seat beside the bride's mother.

With this the minister is ready to begin his part of the ceremony. There is no established order which the minister must follow in his part of the ceremony. There are many suggested forms, some more elaborate than others, but usually each minister has his own form which he reads or gives from memory. It is much more impressive when given from memory. Usually the minister will add a little more to the formal ceremony. We are giving below the ceremony which we have used for a number of years as a mere suggestion and basis for study for those who do not already have a form adopted. It is as follows:

"On an occasion like this we are reminded of the words of Jesus who said, 'For this cause shall a man leave father and mother, and shall cleave to his wife: and they twain shall be one flesh.' Wherefore they are no more twain, but one flesh. What therefore God hath joined together, let not man put asunder.'

"We are gathered in the presence of Almighty God and these witnesses to join *John Jones* and *Mary Smith* in the holy bonds of matrimony. Marriage is a joyous occasion. In our thoughts it is connected with all the magic charm of home, and all that is pleasant and sacred in the most intimate relationships of life. It was sanctioned by our Saviour's presence in Cana of Galilee, and declared by an inspired apostle to be honorable in all. Therefore, if you have appeared before me at the present time for the purpose of being united in holy legal wedlock, will you so signify by joining your right hands? (Some ministers wait until at this point to ask who gives the bride away.)

"Now do you, *John Jones*, take the lady whose hand you hold to be your lawful and wedded wife? (I do) And do you promise to love, honor, and cherish her in sickness and in health, for richer for poorer, for better or for worse, and forsaking all others, keep thee only unto her so long as you both shall live? (I do)

"And do you, *Mary Smith*, take this gentleman who now stands by your side and now holds your hand to be your lawful and wedded husband? (I do) And do you promise to love, honor and cherish him in sickness and in health, for richer for poorer, for better or for worse, and forsaking all others, keep thee only unto him so long as you both shall live? (I do)

"Do both of you mutually agree, in the presence of God and these witnesses, that at all times and under all circumstances you will do your best to conduct yourselves toward one another as becometh husband and wife? (both say I do at the same time)

(At this time the minister takes the ring from the best man according to previously arranged sign.) "This ring which I hold in my hand is an emblem of the love that two have for each other who are thus joined in life. This ring forms an unbroken circle which is a symbol of the unbroken love which, we trust, you will have for each other. The gold of this ring is a token of that which is least tarnished and most pure. May your love for each other be as pure as the gold of this ring!

"And now do you, *John Jones*, give this ring to her who stands by your side as a token of your love and affection for her and to seal the vows you have made today? (I do) (Some ministers have the groom to repeat something like this: With this ring I thee wed, and with it promise to be faithful to these marriage vows.) And will you, *Mary Smith*, receive this ring as such a token of his love and fidelity? (I do) (The groom places the ring on the bride's finger.)

"In like manner do you, *Mary Smith*, give this ring to him who stands by your side as a token of your love and affection for him and to seal the vows you have made today? (I do). And will you, *John Jones*, receive this ring as such a token from her? (I do) (Bride puts ring on groom's finger.)

"Now, therefore, having taken these pledges of fidelity and vows of affection, by the authority of the state of Texas, and by the authority of the Word of God, I do here and now pronounce you lawfully married, husband and wife. What God hath joined together, let no man put asunder. Let us pray." Sometimes the bride and groom kneel at the altar during this prayer.)

After the prayer the bride and groom kiss and march out with a more lively step than they did in coming in. Going out the bride will be on the groom's right. The other attendants will follow in reverse order of their entrance or according to some other order previously planned.

A reception usually follows at which time the guests will congratulate the bride and groom. With this the wedding is over except for a few little details, such as the reception of the fee by the minister, the filling out of a marriage certificate, and the proper return of the marriage license to the county clerk. A further word should be said about the fee. Usually a fee is offered to the minister by the groom personally, or through the best man which is more proper. Sometimes the minister is embarrassed by being asked, "How much do I owe you?" The question is raised as to whether or not the minister should accept a fee. It is our conviction that in the case of a wedding involving members of his own congregation, the fee should not be accepted, if this can be done without hurting the feelings of the groom. There are times when the groom will insist on giving the fee as a token of love and appreciation. In that case the minister will be doing a favor for the groom by accepting it. Some ministers accept the fee from the groom and then give it to the bride. By no means should the minister expect or encourage fees from those who are a part of his own parish. This is only another of the many types of service that the minister can and should render to his own people. If the pastor has been out unnecessary expense, then he should be reimbursed. In the case of those who are not members of his own flock, the minister has a right to expect and accept a fee. By all means the pastor must not become mercenary in his attitude toward the marriage ceremony.

Since the official license is mailed to the county clerk, it is proper and appropriate for the minister to have on hand a wedding certificate to be filled out and given to the bride. These certificates can be obtained at a very nominal cost from almost any religious book store. This certificate may be filled out and given to the best man before the ceremony in order to avoid undue delay after the wedding. Many times the bride will have a bridal book in which is a marriage certificate form. In such case this may be used instead of one furnished by the minister. On the same day or the day following the minister should see that the marriage license, properly filled out, is mailed to the clerk, who, in return, will mail it to the bride and groom after the official recording on the court house books. Most ministers will want to keep a record of their own of all weddings. Such a record will prove to be both interesting and useful in years to come.

AFTER THE WEDDING

The minister's work does not begin with the ceremony; neither does it end with the ceremony. The minister who feels that his job is finished after he "ties the knot" is blind to his own responsibility as a minister. He must have an abiding interest in the welfare of the home which is thus begun with the marriage ceremony. The minister feels a special tie which binds him to the homes of those whom he has united in matrimony and rightly so. And this feeling is mutual. We agree with Dr. W. B. Riley that "in the average church, people married by the pastor are his ardent friends, earnest co-laborers, and if needs be, his ready defenders."[4] There are many things that a pastor can and should do to encourage and strengthen the homes of those whom he has thus united.

First of all, the minister can make a visit in the new home as soon as the bride and groom are settled. This visit from the pastor usually means a great deal to the newlyweds. The visit should not be long, but a few appropriate remarks and a prayer of dedication will greatly inspire the lives of these two in their new relationship. A personal letter from the pastor will also mean much to the bride and groom as they return from their honeymoon to settle down to live. Here is a sample of the kind of letter that could be written:

Dear Mary and John,

I have told you personally, but I would also like to take this means of expressing to you my desire for your happiness and contentment in your new role as Mr. and Mrs. As the new wears off and you get down to bare realities your love for and faith in each other will have many trials, but these trials will ultimately strengthen and sweeten your love for each other.

Your happiness will not come accidentally, but only as you both

4 *Pastoral Problems*, p. 76.

conscientiously work at it. Above all, it is my hope and prayer that
you will put Christ at the very heart of your home life and cultivate
now the habit of daily prayer together. Only this can give to the
home the guarantee of happiness and success.

As your pastor let me assure you that I am interested in you and
your welfare. If at any time I can be of service to you, do not
hesitate to call on me.

Yours for many years of happy and blessed matrimonial bliss,

Many young couples will want to keep this letter as a treasure
and constant source of inspiration. Some couples have been known
to frame such a letter and hang it in their bedroom. Sometimes a
special recognition of this couple at the Sunday worship service following the wedding will add sacredness to their new relationship.

Of course, the minister will want to visit the home when the first
baby arrives. What a happy and blessed occasion this will be!
And a visit from the minister who performed the ceremony will add
greatly to the ecstasy and joy of the occasion and will challenge them
afresh with the added responsibility of raising the child.

Some ministers have the custom of sending a card or letter on
each anniversary. This is not impossible even if there is a long list of
couples. An index system of dates could be set up and kept in order.
A brief reference to this file each day will reveal the anniversary dates.
A personal card or letter is best, but if this takes too much time,
a form card or letter could be kept ready for signing and mailing.
Another helpful custom is that of having an annual recognition at
the worship hour of all couples married by the pastor.

There are many other little things which the minister can do
to inspire and encourage the bride and groom in the building of a
Christian home, but these will give some idea of what can be done.
Whatever the means, the minister must give some manifestation
of a continuous interest in the welfare of the homes of his members.
It is a never ending task, but it pays rich dividends in the contribution which the homes will make to the betterment of the world in
which we live. In closing may we quote an appropriate paragraph
from Dr. Rutledge's booklet: "The minister will certainly in every
way seek to be a true pastor to the couple. He will seek to minister to their spiritual needs in a spirit of true Christian love.
He will seek to win to Christ and church membership those who
should make such decisions. He will seek to enlist in the work of
the Lord and the ongoing life of the church those who are unenlisted.
He will seek to strengthen in the right direction those who already
are devoted and faithful Christians. He may serve well by calling
the attention of workers in the various departments of the church

life to the prospects for membership and service to be found among these young couples. The minister will recognize and emphasize the strategic importance of a couple's beginning their life together with the proper attitudes and practices concerning Christ and the church. Time spent with such young couples will be time well invested for the future of the Kingdom of God."[5]

A LIST OF HELPFUL BOOKS

The following list includes only a few of the many books on this subject. The pastor should be familiar with at least some of these books that he might not only use the suggestions in counsel but also be prepared to make recommendations of a good book to the couples who come to him.

Wood, Leland Foster, *Harmony in Marriage*, Round Table Press, New York City.

Duvall, Evelyn M. and Hill, Reuben, *When You Marry*, The Association Press, New York City.

Dahlberg, Edwin T., *Youth and the Homes of Tomorrow*, The Judson Press, Philadelphia, Pa.

Fiske, G. W., *The Christian Family*, The Abingdon Press, Nashville.

Beaven, A. W., *The Fine Art of Living Together*, Harper and Bros. New York.

Wright, Helnea B., *The Sex Factor in Marriage*, the Vanguard Press.

Royden, A. Maude, *Sex and Common Sense*, G. P. Putman's Sons, New York.

Committee, *Ideals of Love and Marriage*, The Federal Council of the Churches of Christ in America, New York.

Smith, Leslie R., *This Love of Ours*, Abingdon-Cokesbury, Nashville.

Burkhart, Roy A., *The Secret of a Happy Marriage*, Harper and Bros., New York.

Leuba, Clarence, *Ethics in Sex Conduct*, Association Press.

[5] *The Minister and Weddings*, p. 9.

11 | THE FUNERAL

Never is the minister in greater demand than in time of bereavement. People who never think of the minister will want him to come when death comes to a loved one. The preacher's ministry to those who are bereaved is not only a much needed and much desired ministry, but it also gives to him one of his best opportunities for service both physically and spiritually. Such a ministry often serves as a key to unlock the human heart to the minister so that he may introduce Christ as Saviour and Guide. The significance of this ministry, therefore, is not only that of giving immediate comfort to broken hearts, but also that of making possible a wider and more far-reaching service through those who have been thus comforted. "Bereavement brings special pastoral opportunity. — To share with people their greatest sorrows is to come into a soul-communion with them, and to weave one's life in with theirs in an almost inextricable way. The best friendships known to this world are those born of, and bred in, the fellowship of suffering. The man who will not fail you in the hour of your direst need is the one upon whose love and care you learn to lean."[1] The minister must never lose sight of the sacredness and far-reaching significance of this ministry. There is a grave danger that the minister will come to look upon the funeral as just a necessary part of his professional duty. The minister who goes through the activities of a funeral without any feeling of genuine sympathy is not worthy of the title. The shepherd heart of the pastor must never fail to be moved by the grief of loved ones whom death has bereaved. The most vital point in this ministry of which we now speak is the minister's attitude toward it. In these times of crisis in the lives of his people, the minister can render an invaluable service at the time and can make impressions which will serve well in years to come for the advancement of God's Kingdom. Let the minister never lose sight of this. Let not the multiplicity of the funerals lessen his tender feelings and genuine sympathy. Few things mean more to the bereaved than the presence of the pastor, the con-

[1] Riley, W. B., *Pastoral Problems*, p. 88.

88

sciousness of his sympathy, and the consolation of his quiet comforting.

In discussing the more technical phases of the funeral experience, we are not overlooking nor minimizing the importance of genuine feeling and sympathy. These things are basic, but even in such highly emotional experiences definite plans must be made and carried out for the good of all concerned. Genuine sympathy is more than an uncontrolable outburst of tears. It must express itself in some tangible and practical form. Just how the minister can perform this service is the subject of this discussion. For the purpose of clarity and usefulness we are following the same plan which we followed in connection with our discussion of the wedding. There are three main divisions: before the funeral; at the funeral, and after the funeral.

BEFORE THE FUNERAL

There are some definite things which the minister must do before the funeral service. In fact, these things often determine the effectiveness of the funeral message and the ministry of the pastor after the funeral is over. As soon as word comes to the pastor of the death he should leave whatever he is doing and go immediately to the family. His promptness at this point will mean much to the family. The need for pastoral counsel and consolation is poignantly felt during this first shock of the bereavement. Of course, he cannot go if he does not know of the death, but usually someone will call the pastor and notify him of the death. When the pastor comes into the bereaved home, he should not do a lot of talking; neither should his visit be long. A multiplicity of words at this time is neither appropriate nor helpful. Just his presence in quietness will mean more than anything else. After assuring the loved ones of his interest in them and concern for them, the pastor will lead the family in a season of prayer. If this visit is immediately after the death, it is best for the pastor to tell the family that he will return later to discuss with them the plans for the funeral.

After the family has been given time to contact other relatives and discuss plans with the funeral director, the pastor will return to discuss the plans for the funeral. In this conference with the family the pastor should seek to be helpful but not dictatorial. He must always respect the wishes and desires of the family. Many times they will ask him for suggestions pertaining to the funeral and its arrangements. In such cases he should be ready to give helpful suggestions. One of the first things to be decided will be the place of burial. This, of course, will be worked out between the

family and the funeral director. Another initial problem to be settled is the place of the service. If this problem has not already
been settled, the pastor may be called upon to assist in this decision. There was a time when practically all funerals were held in
the churches, but now that most funeral homes are equipped with
chapels, more and more people are going to the funeral chapel for
the funeral service. In most cases this would be the most appropriate
and convenient place to have it for all concerned. If the deceased
was a prominent and loyal church member, it would be appropriate
to have the service in the church. In either case the desire of the
family must be respected, but if the pastor is asked for counsel on
this matter he should very tactfully suggest the funeral chapel unless the service concerns a prominent church member. Another
detail to be worked out is the order of the service. Sometimes the
funeral director may already have this information, but, if not, the
pastor will want to go over the order of the service with the family
which should include a definite understanding as to the arrangements for the music. Before he leaves the pastor should obtain some
facts from some member of the family relative to the deceased for
inclusion in the obituary. Some of these things can be obtained from
the funeral director, but usually the information on the funeral director's card is insufficient. The obituary should not be long, but it
ought to include the following: date and place of birth; place and
duration of residence at time of death; time and place of death; if
a Christian, time of conversion and name of church to which deceased belonged; time of marriage and number of children; a list of
all immediate survivers, such as parents, children, brothers and sisters;
and perhaps the number of other close relatives. In some cases there
may be a few other outstanding facts which ought to be included.

After this visit with the family, a check should be made by the
minister with the funeral director to see that everything is in order.
There must be perfect co-operation and understanding between the
funeral director and the minister. They must work together for the
utmost good of the service to the bereaved. Glaring blunders in the
order of the service only add to the grief of the stricken. Most funeral directors will gladly co-operate with the pastor when they
understand and know what he wants.

There is one other thing to be considered in the minister's
preparation for the funeral and that is his co-operation with other
ministers who may have been asked to have part in the service.
Many times the family will want a former pastor or neighboring
pastor to have some part in the service. In every such case the pastor should gladly and cheerfully co-operate. We have known pastors

who have resented the family's request for a former pastor in such
an hour. Any such resentment should be utterly avoided. In fact,
the pastor will be adding to his own reputation and influence when
he takes the initiative in suggesting to the family that they ask another minister to help in the service, if he knows that the minister
in question is loved and admired by the family. Any minister who
is asked by the family to have a part should be cordially received
and respected. On the other hand, the minister must refrain from
accepting an invitation to conduct a funeral for someone who is a
member of another church without the consent and good will of
the pastor of that church. This is not only unethical, but also hurtful
to both ministers involved. When he does come with the consent of
the other pastor, he should respect the other pastor as the leader
and fit into the program as he may suggest. When an unethical
minister does come into the field of another minister to conduct
such a service, the pastor should realize that he will accomplish
nothing by "tearing his hair" over it. By being gracious and forgiving he will come out winner in the long run.

At the Funeral

Let us come now to a consideration of the funeral service itself.
As the minister comes to conduct the service there are certain things
which he should keep in mind. He should realize that he is there to
try to bring comfort and consolation to the bereaved. A showy display of emotions will not contribute to this purpose. The minister
himself can create an atmosphere at the service which will be conducive to comfort and serenity. The minister also needs to keep
in mind that usually a brief service will do more good than a lengthy
one. Usually the members of the bereaved family are weary from
loss of sleep or long hours of travel. A long service would only add
to their grief. Happily we are getting away from the long drawn-out
funeral service. We have known funerals at which three or four
preachers would preach full length sermons. Those who were already worn out by many hours of sorrow and grief were completely
exhausted at the end of the service. Unless it is a very unusual occasion, the whole service should never last over twenty-five or thirty
minutes. This gives ample time for the minister to do all that he is
able to do toward bringing comfort and consolation to the bereaved.

As to the order of the service, this will vary with the desires
of the different people involved. There is no set order, but here is a
suggested order of service for a simple funeral in the chapel: Pro-
cessional by the organ (as the people come in and the family seated);
special music as previously arranged (this may be solo, duet, quartet,

chorus, or instrumental according to the desire of the family); reading of the obituary and prayer; second special musical number; Scripture reading and message by the pastor (The Scripture reading is suggested here so that it can be woven into the message); closing prayer (This is the cue for the funeral director to take charge for the viewing of the body [if such is desired] and to lead the recessional); Recessional by the organ as people depart. This order may be easily altered or adjusted to fit any situation. If there are other ministers helping in the service, one could read the obituary; another could lead the first prayer; another could read the Scripture. It is usually not best to interrupt the order of the service by giving a formal introduction of those who take part. A written order of service should be handed to each one who has a part. The service, then, can move along smoothly without a break. If the service is in a funeral chapel, usually the family is already seated in the family room when the minister comes in through a side door. If the funeral is in a church, the pastor will march in ahead of the casket and remain standing on the platform until the family is seated. If the casket is placed at the front before the service, the pastor will enter through a back or side door and remain standing for the family to be seated. At the close of the service the minister will march in front of the casket to the funeral coach.

Now let us say a word about the message itself. It is not our purpose to offer here any suggested outlines or thoughts for the funeral message. Many pastor's manuals have suggestions along this line if desired. We do want to make several general observations. First of all, let us insist that the message ought to be limited to about fifteen minutes unless it is the case of an unusual personality. Here is a question which always arises in the minister's mind at the funeral: what should I say about the deceased in the message? Some preachers feel that they should always say something about the personal life of the deceased. And some even take great pains to review certain touching experiences which only aggravate the sorrow and grief of the bereaved. Each minister will formulate his own policy over a period of years, but it has been our policy to say nothing about the personal life or character of the deceased unless he is unmistakably outstanding in his Christian life and character. It is not necessary to say something good about the personal life of the deceased in order to bring comfort to the bereaved. And it is certainly out of place and inexcusable for the minister to encourage hope of eternal bliss in the hearts of the loved ones when there is absolutely no basis for such hope. Even where there is doubtful hope, it is better to say nothing about it. Neither do we need to go to the other extreme and discourage any hope which the loved ones may have felt. If they feel hopeful, well and good. But it seems to us that it is best to say nothing of our opinion or conviction about a man's eternal state unless there is outstanding evidence. Many preachers have sinned by preaching people into heaven who had no ground for any such hope. The minister can be tactful, considerate, and gracious without expressing any word concerning the eternal state of the deceased.

For those who are not Christians, the message should contain something about the inevitable fact of death, the comfort that God gives for all of those who go through the "valley of the shadow of death," and something of the victory over death that can be realized through faith in the living Christ. All of this can be done without any insinuation as to the condition of the soul of the deceased and it can be done with great comfort and profit to those who are bereaved. In the case of the man who is an outstanding Christian, some review of the life can be given as an illustration of the power of the grace of God in a life. Such a life is a sermon in itself, but let us insist that remarks on the life of the deceased should be made only when it is known that there were no glaring inconsistencies of life. Otherwise the service will be harmful. By all means, something should be said in every funeral message which would make clear to the hearers the plan of salvation and the way of victory over death. Many times hearts will be open and receptive to the gospel message at this time that have not been before and may not be again. Of course, he will not give a formal invitation, but at this service he may have his best opportunity to place the seed of gospel truth into some heart.

When the message is finished, according to a previously arranged cue, the funeral director will take charge. It will only detract from the good that may have been done for the minister to say when he has finished his message: "The undertaker will now take charge of the service." It is much better to have a previously arranged signal so that the service may be concluded without a break. Then he will take his place in the funeral procession as directed by the funeral director. Usually the minister's car leads the procession to the cemetery. In such case the minister should take care to see that proper speed is maintained and that the procession is kept in order. The minister then leads the pallbearers carrying the casket to the grave. The minister stands at the foot of the grave while the casket is placed and the flowers banked. At a signal from the funeral director the minister concludes the service with an appropriate quotation of Scripture followed by a dismissal prayer. Some ministers use a more formal committal ceremony. This will be determined by the minister's own desire and custom. In the case of a military burial, a Masonic burial or some other lodge ceremony, then the minister has nothing to do unless he is asked by those in charge to lead a closing prayer. After the grave-side service is ended the minister should extend a personal word of sympathy to the members of the family.

AFTER THE FUNERAL

With this the funeral is over, but the minister's responsibility to the bereaved family is not finished. Perhaps a word should be said just here concerning the minister's attitude toward proffered fees. There are times when the minister will be offered money by a member of the family. Should he accept it? Some ministers do, but we feel that as a rule the minister should politely and yet firmly refuse the offered gift, especially is this true in the case of service rendered to those of his own congregation. There may be a few rare occasions when the donor is so insistent that the minister cannot refuse the gift without hurting the feelings of the one offering it. These occasions will be rare. Sometimes the funeral director gives a fee to the minister which he adds to the funeral bill. When the minister is out considerable expense in travel to and from the funeral service, it would be proper for the minister to accept a reasonable remuneration, though by no means should he suggest or insist upon this. The minister's service to the bereaved and sorrowing should be given wholeheartedly without any thought of any material gain.

The minister's interest in the bereaved must not cease with the benediction at the grave. There will be many lonely hours for the bereaved family in the days and weeks ahead. Perhaps at no time would a visit from the pastor mean more than on the day following the funeral. By that time the other friends and relatives will have gone and there will be a very keen sense of loneliness. Usually it is not best for the minister to go to the home of the bereaved immediately following the funeral, but on the following day or on some day within the week a visit from the pastor would be timely and helpful. Depending upon the attitude of the bereaved, the pastor may feel that another visit should be made, or maybe several in the weeks following. In every case the minister should maintain his interest in the family and visit them as many times as he feels necessary in order to help them to become readjusted to life and conditions.

The most significant thing is that this service to the sorrowing often opens up new avenues of service and evangelistic opportunity. The minister will have an entree into the hearts of some who were cold and indifferent before. The wide-awake pastor will keep his eyes open for these opportunities and follow them up after the funeral is over. Many have been won to Christ and salvation through these open doors. Bereavement is an imperious call to the minister. It is both a challenge and an opportunity in which he must not fail.

12 | ADMINISTRATION WORK

Whether he likes it or not, the modern-day minister is the executive of a growing and increasingly complex corporation, not in exactly the same sense, however, as a business executive in the commercial world. His office carries with it no mandatory authority. (We are thinking in terms of a congregational type church. This would not be true of an episcopal type church.) Futhermore, the minister must work, in the main, with volunteer help. For these reasons the minister cannot employ all of the tactics of a business executive. However, apart from these two things the minister is an executive in every sense of that term. He is recognized as the executive head of a great institution. His is an executive responsibility. The responsibilities of an executive nature are becoming more and more pressing upon the modern minister. The picture is made clear in Dr. Charles Jefferson's description of it: "The minister is an administrator. His church is an organization, and like all organizations it must have an executive head. The minister is that head. It is in one sense a machine, and like all machines must be run. Friction must be reduced, the wheels must be lubricated, repairs must be made, every part of the mechanism must be subjected to constant scrutiny and supervision, in order that the machine may do the work for which it has been created."[1]

There was a time when the minister was almost free from administrative duties. He would spend his time in study and preaching on the Lord's day. There was little or no organization within the church to be cared for. The church was a simple one-room structure and the people came to worship and hear the message of the preacher without becoming entangled in endless organizational details. But this is not true today. With our complex way of life we have developed a complex and highly specialized church organization. And this is not to be depreciated. There was a time when these complicated organizational arrangements were not necessary, but with the

[1] *The Minister As Prophet*, p. 1.

added attractions of our modern civilization we must have them. There is the danger, however, as we pointed out in a previous chapter, that the minister will allow these demands of the administration of the organization crowd out the pristine emphasis which he ought to give to his preaching. But no preacher can ignore the demands of the modern-day church organization without jeopardizing his usefulness as a minister.

The minister has no alternative. He finds himself face to face with organizational and administrative problems which he cannot ignore and expect to succeed in the pastorate. It is unfortunate and regrettable that some exceptionally good preachers do not seem to have administrative ability and because of this their ministries are limited and handicapped. Even in the large churches where there are employed workers to carry out the details of the organization, the minister is still the general overseer and must give considerable attention to the working of the organization. The New Testament term, bishop, suggests the idea of supervision which would include the thing which we are discussing in this chapter. There is only one thing left for the modern minister to do. He cannot ignore his administrative responsibility, neither can he delegate its general supervision to others; therefore, he must diligently train himself to the best of his ability in the art of successful business administration. Even in the case of one who may not have much natural endowment in the realm of administrative ability, he may still achieve a satisfactory degree of success by diligent training and application. Our schools and seminaries are doing more and more in the realm of training ministers in the art of effective church administration. The young minister will do well to take advantage of every opportunity to observe, study, and apply the principles of effective administration. Some denominations offer helpful periodicals on this phase of the minister's task. For instance, Southern Baptists publish a periodical called *Church Management*. Some ministers are natural "efficiency experts" in the realm of organization and administration. Not all ministers can be experts, but any minister can acquire enough of the simple skills of business administration to administer successfully the church organization.

VARIOUS TYPES OF ADMINISTRATIVE RESPONSIBILITIES

If the minister is to be an effective administrator, he must understand the nature of his responsibility and the various aspects of it. To that end let us now make a general survey of the field of church administration over which the pastor must give general supervision. The minister's administrative responsibility may be conveniently arranged for study under four heads: *general, financial, educational,* and *denominational.*

There are certain administrative responsibilities which cannot be classified except as general, that is, they have to do with the whole church organization. Under this head of general administrative duties will come the responsibility of planning and promoting the general church program which ought to give correlation, direction, and unity to every particular field of the church program. There will be certain objectives to be reached, certain emphases to be accented, and certain policies to be followed. An effective organization must have a general pattern, plan, and objective. This is the minister's first duty in the administrative field. He must lead in laying out a blue print for the over-all and long range church program. The definite program will depend upon the particular church situation. The thing we are emphasizing here is that there must be a general plan or program of work and the minister is responsible for giving general direction to this program.

Another responsibility coming under the head of general is that of publicity. A safe and sane program of publicity is essential to the progress of any church. The minister, of course, will not do all of the detail work in connection with the church publicity program, but he will give general direction to it. This publicity program will include an adequate church bulletin or paper, general advertising, news items, etc. It is one thing to make a program, but it is another thing to get this program before the people and to sell them on it. And this is where publicity comes in. The wise pastor will give careful consideration to the publicity program of the church.

Still under the head of general administrative responsibility is the personnel problem. The people constituting any corporation must be kept in proper relation to each other and to the program if effectiveness is to be attained. The church, as a corporation, is made up of people and as the work progresses there will be adjustments to be made in the personnel of the organization. The members must be kept in proper relation to each other and to the whole program of the church. The pastor cannot do all of this single-handedly, but it is chiefly his responsibility. This phase of the minister's responsibility is often a source of much anxiety and sleeplessness. It is this that often breaks the preacher down, though the average layman does not realize the nervous strain of this responsibility.

There are other responsibilities which might be included in this general field to which we will refer briefly. Church building comes in for considerable attention on the part of the preacher. The minister is not an architect or construction expert, and yet he is expected to give general direction to the church building program. Hence he must know something in this field too. The architect may know building construction but he will not know the particular needs of the church program. There are others in the congregation who are qualified to help in these matters, but the pastor will be looked to for general leadership and guidance in the church building program. No period of time is more straining on the pastor's time, energy, and patience than the period of a building program.

More and more our churches are feeling the need for an adequate church-centered recreational program for the young people. In many cases the direct responsibility of this program is placed in the hands of some member or paid worker, but the general plans, objectives, and methods come under the general supervision of the pastor. The pastor will face many problems in the operation of this program to which he must give much thought and consideration.

The financial program is a separate field of administrative responsibility in itself. With our complex and complicated church program the financial burden is becoming increasingly heavy. More and more time is being given by the pastor and others to the promotion of the financial program of the church. Indeed, it seems that in many cases the minister is expected to be a financial wizard. While it is true that in many cases too much is expected of the minister in this realm, yet he must be vitally interested in the financial program and be willing to take his place of leadership in it. There will be, in most churches, finance and budget committees to absorb part of the responsibility of the financial program, but even then the pastor will be sought out, and rightly so, for counsel and guidance in laying plans and setting up policies. Added to this is the minister's never-ending responsibility of stewardship training. He must keep the New Testament stewardship ideal always before his people. This will be done through preaching, teaching, bulletin items, and personal contacts. In and through it all the minister must remember that the financial program is not an end to be achieved in itself, but a means to an end, the advancement of the Kingdom of God at home and abroad.

In the educational field there is the responsibility of giving general direction to the auxiliary organizations of the church, such as: Sunday School, Training Union, Brotherhood, and Woman's Missionary Union. It is not our purpose here to study these organizations separately. Many volumes are now available on the workings of these organizations. The minister will be tempted to lose himself in the maze of organizational details and degenerate into nothing more than an organizer. And yet the successful minister must give some time to the general direction of these valuable auxiliaries. They can and should be used in the carrying out of an adequate church program. When properly related to the whole church program, these organizations will prove to be valuable assets in fulfilling the mission of the church. If the minister is to give general direction to these organizations, he must know something about them. He owes it to himself and to the church to know something of the nature of these organizations and how they work. He cannot possibly keep up with every detail in the educational program, but he can keep in step with the general movements and methods. His chief responsibility in this field is that of correlating these various organizations so that they will fit into a unified program of work. There are almost endless ramifications in this field of ministerial administration.

There is one other field of administration to be mentioned. It is the field of denominational responsibility. Every minister ought to be willing to accept his share of denominational responsibilities. It is possible for a preacher to over-load himself with denominational activity and become nothing more than a denominational agent to the neglect of his own church. Some preachers have been guilty of this. Others have been guilty of going to the other extreme, becoming wholly indifferent to the denominational program. This is more regrettable than the other. The wise and faithful minister will take an interest, not only in his own local parish, but also in the work of his denomination. He will be called upon to serve on committees and boards of various kinds. He will be asked to serve as an officer in some general denominational organization. A reasonable portion of these denominational responsibilities should be accepted gladly and carried out faithfully.

SOME ESSENTIAL QUALITIES FOR ADMINISTRATIVE EFFECTIVENESS

Having seen something of the nature and scope of the administrative work of the minister, let us now give our attention to a consideration of some of the fundamental qualities and virtues which are necessary in successful administration. These qualities can and should be cultivated early in the minister's life. Space does not permit a listing of all the qualities which go into the making of an effective administrator, but we do want to mention a few of the more fundamental virtues which are indispensible and must be cultivated by the minister if he would succeed.

The first quality we name is *honesty*. It might seem absurd to suggest that a preacher should cultivate the virtue of honesty. Are not all preachers honest? We only wish that this were true. However, we hasten to say that most preachers are honest in paying bills, but this is not the kind of honesty of which we are thinking now. It is administrative honesty that we have in mind. It involves the idea of sincerity. People will forgive many blunders on the part of the minister if they believe that he is honest and sincere in his leadership. He must "shoot square" with his people at all times. Deceptive leadership will always have repercussions. Nothing will ruin a preacher quicker than the discovery on the part of the people that the preacher has not been honest with them in his administrative leadership. The padding of reports is one form of administrative dishonesty. This quality is essential in any realm but especially so in the realm of administrative leadership.

A second quality in effective administrative leadership is *humility*. In this respect the minister's position is a little different from that of the business executive. The business executive may be overbearing and domineering and get by with it, since those with whom he deals are salaried people. But even in this case we have a conviction that humility will bring much greater dividends in every way. In view of the fact that the minister is dealing with volunteer workers it is all the more important that he conduct himself in a spirit of humility toward all of those with whom he works. He cannot drive; he must lead his people tenderly and lovingly as one of them. The minister's attitude toward his people will determine the effectiveness of his administration. Most people will resent the pastor who takes the attitude that "I know it all; you know nothing." But the pastor who takes his place along with his people and as one of them will be loved and followed in his administrative leadership.

Tact is another quality which the administrator must cultivate. Many preachers fail at this point. But tact is an art that can be cultivated and the minister who diligently seeks to cultivate it will discover that it pays in every way. Humility and tact go hand in hand. The man who has an humble spirit will usually have little difficulty in developing the art of tact and diplomacy. It is the proud and domineering man who has difficulty in applying . the principle of tact. A man may have ever so good intentions, but if he does not make the right approach to his people his leadership will fail. Tact is simply the application of good common sense and respect in dealing with others.

The element of *conviction* must come in for consideration at this point. By tact we do not mean that the minister should not be definite and firm. Tact is not spinelessness, as some seem to think.

One can be tactful and still maintain conviction and be firm. While the executive must be tactful he must also be firm in his conviction. He must express himself clearly and without equivocation. Some administrators fail because they never seem to put their feet on the ground with any definite, clear-cut plan or program. We must know where we are going, what we want to do, and how we can make this clear and unmistakable to our people. Many programs fail because of a lack of definiteness and tangibleness.

The successful administration must also have *discernment and perspicacity,* that is, the ability to analyze and interpret conditions. He must be able to see what the average man in his organization cannot see. It might also be called vision, foresight, or mental acumen. This, too, can be cultivated. How can the minister lead out in an agressive program if he cannot discern the times, foresee the possibilities, and understand the trends? Happy is the minister who has learned how to analyze and interpret situations as related to future progress. This faculty may be cultivated by mental exercise, close observation, and a study of history.

Along with discernment must come the ability to *systematize and organize.* Many times we fail in administrative leadership because we have no system or order to our work. The minister must have a definite plan and program and he must know where to find what he wants when he wants it. A proper cataloguing of information, records, etc., which he will need from time to time in his work is essential to the success of his administration. An adequate filing system can be set up which will prove a valuable asset to the preacher in his leadership work. Not only must there be system in the arrangement of materials for use in leadership but there must also be system in the work itself. "System is far more than mechanical orderliness. System is an attitude, an ideal, a mark of character. System is a living thing, a junior partner, an office secretary, a second self, a supplement to conscience."[2] A "hit or miss" type of administrative leadership is never effective. The minister must learn to plan and to follow a system. Of course, the system must not be too rigid. There must be room for adjustment and adaptation.

The last quality we mention is that of *confidence,* not a false and superficial self-confidence based upon an exalted opinion of one's self, but a confidence based upon one's faith in God. No executive can succeed who expresses an attitude of uncertainty. He must have confidence in the thing which he is doing and the assurance that it is right and proper. If the trumpet sounds an uncertain sound,

[2] Dobbins, G. S., *Building Better Churches,* p. 383.

who shall prepare himself for battle? As administrators and over-seers in God's house we must sound out a clear call and lead our people with confidence and assurance under the unerring leader-ship of the Spirit of God.

There are other desirable qualities in administrative leadership but these, we feel, are fundamental. Dr. Dobbins lists the following qualities: sincerity, foresight, tact, definiteness, judgment, confidence, and creativeness.[3] Most of the same general ideas are included in this list as in that which we have given. For practical guidance in working out the problems and details of administrative leadership the suggestions made by Dr. Dobbins will prove helpful. They are as follows: "Let action rest on conviction, not on mere consent. Depend more on honest, intelligent prayer than upon human wisdom and shrewd practice. Base decisions, policies, courses of action on facts, not guesses, rumors, gossip, sentimental wishes. Keep upper-most always the eternal value of the individual. Cultivate the spirit of incurable optimism."[4]

[3] *Ibid.*, pp. 378, 379.
[4] *Ibid.*, pp. 422, 423.

13 | PASTORAL VISITATION

The Place of Pastoral Visitation in Ministerial Activity

There was a time when the ringing of the old church bell would bring the people to the church, but this is no longer true. There are too many other bells calling men to other things. The pastor who does not visit will preach to empty pews on Sundays. Not only for the sake of having a congregation, but also for the service he can render through personal contact and in no other way, the minister must visit. We realize that as one critic has said, "Pastoral calling often degenerates into pious loafing,"[1] but we do not agree with this same critic when he says that the average church member would rather have his pastor planning church activities and preparing sermons than ringing door bells and that the honest church member is capable of maintaining interest in the church without frequent persuasion. We do not mean to say that the average church member wants his pastor to neglect his preaching, but he does expect his pastor to visit. In fact, pastoral visitation is a most effective method of preparation for sermon delivery. It will not take the place of study, but it will greatly enhance the effectiveness of the sermon for those who hear if the pastor has had a personal contact with the hearer. Dr. Sockman rightly reminds us that the minister's task is twofold: that of preparing the people for the word, and that of preparing the word for the people. "To say that a minister should prepare his people before his message is somewhat more than to say that pastoral work is the way to open unresponsive hearts."[2]

Few things inspire the preacher more than to look out over the congregation on Sunday and see some person with whom he has had a personal visit during the week. Not only is the preacher inspired in his preaching, but the one who hears will be far more receptive to the preacher's message after such a personal contact. No pastor can do his best work who does not have some personal contact with his people. This does not mean that the pastor should

[1] DeBlois, A. K., *Some Problems of the Modern Minister*, p. 14.
[2] Sockman, R. W., *The Highway of God*, p. 113.

spend all of his time making social calls on his members just in order to keep them in a good humor. But an occasional personal visit, especially in time of need or discouragement, will add much to the effectiveness of his ministry. Most of the time for visitation should be spent in making contact with the unenlisted and unsaved.

Herein is one of the gravest dangers facing our modern churches. Many of our churches are becoming so large in membership that it is almost impossible for the pastor to maintain any personal contact with his members. No matter how good a pulpiteer a minister may be there is something about a personal acquaintance with the minister that means much to the lives of the people. The successful pastor will find that much of his time must be given to personal visitation. Some preachers have tried to make themselves believe that it is not in the realm of their duty to go around ringing door bells. Their philosophy is expressed in this statement: "the people know where I am; they can come to see me if they need me. They know that I preach the Gospel; if they want to hear they know where to come." But this is quite different from Paul's philosophy: "I am made all things to all men, that by all means I might save some." It is not a matter of bowing to the whims and fancies of the people; rather, it is a matter of seeking to do the most good and reach the most people for Christ and Christian service. "It is a bit difficult for the ordinary man in the pew to feel the same interest in what the preacher is saying, when there is no personal acquaintanceship between the speaker and the hearer. It is certain that those who come into the pew, can never feel that the pastor is consciously dealing with their problems, or deliberately attempting to help in their solution if there be no acquaintance. Mutual acquaintanceship, then, is a prime factor in making the pulpit a successful and sympathetic instructor of the pew."[3] The call to personal visitation is an imperious call and the minister must not neglect it. He must lead his workers to visit, but this will not take the place of his own personal visitation, nor will his visiting take the place of the visitation of his workers. We are thoroughly convinced that visitation is an imperative in the minister's work, but it must be the right kind of visitation. Improper motives and methods in pastoral visitation will do far more harm than good. Therefore, the rest of this chapter will be given to a study of proper methods and motives in pastoral visitation.

[3] Riley, W. B., *Pastoral Problems*, p. 137.

TYPES OF PASTORAL VISITATION

In order to get a clearer conception of the task, let us first classify pastoral visitation according to the various types. There are two ways to classify it. First we will classify according to the occasion, and then according to purpose. According to the occasion there are three types of visits which the minister will make. First, there is the casual contact. This may be made on the street or in the store. The wise pastor will keep his eyes open at all times for any opportunity to make a personal contact in behalf of the church and the Lord. Many times the most effective contacts are those which are made casually. One pastor in a small town had the habit of spending about two hours a week on the public square. Many valuable contacts were made in this way. Of course, there were those who, seeing the pastor on the square, would make some remark about the preacher's not having anything to do but loaf on the street. And, indeed, we are afraid that some preachers may have become deserving of that term. Right at this point the minister is in a dilemma. If he spends some time on the streets seeking to make some personal contacts with men, he is branded by some as a loafer. If he never spends any time on the street and in the business places with the men, he is branded as a recluse and because of this he will never be able to reach some of the men that he might be able to reach through such casual personal contacts. We are convinced, however, that a reasonable amount of time spent by the minister in visiting with the men whom he might meet on the streets is time well spent. Especially is this true of the pastor of a small-town church. Such a practice affords the minister many opportunities for personal contact and personal conversion on vital matters which will bear fruit in souls won.

Other casual contacts can be made by the preacher as he goes about his own business in the stores or other places of business. A friendly exchange of greeting with an unsaved man in the store may win the confidence of that man and may ultimately be the means of leading him to salvation in Christ. The minister must not relax a moment in his desire to make every contact, especially the casual contacts. These are golden opportunities which, if neglected, may prove costly to the minister and the church. Another form of casual contact is that which comes with some recreational or social activity. Many times the minister will find that by going fishing with a man he will have an opening into that man's heart which he could not otherwise have. When the minister accepts an invitation to hunt, fish, or engage in any other recreational or social activity with someone else, it is not always for his own personal recreation or is it ever because he has nothing else to do. Many preachers could relate experiences in which they have led men to Christ while on such engagements or as a result of such engagements. This, then, is more than a preacher's avocation; it becomes a part of his task and an effective contact for winning men. Unlike most men, I have no special inclination toward fishing, but on several occasions I have gone with other men simply because I felt that it would afford a means of personal contact which I could not have otherwise. Some of the richest experiences of my life have come while riding in a boat or walking through the woods with some unsaved or unenlisted friend. The heart is more open and receptive under these circumstances than it would be in the case of a planned visit in the home or office. This is not taking advantage of a man. It is simply using the art of personal psychology in evangelism and there is nothing wrong with that. Usually when the visit is planned, and especially when by appoinment, a barrier of resistence is thrown up in the man's own heart which is sometimes difficult to overcome. Henry Ward Beecher very aptly said that "the best of all visitation is that which is casual and on purpose, — that which is apparently off-handed in the freedom of casual visitation, but which in your own secret mind forms a part of the system by which you go through your whole parish."[4]

A second type of visitation according to occasion is the planned visit. By this we mean the planned but unannounced visits of the minister in the homes. Many of the visits of the pastor will be unannounced beforehand to those visited. Some have objected to this type of visitation on the basis that an unexpected visit may find the host unprepared for such a visit and therefore embarrassed. But the minister who uses discretion and diplomacy should not be the cause of embarrassment on any occasion. The minister would not do much visiting if he waited for an appointment for every visit. There are some visits which ought to be made by appointment, but for most of his visits it is not necessary to make previous appointments. Even in the case of the planned visit the minister will be wise to make the visit appear as casual as possible.

The third type of visitation is the visit by appointment. As stated above, there are times when it is both wise and expedient to make the visit by previous appointment. This will depend upon the individual and the occasion of the visit. In such cases the minister should see to it that every appointment is kept promptly on time. There are some visits which cannot be made in any other way. The

4 *Lectures on Preaching.* p. 175 (second series)

minister must not limit his visitation to any one of these three types. He must use all of them if he would have an effective program of visitation.

From the standpoint of purpose there are also three types of pastoral visitation: for comfort, for enlistment, for evangelism. The case of the minister who visits in the home at the invitation of the one visited for the purpose of discussing some personal or social problem comes under the head of pastoral counseling which we will discuss in our next chapter. One visit may involve all three of these, but usually the minister will have one primary purpose in the visit, to bring comfort and consolation in sorrow and distress, to enlist in the program of the church, or to win to Christ in salvation. Of course, the pastor will want to visit the sick and sorrowing. Much of his time will be given in his ministry to those who suffer and sorrow. No visit means as much in time of sickness, distress, or sorrow as a visit from the pastor. He must not neglect this ministry, for the sake of the work and for the sake of the encouragement and help that he can bring in such times. Of course, the pastor cannot afford to use up his time and energy going hither and yonder to see every sister or brother who stumps his toe. Some people are unreasonable in their expectations of the minister's visit at every insignificant occasion. But in times of real need, the pastor cannot afford to be indifferent. A visit to a sick bed may soon be forgotten by the minister, but it will not be forgotten by the one who lies upon that bed. Not only will it bring comfort and strength to the sick, but it will stimulate his interest in the church and thus make for a more effective program of work in the future.

Much of the pastor's visitation work will be for the purpose of enlisting people in the program of the church or in its services. The average pastor will perhaps spend more time in this type of visitation than in any other. Even in the case of the unsaved, the minister will usually find it wise to make an effort to enlist in the services of the church before any definite personal appeal is made for a decision. It is most difficult to make any impression upon the lost man until he has been brought under the influence of the teaching and preaching of the Gospel. Then there are a great host of unenlisted and inactive Christians which need to be contacted. Many of them will never be enlisted until the pastor makes a personal visit. This ought not to be so, but it is and we must face it.

There is also the visit which has as its one primary purpose that of winning to saving faith in Christ. Many souls will not be won unless the minister makes a personal appeal. There are sometimes problems in the mind of the unsaved which never find solution in the sermon. Through a ministry of some twenty years I have known of very few people to make profession of faith in the services with whom I had not had previous personal contact of some kind. The day of mass evangelism is not over, but mass evangelism must be supplemented with personal evangelism if it is to continue to bear fruit. The two are mutually complementary.

SOME PRACTICAL SUGGESTIONS FOR PASTORAL VISITATION

Having seen something of the nature and scope of pastoral visitation, let us now give our attention to some practical questions with reference to it. These are questions which every minister has raised in his own mind perhaps many times. We want to raise the questions and then seek to give a practical answer. The first question to face us is this: How much time should a pastor give for his visitation? This will vary, of course, with the size of the field, the needs of the people, and the season. A few pastors spend too much time in visitation, time that could be better spent in the study. Then there are many pastors who spend too little time in visitation. This is more common. Though it may not seem so at first glance, pastoral visitation is hard work and too many preachers are just too lazy to give themselves to it. It is perhaps safe to say that the average successful pastor will spend on the average of about two hours a day in visitation. Regardless of the amount of time spent in visitation, the minister needs to have a definite plan and schedule of visitation. There will be times when it will be interrupted, but we have observed that the pastor who does not definitely plan a period of visitation each day or each week will neglect it. It has been our custom for years to reserve the hours from 3:00 p.m. to 5:30 p.m. for pastoral visitation. Of course, there are interruptions now and then, but this plan is generally followed. Each pastor will have to make his own schedule to fit with his own program and the particular field in which he is laboring.

A second question is this: What time of the day is best for pastoral visitation? The answer to this question will also vary with different situations. There are some people who cannot be found at home except late in the evening or at night; there are others who may have to be visited in the morning. But in general we have found that the afternoon is usually best for most people. It is not wise, however, for the pastor to begin his visitation too early in the afternoon, especially in the summer while many people are resting. If awakened and disturbed, they may not feel too good about the pastor's visit. The minister should use what he feels is the most convenient time for his visits, always ready to make adjustments for special cases which must be visited at unusual hours. We believe that the late afternoon is best because the people usually have a little more leisure time during these hours. Then from 5:00 to 6:00 p.m. many of the men can be found at home after work hours. The mornings are usually full for the housewife and then, too, the mornings are more conducive to study for the pastor.

Now let us consider another question: whom should the pastor visit? There is a grave danger that the pastor will spend too much time making social calls on the more congenial people of his congregation. Pastoral visitation should never be purely social. Every visit should have one or more of these purposes: to bring comfort to the sick and sorrowing, to enlist in Christian activity, or to win to salvation in Christ. The pastor ought to make at least one visit into every home of his membership as soon as he can after he arrives on the field in order to get acquainted with the home and to understand conditions. After this there is no need for a visit except in case of sickness or inactivity. The pastor's time is too valuable to go around making social calls on his members. After he has made the initial visit in the homes of his membership and after the sick are visited, the rest of his time in visitation should be given to the unenlisted and unsaved. It will save much waste of time if the pastor will keep a little card file, cataloguing the names by streets or sections of the community. This will save endless running back and forth from one end of the community to the other. Here is a sample schedule of visitation for a week: On Monday afternoon visit the sick and sorrowing (Of course, there will be other emergency sick cases to arise during the week.); On Tuesday visit church members who have not been previously visited; On Wednesday visit prospects in prospect file; On Thursday visit any new members who may have joined on the previous Sunday and those who visited in the service on the previous Sunday, leaving a copy of the weekly church bulletin; On Friday visit or revisit the most likely prospects with a view to their decision on the following Sunday. This schedule, of course, will need to be flexible and adaptable as the needs arise. But if the people are visited who need to be visited some plan of work must be followed. In closing this paragraph let us warn the minister against limiting his visitation to a certain class or group of people within his congregation or community. Some preachers have made the mistake of visiting only the wealthy and socially prominent in the community. Others have been found guilty of catering to the opposite group. We must not neglect either class. Both are to be ministered to by the pastor. The advice of Henry Ward Beecher is timely at this point: "Now, for the minister, above all men, it is a necessity that he should sympathize with humanity from the top to the bottom; with all men, not with one class of men; not with the best men, not with men of purest thought alone, because that unfits him to deal familiarly and easily with men who have no such habit of thought. The minister should cut the loaf of society, not horizontally, but vertically and take it with all there is in it, from top to bottom. And you will find — as it is in the housewife's cake sometimes — that the raisins are pretty much all at the bottom."[5]

And now another question: How long should the minister stay in making a visit? This will depend upon the circumstances and the nature of the visit. Ordinarily the most profitable visit will be the brief visit. When seeking to win an individual to a decision for Christ or in dealing with some specific problem, the visit will naturally be longer. But for the average visit to the sick room or for the purpose of enlistment, a brief visit is sufficient. In fact, a brief visit will usually do more good than a long one. There are times when the effectiveness of the visit can be nullified by staying too long. Most people do not have the time, nor do they care, for a long visit from the minister. The thing that impresses them more than anything else is the fact that the minister thought enough of them to make the visit, and this impression will frequently bear fruit. This impression can be accomplished just as well, if not better, by a brief visit. A visit should seldom be over ten minutes and many times less. The minister must learn to apply practical wisdom in this. If he sees that the person visited is preparing to leave for an engagement or busily engaged in the kitchen or at the meal, he should cut his visit to the minimum of time. By so doing he will be enhancing the effectiveness of the visit. If the person visited seems to be unoccupied and cordial, he may afford to stay a little longer. Just plain common sense applied is what the preacher needs in such matters. In all cases the visit ought to be made as brief as possible to accomplish the end desired. The minister's time is too valuable to waste in meaningless stays where it is not necessary.

Another pertinent question is this: How should the minister conduct himself during the visit and what should he say? This question cannot be answered specifically since there will be variety with each particular case, but there are some general suggestions we can offer. In every case the minister must be a real gentleman, giving proper respect and consideration. One preacher raised the question of the propriety of the minister's entrance into a home where there were no men present. Would this not lay the preacher open to criticism? We see no reason for criticism in such cases, unless the

[5] *Ibid.*, p. 150.

minister made a habit of going to the same home frequently or
stayed too long. At all times the minister must retain his dignity
and self-respect. At the same time he must not be too stiff, formal,
and distant. While in the home the pastor will find it profitable
and helpful to enquire as to the welfare of other members of the
family not present. This and other things will let the people know
that he is genuinely interested. And if the visit is to be effective he
must give some indication of his genuine interest in them. However,
the minister should not embarrass the family by asking impertinent
questions. Throughout the conversation the minister must not be
guilty of making any derogatory remarks or pessimistic expressions.
In seeking to enlist people in the church activities, let the minister
always remember that it is not so much a question of what they
can do for the church as it is a question of what the church can
do for them. After building up the proper approach, the minister will
use tact and diplomacy, according to the situation, in making known
his purpose for the visit.

Another closely related question is this: Should the minister
always have prayer in the home? The answer to this question would
vary with different ministers. Some ministers insist on having prayer
in every home visited. Others have it on certain occasions. Still
others never have prayer in the home unless it is requested. Each
minister will determine his own policy. We confess that we are not
absolutely sure as to which policy is best; however, it has been our
practice to have prayer on certain occasions but not in every visit.
A prayer by the minister is always appropriate and helpful in the
sick room. Sometimes this may be a little difficult when visiting
a patient in a ward at the hospital, but wherever possible the minister
should have prayer in the sick room or with those in sorrow. Then
when making a personal appeal to an unsaved person it is always
proper, if possible, to have prayer. In the ordinary visit for the purpose of enlistment it has not been our practice to have prayer in
the home. In many cases the conditions were such that we felt
prayer at that particular time would not be expedient. Of course,
we should make every visit in a spirit of prayer and with a breath
of prayer continually in our hearts, but we are talking now about
having audible prayer in the presence of those visited. While we
do not practice the habit of having prayer in every home visited, we do
not agree with the reason given by R. N. Barrett that "no man can
pray four times an hour for an afternoon without the most miserable formality, and prayer ought to spring out of the occasion."[6]

[6] *Ethics of the Ministry*, p. 163.

Many times the prayer of the minister in the home will mean far more than any thing he may say in the conversation. The minister ought to use it as often as he feels led to use it.

There is one more question to be raised: Should the minister always press for a definite decision when visiting the unsaved? In every visit the minister will have as his ultimate objective the decision for Christ, but we question the wisdom of seeking an "on the spot" decision in every such visit. "Having read appropriate Scriptures and prayed, it is sometimes well to depart and leave the soul to choose its course, but if there is faltering and the danger is pressing, it is in place to urge the immediate acceptance of the terms of salvation."[7] This statement by R. N. Barrett has much wisdom in it. In the average case we have found that it is usually best to give the lost man time to come under the influence of the preaching of the Gospel if this is possible. With this influence the personal appeal will be far more effective. If this does not appear possible or probable, then every energy should be used in pressing for the decision on the spot. Even when the personal appeal is made in the home, we agree with Dr. Barrett that it is usually best to leave the individual to make the decision at the service. Where this seems improbable or where it does not materialize, then all effort should be given to reach the decision in the personal conference. These suggestions are not hard and fast rules by any means, but are simply general observations from experiences in which these policies have proved expedient. Whatever the method, the objective should never be forgotten, the winning of the lost and the advancement of the kingdom.

[7] *Ibid.*, p. 166.

14 | PASTORAL COUNSELING

One of the most vital and far-reaching ministries of the pastor is that of personal counseling. A new emphasis has been placed upon personal counseling in this modern era, but counseling itself is not new, at least it is not new for the minister. Ministers have been giving personal counsel to individuals since the days of Jesus. It has been a part of their ministry. Not every minister, by any means, has been as effective in this as he ought to be or would like to be. And some have even sadly neglected this phase of ministerial responsibility. It is good, therefore, that we have this new emphasis on this phase of the minister's work. Many recent books have come from the press dealing with pastoral psychology and personal counseling. Some of these books the minister will find very helpful in this phase of his work. One of the most recent and best is Dr. Clyde M. Narramore's *The Psychology of Counseling*.

The Need for Pastoral Counseling

It is not our purpose here to give a technical treatise on pastoral psychology or psychiatry. We simply want to give a brief discussion of some of the more practical aspects of pastoral counseling. Our first concern is that as ministers we realize the opportunity for service and helpfulness in this ministry of personal counseling. It is more than an opportunity; it is a responsibility. The minister cannot close himself up to the personal needs and problems of his people. Dr. Tucker has very wisely said that "the preacher who excludes himself from men in the time of their want or necessity is the preacher whose sermons will in time betray this seclusion."[1] The young minister needs to recognize in the very beginning of his ministry the place and importance of personal counseling. Too many preachers never give any thought to this phase of their ministry until they are face to face with some individual with a problem. Preparation and plan should be given to this phase of the ministry as well as to other phases. There are certain fundamental principles and

[1] *The Making and the Unmaking of the Preacher*, p. 71.

114

policies which are indispensible to effective pastoral counseling. Every minister needs to study and understand these. The minister who thinks that he can take care of the counseling problems as and when they come without any forethought or plan is mistaken. Of course, each individual case may present a new problem or a new aspect of an old problem, but still the knowledge and understanding of certain fundamental principles will stand him in good stead. We do not have space in this discussion to analyze and study the various types of problems with which the pastor will be confronted in pastoral counseling. Such a study would be profitable, but we will limit ourselves to certain basic principles and practices in dealing with personal problems. May we remind the reader in this introductory paragraph that these suggestions for pastoral counseling will not be applicable to certain abnormals whose affection or animosity may be transferred to the minister to his great embarrassment and that of the church. Every minister will have a few such cases in a lifetime. In such cases the minister may be forced to use some drastic measure to get rid of the nuisance and embarrassment. Our suggestions apply to normal cases of personal need.

PRE-REQUISITES FOR PASTORAL COUNSELING

The first problem of the minister is that of laying a foundation for pastoral counseling. It is dangerous and unprofitable for the minister to try to give counsel where his counsel is not wanted or invited. Somehow he must create a condition or atmosphere which will make his counsel sought and desired. Some preachers are willing to give counsel, but never give any consideration to the conditions which would make their counsel desired. We knew of one pastor who announced in his church paper that his study would be open during certain hours each day for those who would like to have the pastor's counsel, but no one ever came to seek his counsel. It takes more than an announcement to create the desire on the part of the people to seek pastoral counsel. In fact, if other conditions are conducive, there is no need for any such announcement. How are these conditions to be realized? How can the pastor create the desire on the part of the people for his counsel? Let us answer these questions by offering several practical suggestions.

First, he must manifest a love for and interest in his people. This is the basic principle. It is possible for a pastor to love his people without giving much manifestation of it. No man is going to come to his pastor with a problem unless he is sure that the pastor is genuinely interested in him. Where the pastor's love abounds in unmistakable manifestation the people will seek his counsel. When no one seeks the minister's counsel in his personal problems, then the minister should ask himself, "What's wrong with me?" Thomas H. Lewis has expressed it very admirably in these words: "Love supplies understanding because it begets interest, and you can't understand anything without interest. Love is unselfish, and you study them unselfishly. Love is tactful, gentle, and so gives access to individuals without shutting them up in silence and rendering them impervious to our persuasions."[2]

A kindred principle is this: *The minister must know and understand his people.* If he loves his people, he will want to know and understand his people. This does not mean that he should be a busybody prying into everybody's business. But if he would give counsel in time of need, he must understand something of the need and the conditions underlying it. He must not only know individual persons, but he must also know men. He must study and know human actions and reactions, human customs and motives. He needs to understand the characteristics of the various age groups. Especially is this true in his ministry to young people. However, the minister must not think of his young people abstractly as a society or group, but concretely as definite personalities.

Another related basic principle is this: *The minister must have some knowledge of the principles of psychology and psychiatry.* We do not mean that he must be an expert in technical psychology. In fact, it is not absolutely necessary that he know psychology from the technical and scientific angle, but he does need to know at least a little about practical, applied psychology. The basic principles of psychology will serve the minister well in his ministry of personal counseling. Every minister ought to take at least one course in general psychology in college, or at least give careful study to some acceptable book on psychology or personality.

And finally, if the minister would serve well in the field of pastoral counseling, *he must give evidence in his own life of having conquered problems in the power and leadership of Christ.* He must give evidence of the abundant life which he preaches and claims to have in Christianity. Few people will approach the minister for personal guidance, if they do not see some evidence in the life of the minister himself of that which he has been preaching concerning the sufficiency of Christ in answering all of the problems of life. People seek the counsel of the minister, not only because they have confidence in him, but also because they have confidence in his religion.

[2] *The Minister and His Own Soul,* p. 52.

These things which we have mentioned make possible pastoral counseling; they do not guarantee its success. They merely open the door to the counsel room. And this is necessary before any counseling can be done. The minister may have ever so much wisdom and counsel stored up in his head and heart, but if no one ever comes around to ask for it, it is of no practical value. The first real test, then, in the ministry of counseling is this: Will the people seek the minister's counsel? "The eyes of the people may brighten; they may laugh at his wit and cluster about him to hear his stories. They may wonder at his brilliancy, and feel proud of his friendship. But the test question is: Will they come to him with their doubts, their troubles, their deep trials of heart?"[3] The highest compliment that can be paid to the minister is that which comes with the request for personal counsel and guidance.

SOME PRACTICAL SUGGESTIONS FOR PASTORAL COUNSELING

Let us turn now to a consideration of the counsel itself. When the minister sits in the presence of an individual with his problem (preferably in the pastor's study, though at times it may have to be in the home or at some other place), what is he to do and how is he to conduct himself in the conference room? Of course, each case will have its own peculiarities, but there are some general suggestions which the minister may follow with profit in all of his personal counseling. We give these suggestions with the hope that they will prove especially helpful to the young minister.

First, *never minimize the seriousness of the problem though it may seem trivial to you.* What may seem a trivial problem to the minister may be a mountainous difficulty to the seeker of counsel. If the minister ever reveals a feeling of insignificance toward the problem at hand, immediately his counsel will be invalidated.

Second, *be a good listener.* The first duty of the minister in the counsel room is to listen while the seeker after guidance tells his story. The minister should give ample time without interruption for the counselee to unburden his heart. Many times this is all that is necessary to solve the problem. The problem may be one of trying to hold a burden within the heart that wants to come out. In that case, a mere expression to some one will give relief. Many times the best counseling that the minister can do is to lend a listening ear. It may not always be a grief that needs expression; sometimes it may be a joy. "Joy that is never shared, is never fully matured. A joy that tells its story is like some imprisoned bird that

[3] DeBlois, A. K., *Some Problems of the Modern Minister*, p. 196.

has found the sunny air of larger spaces."[4] Many people experience
what David felt when he said: "When I kept silence my bones waxed
old" (Psalm 32:3). "Unshared troubles bring on premature age.
The trouble we can talk about loses some of its weight."[5]

Third, *do not give counsel until you know and understand the
situation.* Counsel without full knowledge of conditions may be
costly. The pastor, therefore, must guard against being too hasty in
giving his counsel. Let him wait until all of the facts are in, or at
least enough to form a solid basis for counsel.

Fourth, *do not presume to give counsel on matters which are
not in the realm of your familiarity.* It may be that the individual
needs medical care and treatment. In that case the pastor should
recommend a medical doctor or psychiatrist. The minister must not
presume to have knowledge of things which he does not really know.
A confession of ignorance or doubt in the face of some problem
will do far more good than a presumption of knowledge which is
not genuine. He must not attempt to do the medical doctor's work.
He is not qualified for it. Some people come to the preacher when
they ought to go to a doctor. Then some people go to the doctor
when they ought to go to the preacher for counsel. The pastor
and doctor can and should work together in these things. Neither
should infringe upon the other's territory or presume to have authority
on things out of his field of specialty. On several occasions I have
recommended a doctor for those who came to me for counsel, feeling that the doctor could do more for their particular problem than
the preacher. Not long ago a young lady came to my study with
a problem. In the course of the conversation she told me that she
had been to see one of the leading doctors in our city and he had
recommended that she come to see me. He felt that she needed the
counsel and help of a preacher more than she did that of a doctor.
Her problem was primarily spiritual rather than physical.

Fifth, *try to help the individual to overcome the problem rather
than just endure it.* There are some problems which can be solved
only by patient endurance, but there are many other problems that
can be solved and overcome. Many times the minister will be
tempted to take the course of least resistance and urge the counselee
to endure patiently rather than to seek a solution for the problem.
Phillips Brooks is right in saying that "the trouble with much of our
pastoral work is in its pettiness. It is pitched in too low a key. It
tries to meet the misfortunes of life with comfort and not with inspiration, offering inducements to patience and the suggestions of com-

---

[4] Jewett, J. H., *The Preacher: His Life and Work,* p. 191.
[5] *Ibid.,* p. 188.

pensation in this life or another which lies beyond, rather than imparting that higher and stronger tone which will make men despise their sorrows and bear them easily in their search for truth and nobleness, and the release that comes from forgetfulness of self and devotion to the needs of other people."[6] We must look beyond the present condition to the possibilities which will come with the solution of these perplexing problems. Jesus looked for and found the possibilities in the men who came to Him with all of their imperfections and perplexities. So must we.

Sixth, *if there is any correcting to be done, do it cautiously and tenderly.* The minister must not take the role of the scorner and begin immediately to scorn and reprimand the counselee for some misconduct which he has confessed. Many times young people do not come for counsel to the pastor because they feel that he may frown upon them in disdain. We are not suggesting that the pastor should condone sin and wrong at any time. If they have done wrong, he should not try to make them feel that they have not done wrong. Usually there is a need for reprimand and correction, but this can be done tenderly, but just as effectively, if not more so. Before correcting the young man or lady, the pastor could very tactfully suggest that he too has made mistakes in life. Such a confession will add much to the effectiveness of the rebuke.

And last, *always lead the individual to trust God and pray.* Any pastoral counseling which does not include a recommendation of trust in God is insufficient. The greatest help that we can render to troubled souls is to lead them to the Lord. Surely no conference should ever close without prayer. If possible, the pastor should lead the counselee to participate in the prayer season. The minister's final counsel to all people should be a recommendation to the great and all-sufficient "Wonderful Counselor," who knows and understands our problems better than we do ourselves and can lead us out of the mire and haze if we will let Him.

THE REWARDS OF PASTORAL COUNSELING

Few things bring greater anxiety, and yet at the same time greater joy than the work of pastoral counseling. The pastor must feel the poignancy of these problems with his people. He must agonize and sympathize with them. But through the years he will find joy and inspiration in watching the lives of these whom he has sought to help through personal counsel. When the problems of our people become our problems, then the working out of these problems becomes our victory. There is no joy like the joy that comes

[6] *Lectures of Preaching,* p. 79.

when some cherished end is gained through great anxiety, tears, and prayer. And if the minister renders effective service in this realm of personal counseling the problems of those who come to him must be felt in his own heart as keenly as if they were his very own. Then the joys of victory will be felt as keenly as if they were his very own. Besides feeling a sense of joy in the victory which he has helped another to win, the minister will find in personal counseling a source of inspiration and illustration in preaching. Many rich illustrative experiences will come from the conference room, though the minister must be careful not to embarrass the individual by using his name or giving any information which would betray the identity of the individual or the trust which he has placed in the preacher. Warm life-time friendships are won through personal counsel. That individual who has found help and counsel in the pastor's study in time of need will be that pastor's truest friend and defender throughout life.

Part III
The Minister and His Preaching

15 | THE SUBJECT MATTER IN PREACHING

Since preaching is primary in the minister's life and work, it is expedient that we give some further study of it. It is with this in mind that we give this entire division of our study to the subject of preaching. However, this is not intended to be an exhaustive treatment of homiletics or the preparation and delivery of sermons. It is not in the scope of this study to take up the science and art of public speaking or homiletics. Every preacher, of course, ought to make a serious study in this field and he will find much help and guidance in John A. Broadus' *The Preparation and Delivery of Sermons* and others. In this phase of our study it is our purpose to give emphasis to certain fundamental and elementary principles in preaching, leaving the scientific side of sermon preparation and delivery to a separate study and treatment.

THE SOURCE OF THE SUBJECT MATTER

If the minister's primary business is that of preaching, what is he to preach? This is the first question to face us when we think of preaching. Before we can have any adequate conception of the preacher's message, we need to know where he gets it. From what source does the minister receive this message? The answer is simple. He gets it from God. It is God given. A message gotten from any other source is spurious. The minister is not called to manufacture a message of his own concoction. He is called to deliver the message which God has already given. When delivering his great masterpiece on the resurrection to the Corinthians, Paul makes it plain that this message is not something which he himself has thought up, but was given to him of God. "Moreover, brethren, I declare unto you the gospel which I preached unto you, which also ye have received. . . . For I delivered unto you first of all that which I also received, how that Christ died for our sins according to the scriptures;" It is God who calls men to preach and it is God who gives them the message to preach. The minister must never lose sight of this fact. He must look to God for his message rather than to man.

123

The preacher's business is not that of preaching for his church, but rather, that of preaching to his church for God.[1] Dr. Conner has wisely pointed out that, if this is true, "God must be more real to him than the people to whom he preaches."[2] There is this danger into which some preachers have fallen, the danger of formulating a message based upon the likes and dislikes of his congregation rather than upon the inspiration of God.

This subject matter for preaching God has given through His Word, the Bible. It is made clear and understandable through the illumination of the Holy Spirit. God could have used other means of making known His message to the preacher, but in His infinite wisdom this is the means He has chosen. A few so-called prophets have arisen claiming a special revelation in which God has given a message foreign to or adding to that which is found in the Bible. In 1830 a man by the name of Joseph Smith claimed that he had a special revelation from God in which he was given a book, preserved from antiquity, containing a special message from God. This book of Mormon became the basis for a new religion. But we are convinced that the whole message of God is found in the Bible. Nothing else is needed to complete it. Special revelations may be given shedding more light upon that which is already there, but no new revelation containing a new message is to be given. There is a curse pronounced upon those who attempt to add to or take from the message of the Bible (Revelation 22:18, 19). Paul also makes this clear in Galatians 1:8 — "But though we, or an angel from heaven, preach any other gospel unto you than that which we have preached unto you, let him be accursed." We cannot, therefore, accept the pronouncements of councils of men or the so-called special revelations of men as authoritative and coming from God. Our message must come from God, and that message, so far as its content is concerned, is the Bible, no more and no less. But not only has God given the Bible as the substance of His message for man, but He has also given the Holy Spirit to illumine and interpret this message for man. There are, therefore, two fatal mistakes which the preacher can make. Any preacher who departs from the Bible for the subject matter of his preaching has made a fatal blunder. On the other hand, the minister may make the sad and fatal mistake of seeking to preach the message of the Bible without seeking the leadership and illumination of the Holy Spirit. The results in either case are tragic.

[1] Forsythe, P. T., *Positive Preaching and the Modern Mind.*
[2] "The Meaning of a Call to the Preacher" in *Baptist Standard* of March 17, 1949, p. 5.

AN IDENTIFICATION OF THE SUBJECT MATTER

Now we have said that the minister must receive his message from the Lord and that the message of God is revealed in His Word, the Bible. But just what is this message which is contained in the Bible? The Bible contains 66 books and hundreds of pages, but the subject matter of the whole Bible may be clearly summed up in a word — the story of redemption through the death, resurrection, and continuous intercession of Jesus Christ. And this is the preacher's message in a word. There is a wide variety of subjects discussed in the Bible, but running through them all is this golden thread of a crucified, risen Saviour. This is the one paramount theme around which everything else should revolve. The preacher must never lose sight of it; it must be central in all of his preaching. Paul set the pattern when he said, "We preach Christ crucified, unto the Jews a stumbling block, and unto the Greeks foolishness; but unto them which are called, both Jews and Greeks, Christ the power of God, and the wisdom of God" (I Corinthians 1:23, 24). Paul did not say, "Woe is me, if I preach not"; rather, "Woe is me, if I preach not the Gospel." Men are not called to preach anything; they are called to preach a certain thing, the Gospel of a crucified Christ. Go where you will in the Bible and you will find this theme running through it. We are told that when Philip found the Eunuch reading from Isaiah he "began at that same scripture and preached unto him Jesus."

It is both sad and tragic that so many modern-day preachers have substituted their own pet philosophies, political judgments, war strategy, book reviews, or fantastic predictions concerning future events, for the preaching of the simple Gospel of a crucified, risen, and sufficient Saviour. The Gospel of Christ may be applied in every realm of practical living, but the Gospel must be magnified first as the spring in which all ethical conduct must find its source and the basis upon which all moral conduct must be based if it is to be genuine and effective. We agree with Dr. Charles Jefferson that "possibly there never has been a time when there have been so many and such subtle temptations to reduce the Christian religion to an ethical code. Never have there been so many reverent and distinguished and religious men willing to do that as just now."[3] Christianity loses its power only when the Gospel of Christ is replaced with ethical and social platitudes in the pulpit. We have in hand a card advertising a series of sermon subjects by a minister of an

[3] *The Minister As Prophet*, p. 159.

evangelical church in a southern city. Among the subjects listed are these: Les Miserables, Tolstoy on War and Peace, Romola, Quo Vadis, and the Tale of Two Cities. It is obvious that these were simply reviews of certain great literary works. It is no wonder that this church has no spiritual fire or influence in the community.

The minister has but one message for all men, and only as he remains true to this one message will he receive any degree of success. He does not need one message for one situation and another message for another situation. The message of the Gospel of Christ will fit any condition or situation. The approach may be different and the method of presentation may be different, but the content of the message must be the same in every case. Dr. W. B. Riley quotes a wise preacher as saying, "Though I have a scientific mind and a university degree in sociology and philosophy, and although I am an expert in social service and an authority on Browning, and though I use the language of the scientific laboratory so as to deceive the very elect into thinking I am a scholar, and have not a message of salvation and the love of Christ, I am a misfit in the pulpit and no preacher of the gospel."[4]

This one message of the minister is an unchangeable message. It is an old message but ever new. Generations come and generations go, but the message of the cross is still appropriate and sufficient for all generations. Many things change in the course of years, but there are a few things which never change. Sin does not change in its essential nature. We may find new forms of expression for sin, but in essence the sin problem is the same as it was in the days of Moses, Abraham, and Adam. Satan is still in the same business and operates under the same deceptive principles. And since sin is the same, the gospel of redemption is the same. There has never been but one answer to the sin problem, and that is the atoning death of Jesus and its consequent resurrection. Every now and then some popular preacher appears on the scene to inform us that the gospel of redemption in Christ is outmoded and that we must replace it with a more modern and up-to-date message to suit the conditions of this modern scientific era. But, alas, his little light flickers but for a moment and then he is gone and forgotten, having left nothing to make the world better and nothing to solve the ills of a sin-infested world. But those who preach the ever old and yet ever new gospel of redemption in Christ have been and continue to be the most dynamic factors in contributing to the welfare of mankind.

[4] *The Preacher and His Preaching,* p. 49.

THE APPLICATION OF THE SUBJECT MATTER

This does not mean that the minister must preach the same sermon every time he preaches. The one message of the Gospel has thousands of applications and there are many different angles from which the minister may approach it and describe it. There is plenty of room for variety. But the theme of a crucified, risen Christ must saturate every sermon which the minister delivers. This is the subject matter out of which every sermon must come. The tragedy is that in their effort to emphasize the ethical applications of the Gospel, some preachers have ignored or neglected the fundamental basis for all ethical living — the gospel or doctrine of Christ and His atonement. Dr. Jefferson has wisely observed that "applied Christianity has been our theme; but alas, we have too little Christianity to apply."[5] The order of the day is "Ethical teaching without doctrine," but this is essentially contradictory. We agree with Harnack when he asserts that Christianity without dogma, without a clear expression of its content, is inconceivable. This quotation from Dr. A. K. DeBlois is well stated:

> A true theology touches life at all points. More and more in our day it is enforcing its eternal sanctions in the realm of morals. Such doctrines as the immanence of God in human affairs, the worth and meaning of the experience of redemption, the actual union of the Father with the Son and their ministry to man's good, the fellowship of the Spirit, the heinousness of sin, the possibility of a victorious life through faith in Christ's atoning sacrifice, the intimate relationship of the Christ controlled self with all phases of human experience, are interlinked with the problems of everyday living in the closest possible manner.[6]

We are willing to give to every minister the freedom and latitude of the manifold and kaleidoscopic application of the gospel truth, but we must insist that every sermon be explicitly grounded in the fundamentals of God's grace in the atoning work of His Son, Jesus Christ. This is the message of the Christian minister and he must not waver in it.

THE PERSONALITY OF THE SUBJECT MATTER

There is one last word which we would like to leave with the reader concerning the subject matter of preaching: The preacher's message must be predominantly personal and experiential rather than creedal. The creed is only incidental to the person. We preach

[5] *The Minister As Prophet*, p. 173.
[6] *Some Problems of the Modern Minister*, p. 56.

Christ, a person. The effectiveness of Christianity is in the personality of Christ and the possibility of our experience with Him. The preacher who reduces his message to a system of ethical laws to which the individual is asked to subscribe has robbed Christianity of its potency and life. Our message is a personal message and we must keep it on a personal plain. To be sure, there are dogmas, but these dogmas grow out of personal experience with a personal Christ. And this is what gives the message life, animation, and vivacity. In his *Lectures on Preaching*, Phillips Brooks warns against the tendency to take the personality out of our message. These are his words: "To discuss the relations of politics is good. To set Christ forth to men so that they shall know him, and in gratitude and love become his, that is far better. It is good to be a Herschel who describes the sun; but it is better to be a Prometheus who brings the sun's fire to the earth."[7] The minister must come to the pulpit with a fresh experience with the personal Christ to proclaim to his people the sufficiency of this personal Christ to answer the longings of the human soul and to solve the problems of the human heart. In this the minister finds his theme for every sermon, adapting his treatment of it to fit any situation. This is what Phillips Brooks calls Truth and Timeliness.[8] The truth stands without variation and must always be sought first; timeliness is the application of truth to a certain condition. This order must always be followed. There must always be truth before there can be any effective application of truth. And let the minister never forget that this truth is Jesus Christ, who said, "I am the truth." Let truth be always personalized in Christ if we would make it attractive and effective.

[7] *Lectures on Preaching*, p. 21.
[8] *Ibid.*, p. 220.

16 | SCHOLASTIC PREPARATION FOR PREACHING

The Need for Scholastic Training

Since the preacher's message is given to him of the Lord, why is it necessary for him to spend hours of preparation in delivering it? Why not let him just open his mouth and wait for the Lord to fill it with the words He would like for him to deliver? A few preachers have tried this philosophy only to discover (at least the people have discovered) that there is nothing there but wind and hot air. Preaching is not like the mechanical machine which is used for delivering baseballs to the baseball players for batting practice. While it is true that the subject matter of the message we are to deliver has already been given to us of the Lord, yet there are innumerable factors to be considered in the delivery of this message, such as the method of delivery, the attractiveness of the description of the message, and the application of the message to the individual case or condition. The preacher is in much the same position as the baseball pitcher. He doesn't have to worry about what he is going to pitch. The ball is given to him. But much consideration must be given to such things as these: shall he throw it fast or slow; shall he throw an in or out curve or a drop; shall he throw it high or low to the batter? These are things which have to do with the manner of delivery and many hours of preparation must be given to them. It involves a study of the batter as well as the technique of pitching. Even so in delivering the Gospel, the preacher must give much time to the technique of effective delivery and the particular conditions and needs of those to whom he preaches. And this involves much preparation. The minister who thinks that he can succeeed without it is only fooling himself.

There are three kinds of preparation which the minister must make for effective preaching: scholastic preparation; personal study preparation; and spiritual preparation. This chapter concerns the first of these. The other two will come up for consideration in later chapters. Should the minister go to school in preparation for his

ministry? We answer without hesitation that every preacher should
get all of the scholastic training that it is possible for him to get.
In every case he will find it a valuable asset throughout his ministry.
We are not saying that scholastic training guarantees success in the
ministry. Some preachers who have diplomas and degrees from the
best schools in the land are complete failures. That preacher needs
to be disillusioned, and will be sooner or later, who thinks that a
diploma from a college or seminary is all that is necessary for a happy
and successful ministry.

On the other hand, there are a few preachers who have achieved
great success though they never went to a college or seminary. These
are exceptional cases. Only a few men are capable of doing this.
Men like Moody and Spurgeon knew nothing of formal higher education. But these men did not succeed because of their lack of
formal scholastic training; they succeeded in spite of it. Some few
men are big enough to succeed without it, and yet even these men
would have been greater with the advantage of scholastic training.
And, furthermore, these men would be the first to express their desire
for all ministers to have the advantage of scholastic training. Most
of these men would have had scholastic training if it had been available for them. This does not mean that these men are uneducated.
Theirs is a self education. They have applied themselves to study.
After all, it is not the school that makes the preacher. It is the study
and the development of the study habit! A few men are big enough
to develop this without the school, but most of us will never become
students in the real sense of that word without the help and encouragement of the school. It is much more difficult to learn to
study and apply knowledge outside the school than it is in it. This
is why so few succeed without some degree of scholastic training.

Furthermore, there is less excuse for the lack of scholastic
training today than in days gone by. In the days of Moody and
Spurgeon schools were not as accessible as they are today. In
those days very few people had the advantage of the schools of
higher learning. But in these days and in our country, schools of
higher learning are in range of almost every man who really wants
it. There may be a few rare exceptions, but the young preacher who
wants scholastic training can have it, if he really wants it. And with
all of our modern advance in science and art it is all the more imperative that the preacher have the best scholastic training.

THE PLACE OF SCHOLASTIC TRAINING

Having been convinced of the necessity for scholastic training
the next question to face the young minister is this: Where shall I

go to receive this training? We are thinking now in terms of the college and seminary. Schools of higher education have multiplied so rapidly in the last few decades that now there are schools of higher learning within a radius of a few hundred miles of every one who lives within the borders of our nation. There may be a few cases in which, because of limited financial ability and other conditions, the young minister will have to go to the only school available. But in most cases there will be a choice between two or more schools. The young preacher will find it to his definite advantage to go to a Christian school, and if at all possible, to a school of his own denomination. There are many things to be learned in the state school and much profit can come from study in other Christian schools, but the young minister can get all of these things plus an insight into the policies and practices of his own denominational field of labor by attending a school of his own denomination. There may be some advantages in studying first hand the practices and tenets of other religious groups in the schools sponsored by them. We need more knowledge and understanding of what others are doing, but sufficient understanding can be had by an indirect study of these groups through the schools of one's own denomination. Our first responsibility is that of seeking proper grounding in the principles and practices of our own faith. The denominational school will give an interpretation of the general facts in the light of their relation to Christian life and conduct as we accept it and practice it.

Another factor in the choice of a school is the location. If it is possible, would it be wise for the young minister to go to another section of the country for his scholastic training? Some ministers feel that they should get completely away from the environment of their native communities or states for their scholastic training. In so doing they feel that they will receive a broader view and become acquainted with life and habits with which they have not been accustomed all of their lives. This reasoning may have some wisdom in it, but it seems to us that the wisest course for the young minister would be to seek his education in that section of the country in which he expects to labor. Of course, we realize that the young minister does not know with any degree of certainty where the Lord will lead him in the ministry. But as far as this can be ascertained it ought to be a factor in the choice of a school. If it is a case of one who plans to serve on a foreign field, he will be wise to seek at least some additional training in some educational institution in his particular field of labor. There is a definite advantage in having some scholastic training from an institution which has a vital connection with the life of the community or state in which the minister plants his life. This does not mean that all of his training should be in this same section, but at least some of it. We do not want to leave the impression that the minister cannot do a good work who has not had training in some school within the vicinity of his labor, but we are convinced that if this is possible, it will be to his advantage.

THE EXTENT OF SCHOLASTIC TRAINING

In the realm of scholastic training another question faces the young minister: How far should he go in his scholastic training? The answer to this question will be determined largely by the ability of the individual to continue his educational pursuits, the age of the individual, the disposition, and the type of work in which he plans to invest his life. Other things being equal, we would say without hesitation that the minister should get all of the scholastic training that it is possible for him to get. He should be satisfied with nothing less than the best. The price paid for the best training will pay dividends in the future. We are not saying that a man is not qualified to preach until he has reached a certain degree of scholastic training. Some ministers, as we observed above, have achieved great success who have never even been to college. These are exceptions, however. Some religious groups require a certain amount of scholastic training before they will allow their ministers to preach or become pastors of churches. But we are presuming upon the authority of God when we set up laws or policies which prohibit a man from preaching until he has reached a certain standard of scholastic training. If a man feels that he has been called of God to preach, he ought to be given the liberty to preach (or to hold a pastorate if a church wants to call him) whether or not he has finished the first grade. At the same time every encouragement possible ought to be given young ministers in continuing to completion their scholastic training. They should be satisfied with nothing less than the best. Usually the untrained minister will discover before long that his lack of training handicaps his work and that his services are not in demand. These conditions themselves will point the young minister toward the school.

For the most effective work the minister's scholastic preparation ought to include at least the standard courses of study in college and seminary. This will require ordinarily about four years in college and three in the seminary. The college education should include a study of a wide range of the liberal arts and sciences. The ministerial student should get a broad basis of education in a number of fields; however, he should take enough courses in Bible and related subjects to give him a core of religious instruction all the way through his university experience. Studies in english, history, psychology, and social science are always helpful to the young minister in preparation for his life's work. Statistics show that 50% of our college and university preachers never enroll in any of our seminaries. If the minister is uncertain as to the possibility of his seminary training, then by all means he should get all the Bible training he can while in college. For those who go on to the seminary specialized study of the Bible and religion will be intensified in the seminary training. Whether the minister ought to go on beyond the standard seminary course or not will be determined by his age, disposition, and field of labor. It is our judgment that some ministers would be wise not to seek work on a doctor's degree. Others, by all means, should. Each case will have to be studied individually. Many times the school itself determines this. There is little danger that the minister will receive too much scholastic training; but there is grave danger that he will stop short of that which would equip him for the best service in the kingdom.

THE VALUE OF SCHOLASTIC TRAINING

Now let us give some consideration to the purpose and profit of scholastic training for the minister. In what way, or ways, does formal school training profit the minister? The average person thinks of scholastic training as an effort to cram one's head full of facts and information about this, that, and the other. To be sure, some facts are gained through scholastic endeavor, but this is the most insignificant feature of scholastic training. It would really be astonishing if we actually knew how little the student retains of that which he puts on the examination paper. It is doubtful that the average student retains as much as one tenth of that which he goes over in the classroom. If we forget so much so soon, then why go to the trouble? The one tenth we do retain is worth all the effort through which we go to receive it. But this is not the real value of scholastic training. According to Dr. W. J. Tucker, "Education can do these three things to make ready the preacher: First, it can do more than at any previous time to develop and furnish the man, provided he has insight and patience. . . . A second result to be expected from modern education — I cannot overestimate its value to the preacher — is that it can give him contact with the mind of his time. . . . The third result which education ought to be expected to give to the preacher is the clear and sure access to truth. Not possession of it in any large degree, that is the work of a life time, but access to it."[1] All of these things are true, but according to our own experience

[1] *The Making and Unmaking of the Preacher,* pp. 39-44.

and observation the greatest values of education for the preacher are these:

First, it teaches him how to study and cultivates the habit of study. Few preachers know how to study except as they learned it in school. No man can learn all there is to know in four years of college or three years of seminary, but he can during these years learn how to study, and this is what he needs more than he needs the knowledge of facts. Studying is not as simple as it may seem. There is an art to it that must be learned and cultivated. Happy is the preacher who has learned how to study. Scholastic training will do more than anything else in developing this art. There is more to it than holding a book in the hand for two hours. There must be concentration, ability to analyze, creative thinking, and depth of perception. God pity the preacher who goes through college and seminary without having developed at least some of these arts.

Second, scholastic training helps the preacher to know how and where to find what he wants when he wants it. It is not so much a matter of retaining facts as it is a matter of being able to know where to go to find what we want when we want it. Education opens up avenues of access to knowledge and understanding. The minister may not be conscious of it, but he will never be able to evaluate the contribution which education has made in this realm. Education introduces us to the sources, it is ours then to dig into these sources and resources for the food which is there. The room of knowledge, understanding, and usefulness is large and vast; education leads us to the door, unlocks the door, and leaves the rest to us. But how sad would be our plight if we could not find the door, or the key that unlocks the door! This is the plight of most of those who do not have the advantage of scholastic training. Once in a great while a genius finds the door and the key without going through the halls of formal education.

Third, perhaps the greatest value of scholastic training is found in the lasting impressions which are made upon the student by his contact with great leaders. Whether he realizes it or not, the student absorbs through the years the ideals and attitudes of his teachers. The impressions have a tremendous bearing upon the whole life of the individual. As I look back now over my own life I can see more clearly than ever before how many conceptions and attitudes of my life have been formulated from the impressions of my teachers. I cannot put my finger on any one experience or any one thing said, but the whole content of my theology and conception of life is a gradual outgrowth of these indelible impressions of my teachers. No person has as much to do with the shaping and molding of ideals and attitudes of life as the teacher, unless it be the parents, and yet he receives less credit for it than any one else. The teacher is almost a forgotten man except as he multiplies himself a thousand-fold in the attitudes and ideals of his students. We will forget the subject matter of the course of study, but we will not forget the attitudes and conceptions of the teacher. For this reason we must have the right kind of teachers, and for this reason the young minister must seek his scholastic training in schools of genuine Christian atmosphere. From this point of view education can become the greatest destructive force in the universe or it can become the greatest constructive force in the universe. We are dealing now with the very heart of education. Too many people think only in terms of surface facts when they think of education and schools. Dr. Jeff D. Ray has the right idea in mind when he says that "a theological seminary ought not to be a factory where big original independent souls are whittled down to fit a regulation groove. It ought to be rather a temple in whose holy of holies these glowing young souls meet God and on whose altar-stairs they touch the garment-hem of spirit-filled prophets with the gifts of arousing latent powers, and stirring smouldering ambitions and quickening chivalrous ideals."[2] Thank God, we do have some institutions like this. Fortunate indeed are those who are privileged to enter therein. The benefits therefrom are inestimable in value for the minister.

[2] *The Highest Office,* p. 90.

17 | PERSONAL STUDY PREPARATION FOR PREACHING

The Necessity of Study

Scholastic preparation is not sufficient. The minister's life must be one of continuous study. As we said in the preceding chapter, one of the greatest benefits of scholastic training is the development of the habit of study. A few ministers have tried to succeed without study, but no one yet has succeeded in such an attempt. The minister who loses his interest in study will soon lose his effectiveness in the pulpit. Every great preacher the world has known has been a student, whether he ever went to school or not. It is possible, though difficult, for a minister to succeed without scholastic training, but it is utterly impossible for any minister to succeed without consistent personal study. The people may not always know the reason for it but they will immediately sense that there is something wrong with the pastor's preaching when he ceases to study.

Some preachers object to the idea of the importance of personal study on the basis that it precludes the inspiration of the Holy Spirit in the pulpit. They reason like this: if the preacher has the sermon all worked out in his study, there is no room left for the leadership and inspiration of the Holy Spirit in the pulpit. But let us clarify our position by making two things clear: First, even though the preacher has spent hours in preparation for the sermon, there are times when he will be impressed while in the pulpit with a thought which had not been included in his studied preparation. There must always be a recognition of the possibility of added inspiration in the pulpit. And second, could not the Holy Spirit lead and inspire the preacher in his study as he prepares for the sermon just as well as He could lead and inspire in the pulpit? He can and does do both. The preacher's study can and ought to be as much under the leadership of divine guidance as the actual delivery of the sermon in the pulpit. And then, even after thorough preparation the minister must depend upon the leadership of the Holy Spirit in the effective delivery of that which he has worked out in the study. There is absolutely no incongruity between personal study preparation and divine leadership in preaching.

While it is true that the minister must study, the deplorable

136

fact is that so few ministers in our day give the time and energy to the study which is necessary for great preaching. That is why we have so many ministers today who are noted for their organizational ability rather than for their preaching. The pastor's study has been transformed into an office in which the minister goes to transact a multitude of administrative details. And in some cases the pastor's study has been turned into a lounge where the minister idles away hours in social sessions with his special circle of friends. Dr. Jowett very aptly remarks that "if the study is a lounge, the pulpit will be an impertinence. There is no man so speedily discovered as an idle minister, and there is no man who is visited by swifter contempt."[1] The besetting sin of the average preacher of today is his failure to study. Some preachers are just too lazy to study, while others are so preoccupied with countless details of this, that, and the other that there is no time left for study. This condition is distressing. If we are to have great preachers, we must have great students. There are few, if any, modern-day preachers comparable to Spurgeon, Edwards, Wesley, Whitefield, and many others equally great of other generations. These men gave much time to study and meditation. We realize that the modern minister is called upon for many things to which he must give attention, but regardless of other calls if the minister would succeed in the pulpit he must make a place in his busy life for many hours of study. His study must be given priority over most other things to which he is called. It is impossible to have great preaching without great students. The strongest temptation a preacher has is the temptation to neglect his study for other good but less important things. There are times, of course, when because of emergencies the preacher will come to the pulpit without the study preparation he would like to have had. In such emergencies God will bless and inspire with a message. But the man who comes to the pulpit without proper study just because he is careless or indolent need not expect the Lord to bless and inspire. God never endorses or blesses indolence. And usually the preacher has no excuse for lack of study except inertia.

The Plan of Study

The preacher who studies only in his spare time or when he has nothing else to do will seldom if ever study. Study must be planned. There must be a program of study. We never do much at any thing just accidentally. If study is important for the minister, then it ought to be given a prominent place in his daily program. We realize that no minister can follow a rigid schedule. There will

[1] *The Preacher: His Life and Work,* p. 114.

be emergencies to arise and interruptions of visitors seeking help, etc. But in spite of this the minister ought to have some regular schedule of work in which he will include a proper amount of time for study. The minister cannot afford to close the door of his study and refuse to respond to any call. By so doing he will be handicapping the influence and effectiveness of his ministry. The minister must always be accessible to his people. And yet if he has a definite schedule and the people know something of the schedule, they will usually have respect enough to allow him to carry out his schedule with as few interruptions as possible.

Each minister will have to work out his own schedule in keeping with his own taste and the peculiar conditions of his field. However, in most cases the minister will find the mornings best suited for study, especialy the early morning hours. But the important thing is that there must be a time somewhere for study no matter when it comes. A study period once a week for the hasty preparation of a sermon is not sufficient. Study for the minister must be a daily habit. In my own experience I have found that the early morning hours afford the best time in many ways for study. During these early hours the mind is clear and there are no distractions. Because of so many evening duties most preachers are not permitted to retire early at night and many feel that the early hour is too early to permit sufficient night rest. But an hour's rest after the noon meal will compensate for this. Should he go back to his study immediately following the noon meal, the minister will usually find that this is the most difficult time of the day for the best functioning of the mind. And, furthermore, this is usually a most inappropriate time to make pastoral calls in the homes.

Many times the minister must do his best to study in spite of frequent interruptions, but if possible he should have a minimum of interruptions. Uninterrupted study is always better than interrupted study. The first part of the morning should be given to genuine study. The later hours of the morning could be given to counseling and administrative work. "Desultory thinking, and thinking done in fits and starts between the interruptions of intruding visitors and duties, is not the kind of thinking which builds up the preacher's mind."[2] Some preachers, in order to avoid the interruptions at the church office, find it wise and profitable to maintain a study in their homes. This may be advisable under some conditions, especially where there are no children in the home. The practicality of this will have to be determined by each individual case.

[2] Jefferson, C. E., *The Minister As Prophet*, p. 82.

THE RANGE OF STUDY

Having arranged for a definite period of study each day, just what should the minister do during this period of study? What should he study and how should he study? It is not sufficient just to have a time of study. Great care must be exercised to see that this time is spent in the most profitable way for the effectiveness of the ministry. First, from the negative point of view, may we suggest that the minister should not spend all of his time working on sermons and sermon outlines. It is possible for a preacher to spend too much time on his sermon. We say this with fear and hesitation, because most preachers do not spend enough time on their sermons. But some preachers spend so much time on the sermon itself that they spoil it. Dr. Jefferson's warning is very timely: "You may work so long upon a sermon that you spoil it. It becomes too finished and has too fine a polish. It is as beautiful as a statute and as cold."[3] When this is done the preacher becomes overly conscious of the details of the sermon to the neglect of its heart and spirit. Much of our study should be in preparation of our own souls and minds, rather than in preparation of sermons. Good sermons grow out of rich endowments of mind and soul.

From the positive point of view, this is what we are trying to say: Much of the minister's time in study should be given with little or no thought of a sermon or sermon outline. He may not realize it, but such study will have a tremendous effect upon his preaching. Much of what the preacher studies has an unconscious effect upon his preaching. It gives a general background for his thoughts, an authority for his expressions, and impressions and attitudes of soul which are reflected in his sermons though he may never quote exact words. The advice of Dr. Charles Jefferson is so timely at this point that we must quote from him again: "You ought to know ten thousand times more than you ever say. A preacher influences his congregation not simply by what he says, but by what he knows and says nothing about. We are not interested in the man who tells us all he knows. A sermon is only a cup of water, and it tastes better when we know that it comes from an inexhaustible spring."[4] In his lectures to Yale students Dr. Jowett said that "Our very insight into particular truths depends upon our vision of broader truth. Telescopic range gives you also microscopic discernment."[5] Some preachers study little or none at all; others study but only that

[3] *Ibid.*, p. 93.
[4] *Ibid.*, p. 90.
[5] *The Preacher: His Life and Work*, p. 118.

which is directly related to a sermon. In either case the result is poor preaching. The minister must have a broad range of knowledge and understanding for the most effective preaching.

Now let us be more specific. We realize that the minister's study should be broad in range. But just what should it include? We do not have the space or the ability to enumerate all of the things which ought to be included in a minister's study diet. But we can offer some general suggestions. In the first place, we would suggest that most of his time should be given to a study of the Bible and Biblical subjects. After all, if he is to be a minister of the Word, it is only proper that he give his major attention to the study of the Bible. But even in the study of the Bible, the minister should beware of spending all the time just looking for sermon texts. It is well to begin the morning period of study with a devotional reading of the Bible with prayer. Then the Bible should be studied systematically by books, by topics or by periods. Such a study should be made in connection with great works on theology and Bible interpretation. Then, of course, some time will be spent in the study and interpretation of certain texts for the purpose of sermon preparation. If possible, some time should be given to a study of the Bible in the original Hebrew and Greek. It is not in the scope of this study to discuss the details of the process of developing a text for sermon preparation. These are simply general hints for the minister's study.

While the study of the Bible should come first and should always have the pre-eminent place in the minister's plan of study, this is not all by any means. He should give some time to the study of other things, all of which have some relation to Bible truth. Among the things to be included in his study are the following: books on theology, both old and new; history, both secular and sacred (the study of history affords the preacher with many rich resources for ministerial service); biography; philosophy; classic poetry; pastoral psychology and homiletics; and sermons of great preachers. Some reading of good fiction will also be of profit to the preacher. Then there are many periodicals available for study, but these should be studied sparingly. Other things might be added to this list, but all of these ought to be included in a proportionate measure if the minister is to have a balanced study diet.

THE ASSIMILATION OF STUDY

Taking for granted that the minister has given ample time to study, how can he assimilate for practical use the mass of material which passes through his mind in study? Some of that which goes through his mind in study is not worth retaining, except as it helps him to understand what is going on in the thought world of others. Other material will be of no practical value so far as its direct use in the pulpit, but it will do much toward shaping ideas and conceptions. Many times the minister feels that that which he has studied is of no value unless he can quote from it in a sermon. But such an attitude is based on a misconception. Study which impresses itself upon the preacher's ideas and conceptions will unconsciously express itself in every sermon he preaches. Then there is material found in study which can be used directly in the sermon.

For the proper assimilation and use of that which we study let us offer a few suggestions. First, there should be an adequate system of cataloguing and classifying the books and materials which are available to the preacher. We will reserve the discussion of this suggestion until we come to our next chapter on "The Minister and His Library." Second, the minister will find it profitable to study with his pencil in hand, making notes and underlining statements of special merit. The clipping or copying of certain paragraphs and poems for quotation or reading in the sermon may have some value. However, the preacher needs to be warned against making his sermons a compilation of thoughts and expressions of other men. Some preachers are men of thoughts; others are men of thought. There is a difference. A quotation now and then adds to the forcefulness of the sermon, but the sermon itself should grow out of the thought world of the preacher himself and not out of the barrel of classified quotations and illustrations. Too many preachers feed their people on warmed-over hash instead of fresh wholesome food from the life, experience, and thought world of the minister's own soul. Third, in all of his study the minister should seek to relate everything to Christian experience and the Christian message. All reading should be interpreted in the light of Gospel truth. Such interpreting and appropriating will make all of his study more vital and refreshing. Fourth, the minister should seek through study to cultivate ideas and thoughts rather than to memorize statements. Ideas and attitudes are far more important than the memorizing of statements. The ability to analyze the ideas, purposes, and motives of an author is far more valuable than the ability to retain in the mind the words of a certain line or lines. Let the minister resolve, not only to study, but to learn how to make his study genuinely profitable to his ministry.

18 | THE MINISTER AND HIS LIBRARY

The Importance of Books

In the preceding chapter we emphasized the importance of studying for the minister. If the minister studies, he must have books, or at least access to books. There can be little studying without books. A minister's books are the tools with which he works. He should prize them most highly. Few investments will bring greater dividends to the preacher than that which he invests in a book. Every minister should determine early in his ministry to build up a good and usable personal library. Books cost money and some preachers may feel that they cannot afford them, but the minister can better do without butter on his bread than he can without books. He cannot afford to do without books. A preacher can get along no better without books than a carpenter without hammer and saw. Through his books the minister sits at the feet of great teachers. Before any preacher can build a good personal library he must realize the intrinsic value of books in ministerial life.

Now we have said that every preacher ought to have a good personal library, but this is not easily done. There are many problems attached to it. Many questions will arise, such as these: How much money should a preacher spend on books? How many books should he have? What kind of books should he buy? How can he arrange his books so as to make them usable and accessible? These and many other questions will face the minister in the building of his own personal library. In this chapter we hope to face and give some practical answers to these questions.

The Building of a Library

Let us first concern ourselves with the acquiring or building of a library. Our first suggestion is that the young minister should spend every available dollar on books, even to the point of sacrificing other things. A few young ministers are fortunate enough to inherit a large library from some retired or deceased preacher. But most ministers will have to build their libraries from scratch with their own blood, sweat, and sacrifices. Some young minister may ask: Should I not wait until I can accumulate enough money to buy a large quantity of books at one time? The answer is an emphatic "no." In most cases the money would never be accumulated and, furthermore, it is much better to accumulate books little by little, giving time for individual acquaintance and classification, than it is to purchase a large quantity at one time. This does not mean that he should buy a book just when he has an extra dollar that he doesn't need somewhere else. With such a plan the shelves in the minister's study will, for the most part, remain empty. Buying books must be according to a set plan and system. The minister should set aside a certain amount each week or each month for the purchase of books, just as he sets aside a certain amount for groceries and house rent. That which we buy accidentally never amounts to very much. Where the salary is meager the amount, set aside will have to be small, but whatever the amount, the habit should be cultivated of setting something aside each month for books. For some time now it has been my custom to spend from ten to twenty dollars every month for books. This does not mean that the books must be bought the very day the money is available, but for the best results they should be purchased at reasonably regular intervals. With a definite, regular plan of book buying like this, it will be surprising how quickly the books will accumulate in the preacher's library.

The minister needs to learn not only how to build a library but also how to keep his library. It is easy for a preacher to lose valuable books from his library by the practice of loaning them out to Dick, Tom, and Harry. The hardest thing to pay back is a borrowed book. Many otherwise honest people never think of returning a borrowed book. And preachers are greater sinners at this than any other group. They do not intend to be dishonest, but somehow they never seem to think of returning that borrowed book. There are three things that return not: the sped arrow, the neglected opportunity, and the borrowed book! Then even if the book is returned, the minister will often find that when he wants a certain book he will go to the shelf only to discover that it has been loaned out to some brother. The minister will be wise who makes it his fixed policy not to loan a book to just any and everybody who comes along. This may seem cruel and cold blooded, but it is the only way that a minister can keep his library in tact. It has been my policy never to loan a book except on exceptionally rare occasions. I'll loan my shirt and my coat, but I will not loan my books. If some one asks to borrow a book, I simply state my policy and suggest that he sit in my office and use the book if he would like to do so. A minister may not use a certain book but once in three years, but when he does need it he wants it to be on the shelf. And he never knows ahead of time just when he will need a certain book.

Suppose now that the minister has arranged for the money for the purchase of books. Just what books should he buy? Will just any book do, so that he can fill up the empty shelves in his study? Is there any safe plan by which a minister may purchase the right kind of books? In answering these questions we would emphasize in beginning the importance of wisdom and discretion in the purchasing of books. We realize that the young minister may be conscious of this fact and still be at a loss as to what books to purchase. We cannot lay down any hard and fast rule which will apply to all preachers. What may be of interest and help to one preacher may be of no value to the other one, depending on the particular turn of mind of the individual minister. However, there are some general hints and suggestions which will be a help and guide to the young minister in the purchase of books.

First of all, there are certain foundation books which every minister ought to purchase and use as soon as possible. The purchasing of these books should hold priority over any others. They are foundation books without which no minister can effectively function as a preacher. Of course, we are taking for granted that the minister has a copy of the Bible. In fact, he should have several Bibles, including at least two or three different versions or translations. The following is a list of some basic books which every young minister should put on his "must" list for book purchasing even if he has to miss a meal in order to do it: A good dictionary and Roget's Thesaurus of English Words or something similar; Young's Analytical Concordance; A good Bible dictionary or Bible Encyclopedia (such as Hasting's Dictionary or the International Bible Encyclopedia): a copy of the Bible in the original Hebrew and Greek (if the minister has or will have a working knowledge of the original language, and every preacher ought to have this if at all possible); Thayer's Greek Lexicon and Gesenius' Hebrew Lexicon or some other standard Hebrew Lexicon; A Harmony of the Gospels; A standard compendium of Theology (Preferably Strong's); and a general encyclopedia (The Columbia one-volume encyclopedia is sufficient for the average use and is far less expensive than the large sets and takes up much less room on the minister's book shelves.) Beyond these there is no end to the list of good and profitable books which the minister may obtain to his advantage. But these ought to be purchased first. They form a solid basis and foundation for any minister's library.

Now let us pause to give a little warning. Don't fill up your book shelves with too many books of sermons and popular commentaries. It is good for the minister to study the sermons of others, but this ought to be done cautiously and sparingly. It is easy for the preacher to yield to the temptation to duplicate or reproduce a sermon which he has read in a book. The consistent use of such a crutch will weaken the initiative of the minister's mind and will encourage laziness. The same is true of the popular commentaries which throw into the preacher's lap a ready-made sermon or sermon outline which he will snatch up on the run and rehash to his people. This is the unpardonable sin for the minister. No matter how good or how well organized, a sermon reproduced from a book is never as effective and impressive as one of an inferior quality which comes as the product of one's own fertile mind. It is much easier, of course, to find a sermon outline in a book of sermons or a popular commentary and rehash it. And the lazy preacher will always take this path of least resistance. Some preachers may make the alibi that they just do not have the natural ability to "sermonize," but if most of these preachers will be honest with themselves they will confess that their lack of ability grows out of their indolence. They are not willing to pay the price of hard work. Sermons should be studied for the purpose of discovering the technique and the secret of power of the preacher, not for the obtaining of a sermon to be preached. Of course, many things can be found in books of sermons which will be useful in the minister's preaching and we have no objection to their use, but we do object to the wholesale reproduction of sermons found in books.

At any rate, it is an extravagant waste of money for the minister to fill his book shelves with books of sermons and popular commentaries. The minister should be extremely choicy in his purchase of sermon books. And so also with the commentaries. Most of the popular commentaries are of little value to the minister who really wants to do some digging for himself. However, every minister ought to have at least one set of some good commentary on the Bible. For those who know the original language, "The Expositor's Greek Testament" will be found very helpful. The works of Franz Delitzsch on the Old Testament are extremely good for those who know Hebrew, though there is not a complete set of these books covering all the Old Testament. For the English reader the American Commentary on the Bible is about as good as any though there are other good commentaries. What a preacher wants in a commentary is not a homiletical treatment giving ready-made sermon outlines, but a discussion of the background and interpretation of the text. From this the minister can work out his own outline. In the field of Bible interpretation the minister will often find more help in single volumes on particular phases than he will find in the general commentaries. Good books on Bible interpretation are legion, too many to attempt any kind of listing here.

And now from the more positive point of view let us make several practical suggestions. The wise minister, while he is in college and seminary, will become acquainted with many of the books which would be most helpful to him in his work. This is another benefit of scholastic training. The minister will learn very little of the contents of books while in school, but he will become acquainted with many of the books which he should purchase for further study in years to come. The young minister will find it helpful to keep a list of such books, adding to it as he learns of new ones, and then when he is ready to purchase a book he may choose one from this list.

Another good policy to follow in the purchase of books is the habit of giving special attention to authors. Usually the author of a book is more important than the title. Once in a while a certain title dealing with a certain phase of thinking in which he is especially interested will lead the minister to purchase the book, but in most cases the author of the book will be a greater factor in the decision to buy. There are certain authors who have established themselves as being able to give worthy food for thought. Books by such authors should immediately sell themselves to us. For instance, I have been convinced that anything written by G. Campbell Morgan, Alexander Whyte, A. B. Bruce, or James Stewart is worth having. There are other authors in the same category, and when I see books by these authors, regardless of title, I usually buy them.

Another guide in the purchase of books is the recommendation of other preachers and teachers. Many times this may be a personal recommendation. Not long ago I was visiting with a preacher friend at a camp. I discovered that he was reading a book and when I inquired he began to tell me something about it. I had never seen the book before, but his recommendation impressed me and I purchased it and now I treasure it as a valuable addition to my work shop. These recommendations may also come through the official reviews found in the current religious periodicals. This does not mean that a preacher should buy every book reviewed in these periodicals. But a reading of the review may give him some insight into the nature and content of the book and will help him to decide whether or not he should purchase the book. Most of the large religious book houses, like Baker's Book House in Grand Rapids, Michigan, Blessing Book Store of Chicago, and Schulte's Book Store of New York, will gladly send their seasonal catalogue of books, new and used, free of charge. From these catalogues many choice books may be found and sometimes at bargain prices. All of these channels may be used to advantage, but in all of his buying of books through whatever channel the minister must be selective in choice rather than promiscuous, remembering, however, that one thought or idea from a book is worth the price of the book.

THE ORGANIZING OF A LIBRARY

So far we have said two things: First, it is tremendously important that a preacher have books. Second, it is even more important that he have the right kind of books. Now we want to add a third statement: It is supremely important that he know how to organize and utilize his books for the most effective use. There is not much advantage in having shelves full of books if the minister cannot put his finger on what he wants when he wants it. The minister must learn how to make his own library accessible and useable. In order to do this he must have some plan of organization and classification. There are several different systems of classification which the minister may use to advantage. The most commonly known system of library classification is the Dewey Decimal System. This is the plan used in most public and college libraries. It is the plan I have used in the organization of my own library. It is simple and practical. Of course, it will not be necessary for the preacher to go to as much detail as would be necessary in a public library, but the essential principles can easily be followed. Let us take time to explain it.

If the minister waits until he has several hundred volumes in his library it will be quite a task to classify it, but if he will begin when he has only a few books and then keep it up as he adds to his library it will be much easier. I started my classification system when I had only 15 books and have kept it up to date as I have added books. I did not need the classification then, but now with over 1500 volumes it has proven to be an invaluable asset. All told, I have spent many hours in classifying and cataloguing my books but they have been spread out over a period of twenty-five years. When I consider the accessibility of the material in my library at my finger tips through this classification and cataloguing system, I am convinced that every hour spent in such classification work has been well spent. It takes effort and work but it pays great dividends.

Let me explain the plan step by step. Some ministers may not care to go into as much detail as I have done, but at least the general idea could be easily adopted by any minister. First, I take an ordinary note book in which I make a list of every book in my library in the order in which it is added, giving each book an accession number.

Across the page on the same line I list the following things: author, title, publisher, date of publication, source of accession; date received, price of book, and nature of binding (cloth or paper). In this way I can tell at a glance just how many books I have in my library, where they came from and when I received them. This is not at all essential, but I have found it helpful on some occasions and it takes very little time to keep.

Next, I classify the book with a number, according to the Dewey Decimal System. Large classification books can be found in any public library, but for the average minister the little library booklet, "The Church Library Booklist," put out by the Baptist Sunday School Board, Nashville, Tennessee, as a guide in organizing church libraries, is sufficient. This booklet may be had free of charge upon request at any Baptist Book Store. The general divisions of the Dewey classification system will be listed in this booklet with a few examples listed under each heading. The broad, general divisions are as follows: 0-99 General Encyclopedias, etc.; 100-199 Philosophy; 200-299 Religion; 300-399 Social Sciences; 400-499 Languages; 500-599 Science; 600-699 Applied Science; 700-799 Fine Arts; 800-899 Literature; 900-999 History and Biography. It is obvious that most of the preacher's books will come in the 200 classification. A break down of this general division is as follows: 200-209 Religion in General including Philosophy of Religion, etc.; 210-219 Religion and Science; 220-229 Bible Interpretation; 230-239 Theology; 240-249 Devotional Literature; 250-259 Homiletics and Sermons; 260-269 Ecclesiology and Church Administration; 270-279 Church History; 280-289 Particular Churches and Sects; 290-299 Non-Christian Religions. These may be broken down still further for more exact classification.

After the classification number has been determined index cards are made out for each book. The number of cards for each book will vary, depending upon the number of general topics discussed in the book. A separate card should be made out for each general topic discussed in the book, plus one for the author and one for the title. The author card should be made first, on the back of which should be listed the heading for each of the other cards on that particular book. In this way all of the cards in the index for a certain book can be found quickly by looking on the back of the author card. A plain three by five inch card is most practical for use in the index. Below is a sample author card:

270 66	Strickland, Arthur B.
	(The) Great American Revival: Cincinnati, Ohio; Standard Press. 1934.

On the back side of this card I have listed these subjects: author, title, evangelism, history of revivals, church history. For each of these subjects I have a card. If I am studying something on evangelism, I can look in my card index under "Evangelism" and find that I have a book entitled *The Great American Revival*, which includes ideas on evangelism. The same is true with other subjects. It is not necessary to read the book word for word in order to discover these general subjects. A glance at the table of contents will reveal the general ideas treated in the book. A sample subject card is given below:

270 66	Evangelism
	Strickland, Arthur B. (The) Great American Revival: Cincinnati, Ohio; Standard Press. 1934.

In the upper left hand corner of each card is placed the classification number. Just below it I place the accession number. The classification number indicates where the book will be found on the shelf and the accession number indicates where the book is listed in the accession notebook. A perpendicular line is drawn about one-half inch from the left side. The author's name will always be the first word to appear against this line. If it is a title or subject card, the title or subject will be placed on top but always indented about three spaces from the perpendicular line. All cards will have exactly the same wording with the exception of the addition of the subject on the top line of the subject card. The following information should be given on each card: author, title, place of publication, publisher, and date of publication.

When the cards have been properly made up, they are placed in alphabetical order in a card file box or drawer. The word appearing on the top line, whether subject, title, or author, is the determining factor in the alphabetical order. If two cards have the identical word or words on the top line, then the next line determines the order. By the use of this index easy access can be had to every discussion of a certain subject in the library. Many times preachers have valuable information within their own library which is lost and useless to them because they have no system by which they can discover it. When a preacher's library grows to several hundred volumes, he cannot depend upon his memory in locating all of the available material in his library on any certain subject.

I have added to my index of authors and subjects an index of Scripture texts which has proved to be a valuable asset in the use of my work shop. I have made a card just like the others I have described, except on the top line I have a Scripture reference instead of a subject. For every discussion within any of my books on any particular Scripture I have a card. Of course, I do not have a card on Scripture references in general commentaries and such. Nor do I have a card for every reference made to Scripture. But wherever there is any lengthy discourse on a particular passage (including texts for all sermons in books of sermons) I have made a card. If, for instance, I am studying a certain Scripture passage, I can go to my index of Scripture references and find immediately every book in my library that has any appreciable treatment of that passage. There is no way to estimate the value of this index system in the use of my library.

Now a word about the books themselves. All books should be properly stamped with the name of the owner, at least on the flyleaf and title page. After the classification is ascertained, the classification number should be written in white ink on the rib of the book so that it can be seen without being taken from the shelf. If the binding is a light color, it is well to give a black background for the white numbers with India ink. An application of book shellac over the number will protect it from wearing off. Then the books should be arranged on the shelves according to classification number. Where there is more than one book with the same classification number, they should be placed in alphabetical arrangement according to author.

Besides all of this every minister should have a regular letter-size filing cabinet. In this cabinet he will file in the same Dewey Decimal System order all loose material, pamphlets, school notes, sermon notes, correspondence, and any other such material which would come within the realm of ministerial thinking and use. Whether this plan is followed or some other, all of the tools in the minister's work shop should be arranged in some order so that they will be accessible at a moment's notice without unnecessary searching.

Some such arrangement, classification, and index will double and triple the value of the minister's library. The knowledge of this system will be an aid to the minister when he goes to the public library or school library. It is indeed pathetic to see a preacher with a good library but with no plan or system by which he can have access to the full benefit of that library. It is like a man with a gold mine in his back yard, but with no tools with which to dig it out. The minister with a good library has a gold mine in his study, but many times the gold is never fully extracted because there is no adequate system which makes it accessible.

19 | SPIRITUAL PREPARATION FOR PREACHING

In the preceding chapters we have emphasized the importance of scholastic and study preparation for preaching. Lest the reader get the wrong impression, may we hasten to say in the beginning of this chapter that the spiritual preparation is the most vital phase of the minister's preparation for preaching. The preacher may miserably fail who has spent hours in strenuous study. His study is important, but it is of no value if it is not saturated with the proper spiritual attitudes. No amount of study will take the place of spiritual insight and enlightenment for preaching. However, the study will be a valuable asset in the manner of presenting that which has been received by spiritual enlightenment. Dr. W. T. Conner states the case plainly when he says that —

> Preaching depends on spiritual enlightenment. God must give spiritual insight before a man can preach. This is not to disparage intellect in religion or education in the ministry. Such an interpretation of the matter is a one-sided interpretation and a false application of the truth. But it does mean that education cannot take the place of spiritual enlightenment. And if education makes a preacher feel his independence of God in knowing and proclaiming the truth, then education for him is worse than a failure.[1]

A man is not qualified to preach, therefore, just because he has rhetorical ability or scholastic achievement. It is by the spirit of the Lord that a preacher preaches!

Preparation for preaching is more than the preparing of a sermon; it is the preparing of the preacher. The preparation of the preacher is far more important than the preparation of the sermon. Happy is the preacher who has learned this. Preaching involves not only the head, but also the heart and conscience. The head needs to be prepared, but the heart must be prepared if there is to be any effective preaching. Nothing is more pitiful and disgusting than a preacher with a prepared head and an unprepared heart. Preaching under

[1] Article on preaching in *Baptist Standard* of June 9, 1949.

151

such circumstances is nothing more than "the metallic apathy of a record-player, with the cold remoteness of an unappreciative machine."[2] Real preaching must have life and feeling. The world is tired of cold, spiritless, though intellectual, preaching. We do not mean by this that the preaching ought to be of the shallow, superficial, emotional type. It must be full of sound reasoning and logical presentation, but without the presence and power of a spiritual fire it will become nothing more than sounding brass and clanging symbols. Better is it by far to have a preacher with less ability but with the fervor and fire of a spirit-filled life than to have an intellectual giant with nothing more than cold intellect for power and persuasiveness.

SOME PRACTICAL SUGGESTIONS FOR SPIRITUAL PREPARATION

Most preachers realize the importance of spiritual preparation in preaching, and yet so few seem to know how to make such preparation or are willing to pay the price for such preparation. Perhaps the latter is more common. There are no cut-and-dried rules for spiritual preparation, but perhaps a few practical suggestions would be of some help to the minister who is seeking effectiveness in preaching. In preparing the preacher's heart for preaching there are at least four things which should enter into this preparation program. The first is daily devotional study. One of the besetting sins of the average preacher is his failure to study the Bible devotionally. We search the Scriptures for sermon outlines, but seldom sit down to let God speak to our own souls through His Word. How enriching are these moments of private devotional study and meditation! It is possible for the minister to give so much attention to his work and to the application of the Gospel to others that he will fail to make daily application of the message to his own soul. Every preacher will do well to make the habit of spending the first fifteen or thirty minutes in his study each morning in devotional reading of the Word of God with prayer and meditation. This will go a long way toward mellowing and enriching the minister's own soul for a more effective pulpit ministry.

Spiritual preparation for preaching ought also to include personal soul contacts. Few things will give more spiritual fervor and fire to the preacher than a personal soul talk with some unsaved or unenlisted person. The preacher who goes out during the week to make personal contact with those whom he would win to Christ will find fresh inspiration and power in his sermon on Sunday morning. Personal soul-winning experiences just do something to a preacher's sermon. They put life in it. When the minister looks out over his

[2] Jowett, J. H., *The Preacher: His Life and Work*, p. 102.

congregation on Sunday and sees some individual with whom he has talked during the week, his sermon will take on a life and spirit which could not be possible otherwise. The minister who closes himself up in his study until time to go into the pulpit will find his sermons lacking in spiritual power and interest. Personal visitation is not only a means of service for the minister, but it is also a wholesome exercise which prepares him for preaching. I have always found that I have had more spiritual power and freedom in the pulpit when I have had some personal soul-winning experience before coming into the pulpit. After the sermon has been carefully prepared in the study, let the minister leave his books and his pen and go out into the field to find some needy soul and try to win that soul to Christ. Such an experience will put something into the sermon that no amount of study could ever accomplish. It will put real power and effectiveness into an otherwise ordinary sermon. This does not mean that he will, in every case, relate the experience in the sermon. In most cases this would not be wise. But the mere consciousness of the experience will give that mysterious something which makes the sermon live and breathe. The effect of such an experience on the minister's sermon is inexplicable, but also inextricable.

Another effective element in spiritual preparation for preaching is meditation on the sermon's application to the spiritual needs of the people. It is possible that the minister will spend so much time on the rhetorical and homiletical arrangement of the sermon that he will neglect the application of it to the spiritual needs of his people. There is more to preaching than homiletical arrangement and oratorical ability. The sermon must pulsate with the life and needs of the people. After the sermon has been prepared on paper the minister will do well to close his eyes and actually live this sermon in the light of the needs of his people. Many otherwise good and polished sermons are impotent and ineffective simply because they are not adapted to the needs and life of the people to whom they are preached. In that final touch of the sermon preparation the minister needs to visualize his people's needs and polish off his sermon for delivery with this vision in mind. This will give the sermon life and expediency. Good sermons do not come forth like gadgets out of a machine; they must grow up in the life and environment of the needs of the people. When the minister has finished his sermon on paper, it is like the bones of a skeleton. It needs animation and form. This comes only as the preacher opens the door of his heart in meditation and prayer to let the life of the spirit and the needs of his people clothe the dry bones with flesh.

A fourth element which is indispensable in spiritual preparation for preaching is prayer. Every sermon, to be effective, must be bathed in prayer. Prayer must pervade the other three preparatory exercises we have mentioned. Prayer prepares the preacher's heart for preaching, the people for receiving, and the sermon for delivery. Our difficulty is that most of us do more talking about prayer than we do praying. And this accounts for a lot of our puny preaching. Prayer is hard work. It is taxing and exhausting, and all too few are willing to pay the price for the kind of praying that produces great preaching.

Prayer must permeate our whole being. It must be the attitude of our hearts in every moment of the day and night. In fact, if prayer is the attitude of our lives, then it will be less difficult for us to pray when the occasion demands. Certainly the minister should spend some time in definite personal prayer just before going into the pulpit. A pious appearance of prayer before the congregation will not help, especially if there has been no real secret praying before entering the pulpit. A prayerful attitude must be maintained in the pulpit and the minister's prayer before the congregation can mean much, but the real secret of effectiveness in preaching is prayer which rises from the heart of the preacher in those moments and hours while alone in his study before he enters the pulpit. In his book on *The Ethics of the Ministry*, Dr. Robert Barrett has given this practical and timely advice: "Before entering his pulpit the preacher should always contrive to spend a while alone with God. If we are to speak His message it is important to get as much of His Spirit as possible. It is almost sacrilegious for a man to go directly from a playground or a company of thoughtless people, with whom he has been engaged in light conversation, into the pulpit; thus 'rushing in where angels fear to tread.' To kneel on the pulpit steps, or by the chair in ostentatious devotion, on entering, is not so efficacious as closet communion, and may run into formality of the most harmful kind."[3] Real praying is never ostentatious or demonstrative. The preacher does not need to tell his people how much he has been praying, nor does he need to make showy displays of his praying as did the Pharisees. They will know if he has been praying by the power and effectiveness of his sermon. It is nothing short of disgusting to see a preacher who tries to make a great display before his people of his prayer life. The very fact that he does so makes me doubt the genuineness of his prayer life. "The very best equipment for preaching is a private waiting before the Lord when there is no one else in the room save you and Him, and when your deepest secrets can be laid before Him and your crying desires can be

[3] *Ibid.*, p. 110.

poured into His ears."[4] In the light of this it is best, if possible, for the preacher to make no engagements which would occupy his mind with other things just before the sermon. Some preachers teach a Sunday school lesson and go immediately from that into the pulpit. This may be necessary in some cases, but the minister will usually find much more effectiveness in his preaching if he has a time for quiet prayer and meditation before going into the pulpit. He needs this quiet time in which he can open up his soul to God and let the unction of God's Spirit fall on him afresh.

Prayer, as a preparation for preaching, involves not only the preacher, but his people as well. The prayer life of his people is a vital factor in his preparation for preaching. It is not enough for the preacher to pray; his people must pray too. The minister, therefore, must cultivate not only his own prayer life but that of his congregation as well. Time spent in teaching and training his people to pray for him is time well spent and will do much toward preparing the minister for a most effective pulpit ministry.

THE EFFECT OF SPIRITUAL PREPARATION

There are other things which might be included in an adequate program of spiritual preparation for preaching, but we are convinced that if these four suggestions are earnestly followed the minister will find spiritual power in preaching that he never knew he could have. There is no way to estimate the value and influence of the ministry of that preacher who prepares both his head and his heart. Such a minister turns loose upon the world an influence for God and godliness which never dies. The most dynamic force for good in the world today is the preaching of men whose hearts have been filled with the Spirit of God and whose utterances have been inspired of God and bathed in prayer. Thousands of sermons are delivered from the pulpits of our land every day, but all too few of them come from hearts of men who have been touched by the fire from off God's altar. We have gone into our pulpits unprepared, to sound out meaningless words and pleasant platitudes. Our difficulty is not our lack of ability, but our unwillingness to make adequate preparation and to make contact with the source of all wisdom and power. It is really remarkable to observe what God is doing through the puny efforts of God's prophets who are so pre-occupied with a thousand other things that our hearts are seldom really prepared for the pulpit ministry to which we have been called. Just think what could be done if every preacher came to his pulpit every Sunday genuinely prepared in head and heart! The following quotation from

[4] Riley, W. B., *Pastoral Problems*, p. 57.

Dr. Charles E. Jefferson is especially appropriate as a closing thought for this chapter on spiritual preparation:

> A sermon is not a manufactured product, but a spiritual creation. It is not a machine which a man can construct in his sermonic shop, and set running in the pulpit like the electric toys which one sees sometimes on the corner of the city street. A sermon is an exhalation, a spiritual vapor emerging from the oceanic depths of the preacher's soul. It is an emanation, an efflux, an effluence flowing from an interior fountain hidden in the depths of personality. It is an efflorescence, an outflowing of beautiful roses blooming in the garden of the heart. It is a fruit growing on the tree of man's life. "A good tree cannot bring forth evil fruit, neither can a corrupt tree bring forth good fruit." Make the tree good. A sermon is the life-blood of a Christian spirit. A preacher dies in the act of preaching. He lays down his life for his brethren. He saves others, himself he cannot save. The pulpit is a Golgotha in which the preacher gives his life for the life of the world. Preaching is a great work. To do it as God wants it done, the preacher must be a good man, full of the Holy Ghost and of faith.[5]

[5] *The Building of the Church,* lecture VIII.

Part IV
The Minister and Society

20 | THE MINISTER AND HIS PARISHIONERS

In this division of our study we want to look at the minister's place in society. As far as it is possible we want to think of the minister's relation to society apart from his official capacity as a minister. We realize that it is practically impossible to draw a sharp line of demarkation between the minister's purely social relationships and those which involve his official function as a minister. And yet it is our purpose in this study, so far as we can, to put the minister's legal and official duties in the background and look at him from the standpoint of society as such. In order to make this study practical and profitable we feel that the approach should be made from three different points of view: His social relations involving his parishioners; his social relations involving non-parishioners; and his social relations involving fellow ministers. The minister has a distinct social responsibility in each of these three realms. The minister cannot shut himself off from society because he is a minister; in fact, the minister has a more vital connection with society than those in any other vocation. The minister can ignore his responsibility and relation to society only at the price of ministerial suicide. He is an integral part of society.

Our consideration in this chapter is that which concerns the minister and his own parishioners. The minister has a somewhat peculiar social relationship with the people of his own parish which he does not have with those outside his parish. Concerning this relationship there are three things to be considered in this chapter: The parishioners' attitude toward the minister; the minister's attitude toward his parishioners; and some practical hints for a happy minister-parishioner relationship.

The Parishioner's Attitude Toward the Minister

For a happy social relationship there must be a proper attitude on the part of both parties involved. The minister must have a right attitude toward his people; but the people must also have the right attitude toward the minister. It is the people's responsibility to have a right attitude toward the minister, and yet the minister himself has more to do with the cultivation of right attitudes on the part of the people than any one else. In the cultivation of right attitudes on the part of the people there are two important things to be remembered. First, the minister must not be set up on a pedestal out of reach of society in general. There is a strong tendency on the part of many people to circumscribe the minister's life and take him out of society, putting him in a class all by himself. There are those who would classify all people under three heads: men, women, and preachers. And there are some ministers who want to be placed on such a pedestal and looked up to by men. In fact, in some ecclesiastical groups the ministers are required to dress in such a manner that they are immediately conspicuous and differentiated from ordinary people. Such a conspicuous display of ministerial identity tends to keep the minister aloof from society and all but unapproachable. Such a custom not only hinders the influence which the minister might have in society, but also finds no basis in New Testament teaching and practice. The average minister does not want to be so positionized. Dr. Jeff D. Ray has expressed what we are trying to say in these words:

> The manly preacher does not want to be coddled; he does not want to be put on a pedestal; he wants to take his place in the trenches with the rank and file; he has no use for the Pharisee's prayer, "I thank thee that I am not as other men." The genuine preacher knows and wants others to know that he has no sacerdotal accessories that entitle him to respect apart from the respect due to any man of worthy character.[1]

The "holier than thou" attitude never contributed any thing toward the effectiveness of the ministry. There are others who, though they do not idolize the minister, coddle and pet him like a baby. This is as obnoxious to the genuine minister as the attitude which sets him up on a pedestal apart from the general run of society. In speaking to the young preachers of Yale, Phillips Brooks said that "it was not good that the minister should be worshiped and made an oracle. It is still worse that he should be flattered and made a pet."[2] This is only one extreme in the attitudes which people have taken toward ministers.

The other extreme is just as serious. Some have made the preacher so common-place that they lose the respect which they ought to have toward the minister. There is something about the fact that a man

---

[1] *The Highest Office*, p. 228.
[2] *Lectures on Preaching*, p. 66.

has been called and commissioned of God to be a minister of the Gospel which ought to command the respect of all men. There is a difference, however, in having respect for a minister as a minister and in idolizing or worshiping him. He should be respected, first of all, in his own right for his own moral and spiritual integrity. If the minister does not have moral integrity, then he has no right to the respect of men even though he may be called a minister. However, we can safely conclude that ninety-five percent of all ministers do have such moral integrity and, therefore, have a right to be respected. We might also add that every Christian ought to be so respected for his moral integrity. But even beyond this the minister ought to be respected because of the responsibility which has been placed upon him by the Lord. His is a high and holy calling, not that he is worthy of it, but the fact that he has been called into this holy mission ought to demand the respect of men, especially Christian men.

In summing it up let us use the words of Washington Gladden, who said that the minister ought to be regarded by the parishioners "neither as a mere employee, nor yet as a master, but as their spiritual guide and fellow helper in the gospel."[3] There ought to be enough respect on the part of the people to give to the minister sufficient range for real spiritual leadership. At the same time there ought to be enough intimacy and congeniality to give him an entree into the hearts of men. If the minister is to do his best work, he must be looked upon by his people as a true minister called of God to this ministry and also as a man among men with the same problems and weaknesses as other men.

THE MINISTER'S ATTITUDE TOWARD HIS PARISHIONERS

Now let us turn this relationship around and look at the minister's attitude toward his own people. There are two things to be emphasized as we look at it from this point of view. First of all, the minister should look upon his parishioners as a father looks upon his children. By this we are not implying any legalistic authority, nor are we suggesting that the minister should be referred to by the title, "Father." We are simply saying that the minister should feel the same paternal tenderness, love, and compassion that a father feels for his own children. The minister is not worthy of his name who does not have such feelings toward those who constitute his parish. The great Apostle Paul is our best example in this. How tenderly and lovingly he worked with those to whom God had called him to

[3] *The Christian Pastor and the Working Church*, p. 70.

minister! His words to the church at Corinth are typical of Paul's attitude: "I write not these things to shame you, but as my beloved sons I warn you. For though ye have ten thousand instructors in Christ, yet have ye not many fathers: for in Christ Jesus I have begotten you through the gospel" (I Corinthians 4:14, 15). There were times when Paul had to use the rod with severity, but in every case he did it with all tenderness and love as a father would deal with his own son. For the genuine preacher there is a peculiar feeling of paternal love and concern toward the members of the church over which God has called him to be pastor. Especially is this true with reference to those who have been won to Christ, baptized, and enlisted under his ministry. Woe betide the preacher who loses this feeling of sympathetic love and compassion for his people! Ian Maclaren has most aptly described this attitude of the preacher in the following statement:

> His people are ever in the pastor's heart. He claims identity with them in their joy and sorrow and endless vicissitudes of life. No friend is blessed with any good gift of God but he is also richer. No household suffers loss but he is poorer. If one stands amid great temptation he is stronger; if one fails he is weaker. When any one refuses his call, he is dismayed, counting himself less faithful. He waits eagerly to see whether one who groped in darkness has been visited by the light from on high, whether another, who seemed to have gone into a far country, has set his face towards the Father's house. One family he watches with anxiety, because he does not know how they will bear a heavy stroke of adversity, and another with fear lest rapid success in this world may wean their hearts from God. He trembles for this merchant lest he fall below the rules of Christ and do things which are against conscience; he rejoices over another who has stood fast and refuses to soil his hands. He inquires on every hand about some young man of whom he expects great things; he plans how another may be kept from temptation. One thing he cannot do; criticize his people or make distinctions among them. Others, with no shepherd heart, may miss the hidden goodness; he searches for it as for fine gold. Others may judge people for faults and sins; he takes them for his own. Others may make people's foibles the subject of their raillery; the pastor cannot, because he loves.[4]

Along with this feeling of paternal love and devotion there ought also to be a feeling of servitude. Not in any sense of a coerced slavery, but every minister is a servant of the people. We are not called to sit on a throne and rule the people; rather, we are called

[4] THE CURE OF SOULS.

to serve the people. To minister is to serve. The people do not belong to the minister; the minister belongs to the people. There seems to be a natural tendency on the part of preachers to forget this. Preachers are often guilty of looking upon their parishioners as part of their own peculiar possession and ownership. This is evidenced by the common reference of the preacher to "My Church." Some may use this term harmlessly, and yet it often leaves wrong impressions. Every member of a church may rightfully use the term, "my church," but the very tone of the preacher's voice in using this term often leaves the impression that he thinks he owns the whole thing, the building and the people. Not long ago I talked with a pastor of a certain church and in discussing the plans and program of his church he repeatedly used the personal pronoun, I, as if he were going to do it all himself. Of course, I knew that he meant to say that this is what the church was going to do, but I couldn't help but feel an attitude of dictatorial ownership on his part. I was not surprised to learn that the people were wanting to get rid of him.

In all of his relationships with the people of his church the minister should express an attitude of humility and servitude. Paul reminds us in his first Corinthian epistle that all ministers belong to the people. Some of the people at Corinth had been saying, "we belong to Peter"; others were saying, "we belong to Paul" and still others, "we belong to Apollos." But Paul rebukes them for such attitudes and reminds them that "Whether Paul, or Apollos, or Cephas, or the world, or life, or death, or things present, or things to come; all are yours; and ye are Christ's; and Christ is God's" (I Corinthians 3:22, 23).

Christ has called us, not to rule over churches or people, but to serve churches and people. The observation of Dr. Jowett is timely at this point: "I have known many churches where spiritual life has been chilled, and spiritual enterprise has been ruined by the minister's tactless handling of men who were to carry his desires and purposes to fruition. Such ministers treat their fellow officers as so many marionettes, and lo! the marionettes prove to be alive, with very marked and vivacious personalities, and there is consequent discord and strife."[5] And Phillips Brooks has ironically remarked that "there is something remarkable in the way in which a minister talks about 'my congregation.' They evidently come to seem to him different from the rest of humankind. A man begins the habit the moment he is settled in a parish. However young, however inexperienced he may be, he at once takes possession of that fraction of the human

[5] J. H. Jowett, *The Preacher: His Life and Work*, p. 221.

family and holds it with a sense of ownership."[6] Let the minister
never forget that he belongs to the people of his church and not they
to him.

PRACTICAL HINTS FOR HAPPY MINISTER - PARISHIONER RELATIONSHIP

So far we have discussed the basic principles involved in the
proper attitude of the minister toward his parishioners and the
parishioners toward the minister. With these principal attitudes in
mind let us now offer some practical suggestions for a happy minister-
parishioner relationship. These suggestions which we make here are
simply applications of the principles and attitudes which have already
been mentioned. Our first suggestion is a negative one; the other three
are positive.

From the standpoint of the negative we suggest that the minister
avoid too much intimacy with a few. For the most satisfactory relationship the pastor must be equally cordial and friendly with every
member of the church. There is a grave danger that the minister
will form intimate association with a select few of his congregation
to the neglect of the others. Such a practice always results in serious
consequences both for the preacher and for the people. Of course,
no minister can keep from becoming especially attracted by and
attached to certain members of his congregation who seem to have
a better understanding and a deeper interest in the affairs of the
church. And there is nothing wrong with this so long as he does
not make his attraction to these conspicuous to the rest of the congregation. If he is always in the company of these and seldom if
ever in the company of others in the congregation, the other people
will begin to feel left out and will begin to sense that the pastor
does not love them. It may not be always easy, but the pastor will be
wise to avoid a conspicuous intimacy with a few of his members.
Such a practice will eliminate many heartaches and problems within
the church. It will also eliminate many suspicions on the part of the
congregation. Especially is this true of the minister's relation to the
women of the church. Even though he is guilty of no immoral conduct, too much intimacy with certain women will create suspicions
which will prove the preacher's undoing. A timely warning on this
subject is expressed by Robert Barrett in his "Ethics of the Ministry"
in these words:

> The God-fearing pastor will treat them all as "sisters" or as moth-
> ers, and avoid all occasion for scandal. It may be necessary at times
> to seem unnecessarily reserved when in the presence of at least
> certain classes of ladies, but it is better to err on that side than on

[6] *Lectures on Preaching*, p. 180.

the other side of too great laxity. The reputation of the preacher, like that of woman, is easily soiled. It should be unnecessary to say that the minister who will deliberately and repeatedly take advantage of the liberty afforded him and win the affection of a woman's heart, then play the flirt, should be tried for immoral conduct. Scarcely any thing will destroy the good influence of a minister sooner than the reputation of being loose in his dealings with women.[7]

We are not intimating that the minister should be cold and aloof in his relation to his people, but we are suggesting that he should be friendly and cordial to all alike. Dr. Riley was right in saying that

> . . . even when the fellowship is wholesome and confined to brother Christians, the preacher's friendships should be rather extensive than too intensive. The sacred calling creates friends. It does not call for an over-ardent intimacy. In fact, while every pastor will at least discover in his official board certain sane counsellors with whom he will have real occasion for repeated conferences, it is not, however, best, in these instances, to have the public suspect his prejudiced preferences. This applies to his church members.[8]

Our second suggestion is that the minister give evidence of his love for and interest in the people of his parish. It is possible for one to love another without giving evidence, or at least much evidence, of that love. The people must have some evidence of the pastor's interest in them. This is a key point in the philosophy of working with people. Some preachers never seem to realize this fact and wonder why they do not get along with people and why people will not follow their leadership. But how may the preacher manifest his interest in his people? What can he do to let them know that he loves them? There are many things he can do, but we mention here only a few concrete suggestions. The things we do to convince people that we love them are usually the little things which many times we think of as unimportant. One way of manifesting interest is by asking questions concerning the vocation or avocation of the individual with whom we are visiting. Without being officious or impertinent, a question asked will often reveal an interest in what another is doing. Frankly, I am not impressed by the man who begins immediately upon entrance to tell me all about himself and his accomplishments, but I am always impressed and ready to listen to the man who asks me questions concerning my work. For instance, if the parishioner is a farmer, he should spend some time talking

---

[7] *Ibid.,* pp. 173, 174.
[8] Riley, W. B., *The Preacher and His Preaching,* p. 62.

with him about his farming, and by asking questions he can encourage the farmer to do most of the talking which always makes for a more wholesome and effective conversation. As a result, the farmer thus visited will be impressed with an idea that the pastor has a definite interest in him and his welfare. And with this there will come a deeper appreciation for the pastor and a more ready willingness to follow his leadership.

Another helpful suggestion in the manifestation of the pastor's interest in his people is the cultivation of the habit of learning and calling people by their names. There is something about calling a man by his name which is tremendously attractive and impressive. All of us have enough ego that we love to hear our own names called, and when someone goes to the trouble to remember and call us by our names we immediately conclude that he is interested in us, else he would not take the trouble to remember our names. I can already hear some preachers saying, "This is all true, but I just can't remember names." We admit that there is no preacher living who can remember the names of all the people he has met. But we are convinced that all preachers could remember more names if they weren't just too lazy to try. To remember and call people by names takes effort and mental energy. Some think that it is not that important, but it is more important than most people realize. Others simply excuse themselves by saying, "I just can't remember names," so they don't try. Any preacher can remember and use the names of a good proportion of the people whom he meets if he really tries. First of all, he must realize that it is important to remember a name. His influence upon people will be greatly affected by his ability to remember and use a name. In the second place, he must determine that he will remember at least some of the names. Third, he will find much help in the practice of repeating the name as often as he can after hearing it. Upon meeting an individual he should repeat the name in the course of the conversation several times before leaving the individual. And as often as he sees an individual he should call him by his name if he knows it. The only reason that I do not call a man by his name when I see him is that I do not know it. Repetition makes indelible impressions on the mind. Fourth, if it is possible, write the name down on a piece of paper as soon as it can be done. The writing of a name will often aid the mind in retaining it. Fifth, if possible associate the name with some other name or thing. The association of names and ideas is also very helpful. Sixth, if time and occasion permit, inquire of another concerning the name of the one who is approaching and then call him by that name when he comes into the range of conversation. It is not necessary to tell the individual that you had to ask some one for his name. Even if he knows that you did ask for his name, the fact that you thought enough to inquire about his name will convince him that you are interested in him. Time spent in learning and using names is time well spent for any preacher.

There are countless other "little" things that the minister can do to manifest his interest in his people, such as a word of sympathy in time of sorrow and distress, a word of congratulation on occasions of joy, a friendly visit when occasion permits, etc. We realize that the doing of these little things will make quite a demand on the preacher's time and energy, but the minister cannot afford to neglect them if he expects to get along with his people and influence them. We also realize that in many of the large churches which we are growing today it is almost impossible for the pastor to take such individual interest in his people. But this is one of the most serious dangers facing our churches today — that membership is becoming so large in many churches that the preacher cannot know his people nor can the people know their pastor. For the best results and happiest relationships a pastor must know his members individually and they must know him. For the realization of this condition what we need is not larger churches, but more churches. But in every case let the minister do his best to give every evidence possible of his love for and interest in his people.

Our third suggestion for a happy minister-parishioner relationship, which is very closely associated with the foregoing suggestion, is that the minister cultivate the habit of saying all of the complimentary things he can and as often as he can about his people. In other words, learn to brag on people. Every man is human enough to enjoy hearing something good about himself, but it does more than satisfy a man's ego; it inspires him to new and greater endeavor as nothing else will. Of course, there are times when the people need to be reprimanded, but if this reprimand is preceded by some complimentary word it will be far more effective. This is just common sense psychology in dealing with people. Paul understood this principle and used it consistently in all of his dealings with people. Before "eating out" the Corinthians, he made some very encouraging complimentary remarks. In the letters to the seven churches of Asia, the writer began with a word of commendation and followed with a word of rebuke.

We must not be untruthful in our complimentary remarks; indeed, we do not have to be. There is always something good we can say about anyone. The minister should be keenly alert to every opportunity to say something good about the members of his con-

gregation. In so doing he will be enhancing his own influence upon
his people and will stimulate his people with more zeal for labor.
People cannot and will not be "brow beaten" into right activity
and conduct. The preacher who continually "nags" his people will
soon discover that he must move on to a new field without having accomplished any worthy objective. There are a thousand ways
in which we can do and say complimentary things. A note of appreciation for any hospitality while a guest in the home of a brother
is always worth its weight in gold. Dr. Ray's timely advice ought
to be practiced by all ministers: "The fact is mentioned here only
to give an occasion for expressing the hope that every preacher
who hears or reads these words will make it a part of life's program to write a letter of thankful appreciation, immediately on
reaching home, for the hospitality of a brother's house."[9]   Few
things take as little of the preacher's time and yet pay off so richly
as the habit of expressing little words of appreciation and commendation. At every slightest opportunity a brief word of commendation
to some fellow Christian will pay rich dividends in many ways.

Our fourth suggestion for a happy minister-parishioner relationship is that the minister be always ready to take at least part of the
blame for anything that goes wrong. This involves the attribute of
humility. The preacher who is always right, in his own mind, and
the other fellow always wrong, will soon discover that his services
are not wanted. The people will begin to resent his leadership.
The preacher who says, "we made a mistake," when things go wrong
will be loved and admired by his people and the mistake will soon
be corrected. But the preacher who says, "You were wrong; I was
right," will only add to the problem created by any mistake that
may have been made. And no preacher has to pervert the truth to
confess that he is, at least in part, to blame for things which go
wrong. The truth is that in practically every case the minister is
partly to blame for things which do not go right in the church, if
not by definite act, at least by some omission or attitude. The minister who is too proud to admit that he makes a mistake will never
be a successful pastor. He will never have the influence upon people
that he could have with a different attitude. Some people seem to
think that an admission of mistake is a sign of weakness, but nothing is further from the truth than this. The fact is that the admission of a mistake is one of the surest signs of greatness and a means
of greater effectiveness in dealing with people.

We confess that we know very little about the technical side of
the psychology of dealing with people, but from our observation and

9 *The Highest Office*, p. 218.

experience we are convinced that if the minister will follow these three simple rules he will be able to "win friends and influence people": give evidence of your love for and interest in people; cultivate the habit of saying all the good things you can about people; always be ready to take at least part of the blame for any thing that goes wrong. After all, no matter how much we know, if we cannot win friends and influence people, what we know will be of little value to us or to those with whom we come in contact.

21 | THE MINISTER AND NON-PARISHIONERS

In our last chapter we dealt with the minister's social relationships involving the members of his own congregation. In this chapter we want to look at the minister's social relationships involving society in general. We are thinking in particular of the people living in the community who are not members of his parish, and yet in a general sense we are thinking of the minister's relation to society in general including those both inside and outside of his parish. In other words, we are thinking of the minister in his community apart from any peculiar relationships which he may have to the members of his own congregation. In looking at it from this angle there are three aspects of the relationship to be considered: the attitude of men in general toward the minister; the attitude of the minister toward men in general; and some practical hints for effective minister-society relationship.

The Attitude of Society Toward the Minister

Before we can arrive at a proper understanding of the minister's attitude toward society in general, we must see something of the attitude of society toward the minister. And before there can be proper activity on the part of both society and the minister, there must be some attitudes and principles established. Not all men look upon the preacher alike. There are widely differing views of the minister. Generally speaking, however, these attitudes may be summed up under three statements.

First, there are a few who have respect for the minister. We are thinking now primarily of those outside the church. Of course, most of those within the church have at least some respect for the minister as such. Then there are a few outside the church who express confidence in and respect for the minister, giving due consideration to him and his work.

Second, there are many who ignore him. This classification would perhaps include the largest group. This group is composed of those who, though they do not show any avowed or bold disrespect, simply ignore the minister and do not even consider him a part of society. In the eyes of these people the minister is some freak of human nature and may be all right but is not supposed to be a part of the movements of society in general. Thus he is simply ignored and left out of the plans and policies of human society. This attitude seems to be more prevalent now than in generations past.

Third, there are others who despise and vilify the minister. These are not so many, and yet their numbers would be surprisingly large if we actually knew. Such were the people who persecuted and killed the early preachers. Bodily harm is not so prevalent as it was in the first century, and yet even in this present day much mental and social injury is inflicted upon the ministers of Christ by these despisers and enemies of the ministry. And in some respects bodily injury is not more grievous than mental and social injury. The Apostle Paul describes most vividly this attitude in writing to the Corinthians about these agitators and enemies of the ministry: "For I think that God hath set forth us the apostles last, as it were appointed to death; for we are made a spectacle unto the world, and to angels, and to men. We are fools for Christ's sake, but ye are wise in Christ; we are weak, but ye are strong; ye are honourable, but we are despised. Even unto this present hour we both hunger, and thirst, and are naked, and are buffeted, and have no certain dwelling place; and labor working with our own hands; being reviled, we bless; being persecuted, we suffer it; being defamed, we intreat; we are made as the filth of the world and are the offscouring of all things unto this day" (I Corinthians 4:9-13). The true minister will soon discover that there are those in the world who continuously seek to defame and discredit the minister and his holy calling. Our joy is that not all men are like this; nevertheless, we must face the fact that these, though they may be few in number, must be confronted and their calumnies faced.

THE ATTITUDE OF THE MINISTER TOWARD SOCIETY

In looking at it from the other end of the line we would emphasize two fundamental principles concerning the minister's attitude toward society or men in general. First, the minister at all times should maintain genuine love and respect for all men. The attitude of any man toward the preacher should not alter in any way this attitude on the part of the minister. The idea of retaliation must be forever kept out. This is the spirit of Christ, and to some degree at least we are convinced that this is the attitude of most ministers toward all men. Paul expressed it for us when he said: "being reviled, we bless; being persecuted, we suffer; being defamed, we intreat" (I Corinthians 4:12, 13). While there is a peculiar feeling in his heart for those who are under his pastoral care, the minister's love for man must not stop there.

In the second place, the minister must learn to look upon all men for what they could be and not for what they are. We must see in every man the potential values and virtues. No man is an impossibility in the light of God's grace. This is the way Jesus looked at men. He saw something in every man. He looked upon unstable and repulsive Simon and called him a rock, because he saw in him the potential stability of a rock. The minister must see all human nature as of inestimable value. We must not sell men short in what ever condition they may seem to be. All human life is valuable and precious in God's sight. The minister is not worthy of the name who does not recognize the potential value of every man with whom he comes in contact. Dr. W. J. Tucker has very aptly expressed it for us in these words: "The first thing, then, which the preacher owes to men is the clear understanding and unconditional acceptance of Christ's view of humanity. Christ's estimate of men, his way of looking at men, his whole conception of humanity, must become a part of the preacher's thinking, the very habit of his mind."[1]

This recognition of the value of human life, if genuine, will express itself in respect, interest, and a desire to bring out the best which is in man. Again the words of Dr. Tucker are appropriate: "The preacher will certainly come short of fulfilling his obligation to men if his love for them does not rise to the strength of a spiritual passion for them. It must be utterly devoid of sentimentalism. That is too weak a thing to speak about. It must be a strong, manly passion, but it must have the ardor of the soul in it. And this alike in public and private, when the preacher is dealing with men under conditions which invite it."[2] Thus the two things mentioned here are mutually complementary. Our love for men will increase our appreciation of human value and our recognition of human values will increase our love for men.

Some Practical Hints for Minister - Society Relationship

Having established these principles, let us now turn to the more practical side of this minister-society relationship, with the hope that we may be able to offer some helpful suggestion for the minister's conduct in society as such. First, let us study it from the standpoint of the business world. The minister will have many contacts with society in the business world. Though he is not a "busi-

[1] *The Making and the Unmaking of the Preacher,* p. 146.
[2] *Ibid.,* p. 155.

nessman," he will have many contacts with the business world because of his own personal needs and the needs of his church organization. In all of these contacts he should maintain the most cordial relationships. Even though it may involve a business proposition he has no right to lay aside the principles of cordiality and respect. On the other hand, just because he is a preacher he does not have to let men take advantage of him in a business way. But he can exercise his right for a fair deal and at the same time maintain a spirit of cordiality and respect. Besides this there are two other things which are extremely important for a preacher in his dealings with the business world.

First, he must keep his obligations paid up to date. Carelessness in paying bills will finally lead to the ruin of a preacher and great injury to the cause of Christianity in the world. We believe that it is a safe assumption to say that ninety-eight percent of all preachers are honest, and yet some of those who are honest may allow themselves to be careless and negligent in paying their obligations. As nearly as possible every minister will do well to take Paul's advice to "owe no man anything save to love one another." If ministers maintain their integrity and influence in the community, they must keep their slates clean with the business world. Better is it that he do without butter for his bread than that he should jeopardize his whole ministry by loose business dealings.

Second, the minister should never cheapen the ministry by requesting or even hinting for ministerial discounts. Few things are more disgusting than the minister who goes around requesting discounts because he is a minister. If a discount or gift is offered voluntarily, it may be received graciously without injury to anyone, but a request for such is a ministerial abomination. The preacher who insists on making such requests or hints will do so at the cost of losing the confidence and respect of the people of his community. Let the minister take his place in society along with other men and carry on business relationships as other men do in his community.

In the political field the minister also has a responsibility. What part, if any, should the minister take in politics? This question every minister must face. Some feel that the minister should close the door completely and have absolutely nothing to do with politics, in private or in public. Others have taken the other extreme and have made politics the major concern of their ministry. Somewhere in between these two extremes is the proper attitude for the minister to take. As citizens we cannot ignore our responsibility in the political world. Politics is the science of government. If the minister is a man and a citizen, he cannot ignore his responsibility to politics and government. Dr. A. K. DeBlois has raised these timely questions:

> . . . has the minister ceased to be a citizen? If not, he must do a citizen's full duty. He is more than a private citizen, however. He is a public man, a people's leader. Should he use the pulpit as a means of furthering those moral reforms which are at the bottom of political reconstructions? Yes, he should use the privilege of the pulpit; but he should not misuse or abuse that privilege. This distinction is most delicate and important. He must never be a party politician. Let him remember that he is a practical philosopher and a prophet with a message. If he remembers this he will not deteriorate into a demagogue, a fanatic, a partisan, an agitator or a common scold. His words will be well thought out, and good men will follow him.[3]

The principles of good government must always be championed by the preacher in pulpit and in private life. There is absolutely no place for an official alliance of church and state. Such a tie up would be disastrous in every way. And yet if our churches and our Christian people do not have an influence upon politics and government in the establishing of sound principles and practices, then our government is doomed. The minister should lead out in this program, both by private example as a good citizen participating in the ordinary responsibilities of citizenship and politics, and by public proclamation of the principles of right living and right treatment of one another as set out by Jesus Himself. The minister can do this without becoming involved in party politics or political personalities as such. The preacher who uses the pulpit to parade political personalities or who enters into promiscuous political personality debates with the people of his community is cutting his own throat and jeopardizing what little influence for good he may have had. Here is the safest and wisest policy for every minister in the political world: Be a good citizen privately by taking part in the privileges and responsibilities afforded every citizen and take every opportunity to magnify the principles of good government in public and private as interpreted by Christ and Christianity.

There is one other realm of society in which the minister is involved. It is in the realm of social activities, that is, community activities which are of a purely social or fraternal nature. How much part, if any, should the minister take in the social and fraternal activities of his community? Of course, there are some social functions of a questionable moral nature with which the minister should have no part. One of the quickest and surest ways for a

[3] *Some Problems of the Modern Minister,* p. 167.

minister to ruin his reputation as a minister is to participate in or be a spectator of functions which are of questionable moral caliber. There is nothing to be gained by such participation. But there are some general functions and activities within the life of the community which are decent and honorable. The minister will do well to have a reasonable association with such activities. We use that word, reasonable, because there are two extreme dangers to which all ministers are exposed. Dr. Jeff D. Ray quotes Dr. Hopping as saying that

> . . . there may be two opposite errors in ministerial conduct in regard to society: a minister may have so strong a desire to separate himself from worldly things and worldly men as entirely to lose the social spirit; or, on the other hand, he may have so intense a desire to smooth the way for good influence among all men, and to come down to the level and sympathy of all, that he may not only thereby lose his dignity, but may compromise his principles; and he may unconsciously adopt the principles of the world and of the evil there is in the society. He may go so far as to open the ground of doing evil that good may come.[4]

Some ministers err at one extreme and others err at the other. All ministers need to take warning. Even though a minister may keep all of his social activities in the realm of decency and order, there is the danger that he will spend so much time in his social activities that he will neglect the more important aspects of his spiritual ministry. This temptation is stronger today than ever before, with our modern-day community emphasis upon fraternities, service organizations, and humanitarianism. Right at this point a serious question arises: Should the minister become a member of the service organizations or fraternities in his community? This question is more keenly felt in the small town than in the suburb of a large city. In most cases we can see no moral wrong in the minister's participation in such organizations. In fact, we can see some advantages. It offers him a good opportunity of getting acquainted with more men in his community. But we can also see some dangers. There is a growing tendency on the part of many men to look upon these service and fraternal organizations as being as important as the church. In fact, for many men, the service or fraternal organization takes the place of the church. Its humanitarian and benevolent program seems to satisfy their religious inclinations. Many people who feel this way do not express it in words. This is no fault of the organization itself. It is the fault of those who so misinterpret the

[4] *The Highest Office*, p. 208.

meaning and purpose of the organization. The preacher's presence
and participation often confirm this feeling on their part. Because
of this danger it has been my custom to visit these organizations on
occasions but not to become an active part. To sum it up, our advice would be that the minister cannot afford to ignore these organizations, but at the same time his participation in them should be
with reservation and great caution.

Not only with reference to these organizations, but in all of the
social life of the community, there is the danger that the minister
will lose sight of his major responsibility while going about over
the community patting people on the back and trying to create social
impressions. God pity the preacher who becomes nothing more than
a society bug who had rather make social impressions for himself
than to win people to Christ. On the other hand, we are not suggesting that the minister close the door to society and social activity
in his community. He cannot do this and accomplish his mission.
He must be willing to make a reasonable contact with the social
life of his community and be wise enough to utilize these contacts
in the fields of evangelism and Christian training. Every preacher
will do well to consider the words of the great teacher of preachers,
Dr. Jeff D. Ray, who said,

> While it is important that the preacher should be a gentleman
> both by instinct and training and should be able to conduct him-
> self with propriety in any social circle a word of warning needs to
> be spoken. A preacher with social instinct and qualified to move
> easily in social circles is in constant danger of yielding too much
> time to the social demands of the community. It is glorious if
> he can make social functions contribute to the spiritual success
> of his ministry, but it is nothing short of tragic if he makes his
> ministry subservient to social functions.[5]

Paul's motto for social relationships ought to be accepted by every
minister: "I am made all things to all men that by all means I
might save some" (I Corinthians 9:22).

[5] *Ibid.*, p. 214.

22 | THE MINISTER AND HIS FELLOW MINISTERS

An Approach

The minister has a peculiar relation to his fellow ministers, therefore, a separate treatment of this relationship is necessary. A vital part of the minister's social relationships is that which involves his fellow ministers. In this realm he often finds some of life's happiest hours, and in this same realm he also finds, much to our regret, some of life's most distasteful experiences. One might suppose that the minister's homologous relation to other ministers would always guarantee the very happiest of associations. But this is not true. Preachers have difficulties of fellowship just as others do. It ought not to be so, and yet the preacher is human just like other people and he is subject to the same weaknesses which mar fellowship in any realm. In the main, the fellowship of ministers with other ministers is of the most wholesome variety, but here and there black splotches appear on the horizon of ministerial fellowship. And when they do appear it has a more disastrous effect upon society in general because so much more is expected of the minister in every way. The wholesomeness of ministerial relationships could be greatly enhanced if every minister would think through seriously and with open mind the principles, practices, and problems involved in such relationships. And this is the purpose of this study — to rethink the whole question of ministerial relationships to the end that we might arrive at a more satisfactory and mutually helpful relation to our fellow ministers.

Some Suggested Principles

In approaching this subject let us first call attention to some general principles which are essential for a happy relationship between minister and minister. For the sake of clarity it seems best in this case to express these principles in negative form. There are three exhortations we would make.

First, do not think of other ministers as competitors. Ministers are not in competition with each other; they are complementary to each other. And yet there are times when the idea of competition seems to creep into the minister's heart. There is nothing particularly wrong with a little friendly competition between neighboring churches with reference to attendance. This often stimulates more enthusiasm, and yet there is danger that even this may have serious consequences if not carefully directed and guided. But the idea of competition on the part of one minister as over against another minister is entirely foreign to genuine Christianity and always results in tragic consequences for the minister and for the church. Paul expressed the right idea when he described ministers as "God's fellow laborers" (I Corinthians 3:9). He illustrates this idea by referring to himself and Apollos with these words: "I have planted, Apollos watered; but God gave the increase. So then neither is he that planteth any thing, neither he that watereth; but God that giveth the increase. Now he that planteth and he that watereth are one" (I Corinthians 3:6-8). The minister is doomed who comes to think of himself as in competition with some other preacher. Even though there is the closest proximity geographically, we are not competitors but "workers together with God."

Second, do not become overly critical of a fellow minister. Most ministers are easily tempted to become excessively critical of their fellow ministers. But in yielding to such temptation difficult problems are created in ministerial fellowship and effectiveness. Constructive criticism given direct is always helpful, but the criticism of which we are thinking is that cheap criticism which is done behind the back. And the lowest form of this criticism is that which is expressed on the sly to some member of the other minister's church. This does not mean that a minister should try to cover up for the other minister's errors or sins. We are never justified under any circumstances in condoning or covering sin and wrong. But most ministerial criticism is that which concerns some little unimportant method of work or some insignificant idiosyncrasy. Great injustices have been done by such base criticism. A minister should always look for and magnify the best qualities in the lives of his fellow-ministers. We could use some of the professional ethics of the medical world in the ministerial life of our day. It is seldom if ever that a doctor will "run down" another doctor before a patient. How much more careful ought ministers to be in this matter! Dr. A. K. DeBlois offers this timely observation and warning:

> It is possibly not good policy to expose any weakness of the craft to which we belong; but those of us who have had a good deal to do with ministers realize how prevalent is this unfortunate habit. Have we not ourselves yielded at times to its lure? Self-respect and

brotherly kindness should alike prevent its presence in the life of a man set apart in God's name for holy ministration. Do not "run down" your fellow ministers! Such ill-natured personal censure is unfair. A sincere heart and sterling common sense will eliminate all such tendencies.[1]

Third, do not allow jealousies to creep in! This is the minister's gravest danger — ministerial jealousy. "Nothing is more insidious than ministerial jealousy and no refined frailty more despicable and none more fatal ultimately to both happiness and usefulness."[2] Many a preacher has been ruined and his usefulness hindered by jealousy. Of all people the minister, it seems, ought to be the least jealous. And yet experience and observation reveal that it is all too prevalent in ministerial relationships. The bane of the modern ministry is jealousy. May God deliver us from it. The human element in the minister often expresses itself in a feeling of jealousy at the sight of another minister who seems to climb the ladder a little faster, becomes more popular, and is called to a larger church. Perhaps the most common form of jealousy among preachers is that which is inspired by an apparent love of the people for a former pastor. Some preachers just can't stand to see their parishioners express any love for a former pastor. From whatever source, jealousy is not only ugly but detrimental to every aspect of kingdom work. Pray to be delivered from ministerial jealousy and sensitiveness. Happy is the preacher who has learned to rejoice wholeheartedly and unselfishly in every evidence of personal or Kingdom victory in the lives of his fellow ministers. There is absolutely no reason for jealousy on the part of any minister under any circumstance. And the tragedy is that the minister who is jealous is usually the last one to suspicion or admit that he is jealous. Somehow jealousy is blind. Love may be blind, but jealousy is more so. Usually the man who talks the most about not being jealous is the one who is most jealous. If we are not jealous, it will not be necessary to publicize the fact that we are not jealous. It will be obvious by our actions. I have always been a little skeptical about the preacher who is continually reminding people that he is not jealous, just as I am skeptical of the man who is always talking about his great forgiving spirit. These things are attitudes which need little or no expression in words. The fact that a man always talks about not being jealous makes me believe that he is jealous, else he would not be trying to convince others by words that he is not jealous.

[1] *Some Problems of the Modern Minister*, p. 236.
[2] Ray, Jeff D., *The Highest Office*, p. 241.

SOME SUGGESTED PRACTICES

Now let us make some practical applications of these principles. There are several different kinds of minister relationships, such as: the minister's relation to the visiting minister, to the adjacent minister, to the minister of another denomination in the community, to the succeeding pastor, to the preceding pastor, and to other ordained ministers within the congregation. In each of these cases there is a peculiar relationship which we shall discuss separately and in this order.

There will be many occasions in which one minister will be the invited guest of another minister. In most cases this will take place on the occasion of a revival meeting at which time the visiting minister will be evangelist. Whether for a revival meeting or for some other meeting or series of meetings the conditions will be practically the same. In every case the visiting minister ought to be treated with the greatest courtesy and hospitality. Sometimes, without intending to do so, the host minister has taken undue advantage of his visiting preacher. First of all, he should see to it that the visiting minister has a comfortable place to stay. If it is possible and available, a room in a hotel ought to be arranged for the visiting minister, not that he is too good to stay in a private home or that he would not enjoy it, but often when staying in the private home he must give much of his time and energy to entertaining and being entertained. To do his best he needs much time for meditation, prayer, and study. In some homes this could be done, and if placed in a home, the host minister should see that it is such a home as would be conducive to these things. Many times the minister will want to entertain the visiting minister in his own home. This is all right except that it sometimes puts an undue strain upon the pastor's home at a time when he, too, needs to put everything he has into the special program at hand. By all means, do not have the visiting minister moving from house to house each night. No man can do his best who must move every night and sleep on a different bed every night.

The matter of entertainment at meal time is also important. One of the most common sins of the ministry is that of over eating and jeopardizing the usefulness of the mind and body at a time when it is needed the most. But the visiting minister is not wholly to blame for this, nor is it always the fault of the host minister. It is easy for any man to gorge himself when he is set down three or four times a day to a table full of super-delux delicacies. However, the host minister can avoid a lot of this. The idea of visiting in the homes for meals is good and the contacts which are made by such visits can be valuable, but if at all possible the visiting minister should not be expected out for a heavy meal just before the evening service. After a heavy meal the breath is short and the mind is dull. I have the habit of asking the host pastor to arrange for no evening meals in the homes. A light meal is much better. Some prefer to eat nothing until after the service. Do not allow your people to gorge the visiting preacher to the extent that he cannot give his best in the pulpit.

Then there is the question of visitation. The pastor will and should make many visits and personal calls during the course of a revival meeting. Should he ask or expect the visiting minister to make all of these calls with him? The answer is an emphatic "no." Some preachers want the visiting evangelist to make every pastoral call with him, go with him to visit all of the sick, and meet many of the members. This may be all right, but it saps the energy and strength of the evangelist at a time when he needs to concentrate them upon the preaching of the Word and winning of the lost. Of course, the visiting preacher should be ready and anxious to make any personal contact with those who might be won to Christ. I want my evangelist to be willing and ready to go out with me to make personal contact with certain individuals who might be helped by the evangelist's personal work. But I do not expect the evangelist to make every visit that I make during the meeting.

On the other hand, the visiting minister should know and use wholesome ministerial ethics in his relation to the host pastor. May we offer several brief suggestions. First, he should not try to steal the affections of the people from the pastor. Some ministers have been guilty of this. But the wise minister will seek to strengthen the tie between pastor and people. The visiting preacher has an opportunity and responsibility to solidify and sweeten the relationship between pastor and people. Second, and closely related, he should not listen to nor encourage criticism of the pastor by the people. Under any circumstances it is never good ethics in any realm to listen to and encourage criticism of the host. Third, he should always think to give definite expression of appreciation for all hospitality given. A letter should be written immediately upon arrival home to the host pastor expressing appreciation and gratitude. This may seem unimportant and insignificant to many, but it has more weight and carries more importance than most of us think.

Now let us consider the relation of the minister to an adjacent minister, that is, one who is pastor of an adjacent parish or territory. In this case especially the minister must guard against any feeling or act of competition. The relationship should be always most cordial and it will be if each pastor will use good ministerial ethics. In the first place, friendship should be cultivated with occasional visits. Many problems would never arise if we knew each other better. There is the danger that we will become so engrossed in our own field of labor that we do not meet or cultivate friendship with our neighbor ministers. This is often true and lamentable. Time spent once in a while cultivating these friendships is time well spent. In the second place, the minister must refrain from all "sheep steal- ing" activities. Nothing disrupts ministerial fellowship more than this. "Sheep stealing" is both unethical and unchristian. If a person is a member of a near-by church and attends that church, he should not be invited or urged to attend another church. If he is inactive, that is a different question. Any preacher has a right and a responsi- bility to reach and enlist those who are inactive or lost. But the practice of trying to enlist people who are already actively engaged in some other church is "sheep stealing" and will be avoided by all honest and fair-minded ministers. Now if the individual in question voluntarily expresses a desire to change churches, then the minister should do his best to make him feel welcome and wanted. I have a next door neighbor who attends church across town from our com- munity. I have never asked him to join our church and never will so long as he is active and faithful to his own church. If the time should ever come that he becomes inactive and irregular in his own church, then I will do my best to enlist him in regular Christian activity through the program of our church. It is my custom at some time during the week to visit in the home of every new visitor who has attended our services on the preceding Sunday. If I learn that the individual being visited is an active member of another church, I do not insist on his coming to our church but simply try to express our delight in having him visit our services. Many serious injuries have been inflicted upon ministerial fellowship by some unethical ministerial "sheep stealer." In the third place, if a member of a min- ister's congregation moves to another field and, because of the dis- tance, becomes irregular and inactive, the minister should be un- selfish enough to give the name and address of this person to the minister in his immediate vicinity with the hope that the person will be enlisted in active Christian service. Selfishness on the part of preachers often is the cause of continued inactivity on the part of some Christians who move to adjacent fields.

There is also the question of the minister's relation to ministers of other denominations in his own community. The relationship in such case most likely will not be as intimate as in the case of a min- ister of the same faith, but it can be, and should be, just as wholesome and cordial. Though there are differences of conviction which make impossible some organic ties, yet the very highest form of ministerial ethics should be employed. First, a minister should get acquainted with the other ministers of his community. When a new minister moves into the community a word of welcome from a fellow minister would be both becoming and helpful to all concerned. Second, the minister should co-operate and work with the other ministers of his community in matters which concern the well being of the community as a whole. He can do this without becoming involved in any activity which would necessitate a compromise of convictions. Third, the minister should avoid personal controversy with other ministers of his community. Of course, he will preach his own doctrines without compromise from his own pulpit, but there is no advantage in engaging in personal controversies with the other ministers. Such personal squabbles between ministers of opposing faiths are always hurtful. Fourth, in his visitation, if the minister runs across those who have definite preference for a church of another faith, he should report these prospects to the minister of that church. This is not only a matter of common courtesy but also a means of strengthening fraternal feelings and of enlisting more people in Christian service.

Perhaps the greatest strains on ministerial fellowship come in the relationship of predecessor and successor. This relationship needs to be carefully reconsidered by every minister. First, let us consider the relation of the minister to his successor. At this point many preachers are guilty, whether intentionally or not, of committing grave injustices to their fellow ministers. Though he cannot expect the people to terminate their love for him immediately upon his departure, the departing pastor can explain to his people that he is no longer their pastor and should not be so considered by them. He can also encourage his people to give their fullest co-operation and loyalty to the succeeding pastor. A few timely remarks like this by a departing pastor will do much toward paving the way for an effective ministry by the successor.

After the new pastor moves on the field, it would be wise and helpful for the predecessor to write a personal letter to his successor expressing his hope and prayer for a happy and successful pastorate. Such a word often relieves the strain that might exist between successor and predecessor.

Perhaps the most common sin in this relationship is that of too frequent visits of a former pastor to his previous field of labor. There is absolutely no excuse for the oft repeated visits of a former pastor in the homes of members of a former church, with the idea of holding the affection of former parishioners against the love and loyalty due to the new pulpit occupant. This is about the most unkind, unethical, and unchristian thing that a minister can do in his relation to his fellow ministers. A visit on rare occasions is certainly not out of order, but even in such cases it is best to visit the pastor first and let him know that you are on the field for a brief visit with old friends. Then he will know that you are not trying to slip in behind his back and do something which might be detrimental to him and the church. If he hears after you are gone that you were on the field, he might suspect as much.

Then there will be times when the former pastor will be called back for various occasions, such as funerals, etc. In this realm great caution should be exercised. In times of sorrow and bereavement when the people request the services of a former pastor, no one has a right to deny them this request. However, the pastor involved should use the utmost caution in the acceptance of such engagements. Never should he accept such invitation without first talking with the present pastor. He should come only with the cheerful consent of the pastor. And even then he should never have charge of the funeral service, unless it is impossible for the pastor to be present. The former pastor may have some part in the service, but he should never consent to have full charge if the present pastor is available. These things should be carefully understood between former pastor and pastor. The same is true in the case of weddings. Many strained relationships are created by unethical conduct in these two realms. Someone has accurately observed that weddings and funerals are the most prolific source of misunderstanding among ministers. And yet all of these misunderstandings could be so easily avoided if ministers would stop and think before acting, if they would just use a little common sense, courtesy, and respect. These timely words from the pen of Dr. A. K. DeBlois will shed light on this phase of ministerial relationships;

A minister's relation to his successor involves delicate and important considerations. It is easy for him to work harm at this point. For a number of years he has been directing the spiritual energies of a company of people. His duties have frequently brought him into more or less intimate personal fellowship with certain individuals and family groups. His ministry has been a dismal failure unless a few at least of such associations have been formed. When he takes a pastorate elsewhere these old associations are by no means severed. Another man has, however, been called to the pastorate of the church he has left. This new man needs, and ought to have, the undivided loyalty of the entire membership. The former pastor may, and should, remain a true and trusted friend of all his old parishioners, but he must bear clearly in mind the fact that he now ministers to another congregation. He is the responsible head of an entirely distinct group of people. Or, if he has taken no new pastorate, he has none the less definitely resigned the old one. In other words, he has no pastoral relationship whatever in that parish. [3]

Now let us consider the relation of the minister to his predecessor. Right at this point is where most jealousy arises on the part of preachers. It is true that the predecessor may do things to injure his successor; but it is also true that the successor can do things to injure his predecessor. This relationship must be right on both ends of the line. Right now we are looking at it from the standpoint of the minister's attitude and conduct toward his predecessor. First, he should not be surprised or disappointed if he finds that some of the people of his parish have an expressive love for and attraction to the former pastor. If the pastor has done a good work, it is only human that the people love him, especially those who have been won to Christ through his ministry and those who have been comforted in times of sorrow by his ministry. The love and friendship ties which are thus developed cannot be suddenly cut off at the going of the pastor, nor should they be. It is nothing but right that people continue to remember with love and affection a pastor who has served faithfully as God's undershepherd, so long as they do not allow their religion to become nothing more than a sentimental attachment to a man. The wise minister will expect and encourage his people to love and appreciate a former pastor. Even from a selfish standpoint any pastor will be wise to encourage and delight in the love of his people for a former pastor. It is only reasonable to suppose that if we express delight in the affections of our people for another, this expression of delight will cause the people to love us the more. The surest way for any preacher to work injury to himself is to express resentment at the expressed love of the people for a former pastor, even though the former pastor may have unethically encouraged such. No preacher can ever win the affections of any people by scolding them for loving another preacher. Even though a member may be ever so loyal to the present pastoral leadership, he should not be expected to give up completely any feeling of love and affection for a former pastor.

If the former pastor is loved by the people, the wise pastor will capitalize on this condition to his own profit and the profit of the church by taking occasion publicly to commend and compliment the brother who is thus loved. By so doing he will weld the people

[3] *Some Problems of the Modern Minister,* p. 225.

to himself. The preacher who becomes resentful and jealous is not only little but foolish. If the former pastor is the right kind of a man, an occasional invitation to revisit his former field for some special service will not only sweeten the fellowship between the two ministers, but will also strengthen his own influence in the hearts of his people. We agree with Dr. W. B. Riley that —

> . . . to object to having a member call a loved ministerial friend, from within or without the fellowship of the church, to pray with the sick, to comfort in the hour of sorrow, to participate in a funeral service, or to perform the wedding of a son or daughter that perhaps had been baptized in a former day by him — resentment at such procedure would indicate that in the pastor's mind these members are no longer free men and women permitted, therefore, to exercise personal judgment and preference, but are his vassals and can neither serve nor be served by other than himself.[4]

There is one other ministerial relationship to be mentioned, and that is the relation of the pastor to other ordained ministers who might be in his congregation. In many congregations there are disabled and retired ministers. It is thought by many that the presence of such ministers within the congregation always constitutes a problem for the pastor. But we beg to disagree with any such thought. It is true that some ordained ministers in the congregation have caused trouble for the pastor, but such cases are exceptions and not the rule. In most cases the minister will find his most staunch supporters in these other ministers within his congregation. And indeed, if the time should ever come that we must take our places in the pew, may God give us grace to be the kind of members any pastor would like to have. Sometimes the pastor himself is the cause of ill-will and dissension in relation to these other ministers by expressing a feeling of resentment and jealousy. These men, most of whom are retired ministers, have a right to some attention and the wise pastor will not ignore them. In my own experience I have had a number of other ordained ministers in the churches I have pastored. In no case have they ever given me cause for alarm or discontent. They have been a boon to my ministry. My own life has been greatly enriched by my association with these great men of God. Never shall I forget the inspiration and profit that came to me through contact with such men as B. B. Blaylock, W. H. McKenzie, and J. P. Boone. I count it a privilege indeed to have been pastor of these men and others, who, having blessed multitudes with their ministries through the years, gave to me many of the benefits of their

[4] *The Preacher and His Preaching*, p. 65.

sound judgment and long and rich experiences. I would say to every young pastor: cultivate the friendship of those dear men of God who may be found in your congregation in the closing hours of their ministerial day. You can be a blessing and comfort to them and they will prove to be a rich endowment to you. Dr. Robert Barrett has summed it up in these words: "Not every pastor is blessed with the privilege of 'dying with the harness on,' but many find it necessary to retire on account of growing infirmity. Sad to say, it is generally understood that the pastor who has other ministers in his flock will have a stony road to travel. The reverse should be true. A number of godly, experienced veterans should be a bulwark of strength to the pastor."[5]

[5] *Ethics of the Ministry,* pp. 191, 192.

Part V
The Minister
and His Personal Life

23 | THE MINISTER AND HIS FINANCES

In this part of our study we are dealing with matters pertaining more particularly to the minister's personal life. Many laymen never seem to realize that the minister has financial problems and responsibilities the same as others. And some preachers do not give enough consideration to the financial side of living. A serious reconsideration of the financial side of ministerial living is greatly needed at this time both by the laity and by the ministry. It is our purpose in this chapter to face the problem of the minister and his finances from every angle with fairness, clarity, and reason.

THE NECESSITY OF FINANCIAL SUPPORT

It is hardly necessary to remind the reader of the necessity of some kind of financial support for the minister and his family. Even though he gives his time and energy to spiritual endeavors, he must eat, sleep, and be clothed as any other man. No matter how great the preacher, he must maintain his existence on earth by the material substances of life. There are a few people who seem to think that the minister lives on such a plane of life that he does not need the material things of life. But those who have had experience know that a preacher can no more live physically on the spiritual elements than a bride and groom can live on love. Therefore, some means of material support and sustenance must be arranged.

THE SOURCE OF FINANCIAL SUPPORT

Having recognized the necessity of some kind of financial support, from what source should the minister's financial support come? Some few ministers receive financial aid through inheritance. These are very rare cases. Most ministers come from poor families, and, as a rule, those who do so make better preachers. There is something about poverty that prepares a preacher for a more sympathetic ministry. Then there are a few other preachers who receive financial aid by engaging in some business enterprise along with their preaching. But the effectiveness of any ministry is jeopardized if a good part of the attention and energy of the minister is occupied in some worldly pursuit. A few others receive financial aid by taking the role of beggars and becoming objects of charity. Such practice not only embarrasses the ministry but also cheapens it.

There is only one proper source for the minister's financial support. He should receive his financial support from the people whom he serves. This is not only reasonable but also Scriptural. Though he waived this right because of the peculiarity of his own case, Paul makes a lengthy, elaborate, and logical defence for the minister's right to be supported by the people whom he serves. Here are his words: "Or I only and Barnabas, have not we power to forbear working? Who goeth a warfare any time at his charges? Who planteth a vineyard, and eateth not of the fruit thereof? Or who feedeth a flock, and eateth not of the milk of the flock? Say I these things as a man? Or saith not the law the same also? For it is written in the law of Moses, Thou shalt not muzzle the mouth of the ox that treadeth out the corn. Doth God take care for oxen? Or saith he it altogether for our sakes? For our sakes, no doubt, this is written: that he that ploweth should plow in hope; and that he that thresheth in hope should be partaker of his hope. If we have sown unto you spiritual things, is it a great thing if we shall reap your carnal things? If others be partakers of this power over you, are not we rather? Nevertheless we have not used this power; but suffer all things, lest we should hinder the gospel of Christ. Do ye not know that they which minister about holy things live of the things of the temple? And they which wait at the altar are partakers with the altar? Even so hath the Lord ordained that they which preach the gospel should live of the Gospel" (I Corinthians 9:6-14). Paul proves his argument by natural analogy, Scripture, intrinsic justice, common practice, Old Testament custom, and the express commandment of the Lord. It is evident from this passage and others that preachers should receive their financial support from the people whom they serve. That preacher's work is vitally hindered who relies, by choice or by necessity, on outside sources for his financial support. There are rare cases, of course, in which the preacher must depend upon some outside source for financial support. This was true in Paul's case. In purely missionary work, such as Paul's, it is not only necessary but also wise to seek financial support elsewhere. In Paul's day the churches already in existence were hardly strong enough to support a vast missionary program, thus Paul worked on the side. In this day our churches participate in a Co-operative Program which enables even missionaries to serve without being encumbered by the worry of seeking financial support from outside activities. No minister can give his best if he must divide his time and attention by seeking financial support outside the field of his ministerial labors. The pastorate of the smallest church is a full time responsibility and needs the full and undivided attention of the minister. It is the church's responsibility to see that this is possible.

THE METHOD OF FINANCIAL SUPPORT

If we are agreed that the preacher should be supported by the church, how should this support be given? In days gone by it was the common practice for the preacher to receive from each individual in the church just what he cared to drop in his hand either before or after the service. In most cases the preacher went home empty handed. In my first pastorate the senior deacon would arise at the close of the service and announce that he would be at the front at the close of the service and if any body had any money for the preacher he would receive it. This method of individual spasmodic giving has never been very adequate in the support of the ministry.

A few churches practice the method of giving to the preacher a certain per cent of the total income of the church. In such a case the preacher's income would vary with the income of the church and it would become difficult for the preacher to make definite plans, for he could not anticipate the amount of the income. Furthermore, under such an arrangement the minister is made liable to much criticism when any mention is made of church finances.

The most common and adequate method of ministerial support is the specified salary. In this way the preacher knows what to expect and can plan his own financial obligations accordingly. No matter how small or how large the salary, there ought to be a definite salary set; otherwise, the preacher will find himself in unavoidable financial embarrassments.

THE AMOUNT OF FINANCIAL SUPPORT

This method of financial support for the minister involves another question: How much should the minister receive? What should his salary be? These questions should be thoroughly thought through and understood by all who have a part in the life of the church. Let us observe in passing that a few preachers are adequately supported. Most of these, of course, are in the large churches. But the vast majority of preachers are very inadequately supported. The average minister's salary is below the average of any other professional group. According to Porter Routh in the Southern Baptist

Handbook[1] the average salary of a Southern Baptist full-time pastor in 1959 was approximately $3,000. The average salary of pastors in other denominations would most likely be somewhere in this same neighborhood. This means that some are above this and many are below it. Nor does this take into consideration the many part-time churches which usually pay very meager salaries.

In fixing the salary of the minister it should be remembered that the minister must live on an economical plane comparable to that of the people whom he serves. Most preachers could live on less than they do, and would be cheerfully willing to do so, if it were necessary and expedient, but when a minister cuts his living to the extent that he must live in an altogether different realm of society and economics from that of his church members, that moment he begins to be a target of criticism and ridicule and soon he will be forced to leave for another locality. People expect their preachers to live on their economic plane and yet often they do not give them the support to live on such a plane. Every preacher is expected, and has a right, to live as his people live; therefore, he ought to have a salary on a par with the average of his people, remembering that his expenses in connection with his work are usually more than that of the average businessman. Ordinarily he should not live on an economic plane above that of his people. In such a case the minister will find it difficult to win the love of the people or to do his best work. The salary, therefore, will vary according to the ability of the church, living costs, economic conditions, and living customs.

Preachers themselves are partly to blame for an inadequately supported ministry. In many cases the people have not been taught. Of course, the preacher must not embarrass himself and disgrace the ministry by constantly complaining of his poor salary. Nor must he ever resort to trickery or chicanery in order to get a raise in salary. We have known of preachers who would go before pastorless churches just to prize a raise in salary out of their own people by a threat of leaving. God pity the preacher who is guilty of this! Surely no genuine preacher would stoop this low. However, a timely word of instruction from the pulpit on the Bible teaching concerning ministerial support will help greatly in solving these problems. At the opportune time a friendly, fair, thorough, and frank discussion of the problem of ministerial support with the church leaders will also help. A few ministers who have lucrative incomes from other sources have hindered the cause of adequate ministerial support by giving their services to the churches as pastors without pay. No matter how much

[1] *Southern Baptist Handbook* for 1959, p. 32.

money a preacher makes from other sources he ought to lead his
church to pay an adequate salary. He may in turn invest it in missionary projects, but, by all means, the church needs to be trained
in the responsibiliy of ministerial support. It not only develops the
grace of giving, but it will prepare them for the next pastor who
may not have any other source of income.

THE ADMINISTRATION OF FINANCIAL SUPPORT

The problem of getting sufficient financial support is serious,
but the problem of the proper administration of finances available
is more serious. The minister has been unjustly accused by many
as being a poor businessman. But the facts of the case prove the
contrary. There is no other group of men on earth who can do as
much on as little money as the preacher group. This fact commends
the minister as a most efficient businessman.

> Popular opinion has it that the minister is of necessity a poor busi-
> nessman, particularly impractical in the matter of money. The fact
> that he lives within his income and maintains a standard expected
> of him and his family usually contradicts this tradition. The minister
> and his wife must be expert economists in order to get by. The
> minister must not be unduly concerned with money matters, yet
> no man in the community should be more careful than he in the
> getting and spending of money. Carelessness and looseness at this
> point may undo him.[2]

There are a few exceptional cases in which a minister has been
found careless and loose, even dishonest, in business matters. These
cases are always publicized out of all proportion to the ratio of ministers who are guilty. At least 95 percent of all ministers are honest
in their business relationships, and yet sometimes ministers allow
themselves to get into financial embarrassments because of a lack
of care and training in the administration of business matters. In
his book on ethics, Dr. Barrett has pointed out that "the time is past
when a preacher is considered 'too holy' to look after his business
affairs. It is no credit to a minister to have it said that he is so engrossed in his studies that he never thinks of his accounts, and so
leaves every town in which he preaches with a long list of unpaid
bills. Besides the crime of dishonesty thus committed, and for which
he must answer before God, such a man also kills his influence in
the community."[3] May we, therefore, offer a few practical suggestions
for the minister in the administration of his own finances. *First, have
a definite understanding as to the amount of salary you are to re-*

---

2 Dobbins, G. S., *Building Better Churches*, p. 396.
3 *Ethics of the Ministry*, p. 176.

ceive from the church and the date it is to be paid. It is extremely
difficult to carry on a sound financial program without a knowledge
of the amount of salary to be expected and the time of its payment.
It is nothing but right that the minister know these things. *Second,
determine to live on the amount of income received.* Any man can
adjust his living to fit his income if he really wants to do so. He
may have to leave some things out, but better is it by far to leave
out some desired things than to leave his life open to suspicion in
the realm of honesty and integrity. *Third, keep a complete record of
personal finances.* Sometimes preachers over-spend unintentionally
simply because they have no records to keep them informed as to
their financial condition. System and order are essential to efficient
operation in any realm, and this certainly applies to a minister's
personal finances. A family budget should be set up and an account
of all spending and receiving kept. By such a system the minister
will avoid many financial embarrassments. *Fourth, beware of too
much installment buying.* Many a man has been ruined financially
by over-indulgence in installment buying. We are not saying that
a minister should never buy anything on the installment plan or
establish credit accounts. Most of us would have little or nothing if
we were not privileged to buy on the installment plan. And yet it
is easy to over-indulge, and preachers are not invulnerable at this
point. *Fifth, take advantage of the markets.* A preacher's dollar can
go much further if he will watch for the bargains on the markets
and take advantage of them. Buying ought to be planned so as to
take advantage of these. We are not referring to ministerial discounts. We have no patience with ministers who cheapen the ministry by expecting or asking for ministerial discounts. But careful,
planned buying will result in savings. *Sixth, save a little for the
"rainy day."* The family budget should be worked out so that it
will not tax every penny of the total salary. Some margin should be
left. The Lord will take care of His own, but, where it is possible,
a sensible saving for financial emergencies is both wise and religious. The Lord expects His ministers to use common sense in
financial matters. Few people are able to put money away in a saving account. *But practically every one can save through the medium
of life insurance. The best investment of savings for the average
minister is in life insurance.* Life insurance is not only protection,
but a savings account as well. Any minister will do well to consult an
experienced insurance specialist early in life and plan a sensible insurance program which will afford him some savings and at the
same time take away much of the anxiety of old age. And by all
means, every minister ought to take advantage of the minister's

retirement plan offered by his denomination. Most denominations do have some kind of a plan. It is to his definite advantage that the minister get into this plan as early as possible in his ministry. It is a source of great comfort to know that provisions have been made for those sunset days without having to be thrown out upon society and the mercy of charitable people. The time to make these arrangements is in the early part of one's ministry.

THE CHRISTIAN ATTITUDE TOWARD FINANCIAL SUPPORT

The closing thought of this chapter concerns the attitude of the minister toward his money. What attitude should the preacher take toward his own financial support? According to some, a preacher ought never to consider the financial end of his task. Some people even go so far as to lose confidence in the preacher when they learn that he had given some consideration to the finances involved in a move from one church to another.

In regard to this question two things ought to be made clear: First, preachers do consider the financial side of the ministerial service. Whether we like it or not, ministers are human and as such they cannot help but give some consideration to the financial side. The minister who tries to impress a people with the idea that he has given absolutely no consideration to the finances involved in making a decision, is misrepresenting the facts. He is not giving a true picture. In fact, usually the preacher who says the most about not considering the finances is the one who gives the most attention to it. Frankly, I give some consideration to the financial angle of every move I make.

Second, preachers not only do consider the financial side of a move, but they have a perfect right to do so. A minister ought to give some consideration to the finances involved. I hasten to qualify that statement by adding that the finances must never be the sole and determining factor in any move the minister makes. But the fact that it should be given some consideration no reasonable man will deny. When a preacher makes a move from one church to another which involves an increase in salary, someone is always ready to say that he moved just because he could get more money. But why can't a preacher be just as divinely led when he makes an increase in salary as when he takes a cut in salary? Why can't a preacher do just as much good, and maybe more, in a church which pays a little more salary? Why must a preacher be branded as dishonest and unholy just because he goes to a church that pays a little more? If a preacher makes a move which involves an increase in salary, he is in it just for the money, but if a preacher makes a move which involves a decrease in salary, then he is slipping; he's no good. This is the minister's dilemma.

Lest some one get the wrong impression, we are not suggesting that a preacher ought to move every time he is offered a better salary. This would be a colossal mistake. Usually an increase in salary is involved when a preacher makes a move and this is to be expected. Suppose a preacher only moved when he could take a cut in salary! But in the experience of nearly every preacher there are times when a move was not made even though it involved increase in salary. Most of the moves I have made have involved increases in salary, but not in every case. I have made some moves involving decrease in salary. This leads us to the principle underlying all of these questions: A minister ought and must consider the financial side of any move so long as this consideration does not become the determining factor in the move. Certainly, the finances are to be considered, but this is not the chief consideration. There are other things which are more important. The financial end may have some bearing upon the move, but never the ultimate motive. If a preacher will make any move just because it involves an increase in salary, that man is not worthy of the name of a Christian minister.

Perhaps a word of warning should be offered in closing. One of the grave dangers faced by the minister is that of becoming money conscious. Some men refuse to give themselves completely to the ministry just because of a fear of not making enough money. Nothing is more certain than the fact that God will supply the needs for those whom He has called into His minstry. On the other hand some preachers have been guilty of making unwise and unholy moves just for the sake of more money. "The money heart is the preacher's ever-present menace. It blasts the brightest prospect, blights the noblest plans, and mildews the rosiest dreams. It saps preaching of its romance, service of its knighthood, and sacrifice of its chivalry. It debases ideals, attentuates vision and emasculates heroism. It clogs prayer, clips the wings of faith and defiles meditation."[4] A wise and sensible attitude ought to be taken by the preacher and also by the laity toward the preacher, one which recognizes the necessity of financial considerations but at the same time one which recognizes the supremacy of the will of God in the directing of our lives to the most useful ends.

---

[4] Ray, Jeff D., *The Highest Office*, p. 102.

24 | THE MINISTER AND HIS HEALTH

THE NECESSITY OF GOOD HEALTH

The minister's health has much to do with the efficiency of his work, and the condition of the minister's health is determined largely by the minister himself. There are some deficiencies of health, of course, over which the minister himself may have absolutely no control, but we are convinced that at least eighty percent of health deficiencies are caused by the minister's own habits and practices. That is why we write this chapter — a study of the minister's health and what he can do toward maintaining good health for a more effective ministry.

We cannot overestimate the importance of good health for the best ministerial service. Dr. Jefferson makes this significant comment about the minister's health: "A minister cannot preach without his body, and, other things being equal, the sounder his body, the more effective will be his preaching. Indeed, the body is more implicated in the work of the preacher than in the work of many a man who seems to use his body only. A minister is subjected to a nervous strain which is continuous, and which at times becomes terrific. Heavy weights hang on all his nerve centers."[1] While most of us realize, at least theoretically, the importance of a sound body for ministerial service, very few ministers give any serious consideration to the study of proper habits and practices which would contribute to a sounder body. It is hoped that this study will provoke some serious thinking along this line, especially for the young minister who has his life before him. Dr. Barrett has correctly pointed out that the physiology of preaching is a neglected department of homiletics.[2]

STRAINS ON THE MINISTER'S HEALTH

The average layman, and sometimes the preacher himself, does not realize the strains which are constantly being brought to bear upon the minister's physical nature. Though he does not use the

[1] *The Minister As Prophet*, p. 40.
[2] *Ethics of the Ministry*, p. 113.

199

muscles of his body as much as the man who digs a ditch or works at some other form of manual labor, yet the body itself is under frequent strain, because of a lack of sleep, the lack of muscular activity, and the lack of outside fresh air. The minister who does his work well must be at it early and late.

Even more serious is the mental strain. Some people seem to think that the man who doesn't do some form of manual labor doesn't really work. Such people need to be disillusioned. There is nothing more taxing and exhausting on the body than mental work. And if the preacher is a successful preacher he must spend many hours in mental activity which will tax his strength and wear his body.

But most serious of all is the nervous strain. The anxieties which come with working with people and ministering to people make a tremendous drain upon the preacher's nervous energy. When a preacher's body breaks down it usually comes through the nervous system. There is no vocation in which nerves are more seriously strained than in the ministry. The sincere preacher is touched constantly with the feeling and needs of his people. The problems, needs, and anxieties of his people create a continuous tension on his nervous system. Some men punch the clock at a certain hour and go home, forgetting the responsibility of their jobs until the next morning. But not so with the preacher. He goes home only to be repeatedly disturbed by telephone calls from parishioners with their problems. When he goes to the neighborhood grocery his nervous tension is not relaxed, for he must be constantly on the alert lest he overlook some brother or sister who might go out to criticize the pastor for not speaking. These and a thousand other things keep the minister in a constant state of nervous strain. Dr. Jeff D. Ray points out that "the preacher makes more speeches than a lawyer, more visits than a doctor, does more studying than a college professor, writes more copy than an editor, loses more sleep and has more irregular hours than a trained nurse."[3] Add to this the nervous strains that come with the rapid pace of our modern machine age and we wonder how any one of us lives long. It is no wonder that many preachers break down, but many of these break downs could be avoided if ministers would give more serious consideration to the essential and basic elements of good health. In spite of these strains there are some things that can be done to strengthen and fortify the body if the minister will determine to do them. Some ministers may feel that there are so many other things of so much greater importance that we must neglect the matters which have to do with the physical. But one of the first lessons the

[3] *The Highest Office,* p. 130.

preacher needs to learn is that the care of his body is a religious necessity and ought to be done religiously. In lecturing to Yale students Phillips Brooks gave this timely advice: "Remember that the care for your health, the avoidance of nervous waste, the training of your voice, and everything else that you do for your body is not merely an economy of your organs that they may be fit for certain works; it is a part of that total self-consecration which cannot be divided, and which all together makes you the medium through which God may reach His children's lives."[4]

SOME HEALTH HINTS FOR MINISTERS

The author is not intimating that he has kept all the rules for good health. In fact, I am embarrassingly conscious of my failure at this point. God has blessed me with a good body. There are some things I have done toward the strengthening of it, but there are many things I have neglected to the injury of it. It is my hope and prayer that many young preachers will take advantage of a few of these hints for better health to the end that they might have a more effective ministry. In spite of many strains, ministers can, if they will, do much toward the building up of stronger bodies for better service. There are a few basic principles which, if followed, will contribute much to the health of any individual. We do not claim any knowledge of medical science, and if serious complications set up in the minister's health, certainly he should consult a good physician. But experience and observation have revealed certain fundamental principles of good health. These might be classified in different ways. Dr. Ray names seven elements necessary for the maintenance of good health: sleep, food, fresh air, clothing, exercise, a bath, mental recreation, including laugh provoking amusements.[5] In our discussion here we are mentioning only four fundamental principles which are necessary for the maintenance of good health. These either include or imply all of the items mentioned in Dr. Ray's classification. These four health principles are as follows: the proper quality, quantity, and regularity of eating; the proper amount of sleep; the proper kind and regularity of exercise; and the proper relaxation of mind and body. Let us consider the application of these principles.

Eating habits have a tremendous bearing on health. Proper eating habits must include three things: quantity, quality, and regularity. We must eat the right amount of food. Most preachers are proud of the fact that they are total abstainers so far as liquor is con-

[4] Lectures on Preaching, p. 41.
[5] The Highest Office, p. 131.

cerned, and this is good, and yet few people are greater sinners than the average preacher in the matter of over-eating. It has been our observation that most preachers eat too much. The habit of over-eating is not difficult to cultivate, especially when we are frequently invited to a table of elaborate delicacies. The preacher must constantly be on his guard against temptation. Over-eating is the prolific cause of innumerable diseases. And by all means, the minister should eat a light breakfast if he plans to spend the morning in study. Dr. Jefferson is right in pointing out that "you cannot fill the stomach with a huge breakfast and then have enough blood in your brain to do successful mental work. The students of all lands have learned by experience that to study in the morning the breakfast must be light."[6] If a man is to dig a ditch, he needs a heavy breakfast; but if he is to use his brain, he needs a light breakfast. I have found that my mind is much clearer after drinking a glass of pure orange juice for breakfast.

Proper eating also involves quality. We must eat the right amount but we must also eat the right kind. It is not in the realm of our knowledge to say with any assurance what ought to go into a balanced diet. I do know that one can eat too much starchy food and too many sweets for the maintenance of good health. The minister will do well to learn from some good physician what kind of food ought to be included in a balanced diet, one that will do most toward the building up and maintaining of the body. The minister does not need to be a crank in his eating, but the use of some reason and discretion in the type of food which he takes into his body is imperative.

Regularity is also important. Between-meal eating is never good for the body. The minister cannot have any kind of a definite schedule without some interruptions, but so far as it is possible, he will do well to have a regular time for the eating of each meal. In Gaylord Hauser's book, *Look Younger; Live Longer* (Farrar, Straus and Co., N. Y.), will be found some helpful hints for the diet.

Our second health hint concerns sleeping. For the welfare of any body there must be a proper amount of sleep. Some people do not get enough sleep, while others get too much sleep. The amount of sleep necessary will vary with different individuals. Some natures demand more sleep than others. In delivering the Yale lectures to preachers Henry Ward Beecher makes the following interesting observation: "Now it may seem a little singular, but it is true, that if you are possessed of a very nervous organization you will need less sleep than if you are a phlegmatic temperament. If a man is dull,

6 *The Minister As Prophet*, p. 47.

lethargic, slow, eight or nine hours of sleep is necessary for him."[7]
For most adults I would say that seven or eight hours would be
sufficient. For the most part this sleep ought to be gotten at night.
God made the night for sleeping. We realize, however, that in this
modern era it is practically impossible for the minister to retire early.
There is some meeting nearly every night which he must attend.
But he ought to retire as early as possible at night. We still believe
that there is some wisdom in the old adage: "Early to bed, early
to rise, makes a man healthy, wealthy, and wise." We are not sure
about the "wealthy and wise," but we do know that a good, sufficient
sleep is conducive to good health. Because of the late hours he
must keep, the minister may feel that he cannot rise at an early hour.
It may be necessary for him to sleep later than some people sleep,
and yet there is no excuse for the habit of lying up in the bed half
the morning. The best time for mental work is early in the morning.
Some ministers may not find this convenient, but whatever his schedule, the minister should arrange for the proper amount of sleep, not
too much and not too little.

Our third health hint concerns exercise. The human body must
have a reasonable amount of regular exercise if it is to function at
its best. Perhaps more people err at this point than at any other.
Many bodily weaknesses and defects come from a lack of exercise.
Exercise habits may take many different forms. But whatever the
form, every preacher needs some exercise for the maximum usefulness of his body. This, of course, will involve fresh air. If possible
exercise should always be taken in the open air. For a preacher, this
exercise does not need to be strenuous. In fact, he will make a mistake if he indulges in strenuous exercise. A man who is engaged in
mental activity primarily does not need to spend too much time
building muscles. But he does need enough exercise to keep the organs of his body operating efficiently. Again may we quote from the
advice of Henry Ward Beecher to the Yale students of 1872: "When
I first began, I had an impression that if I had good bone and muscle
I should be all right. I very soon learned that it was possible for
a man to take too much exercise, and that a man could be built up
physically at the expense of his brain. Now, if you undertake, as
scholars, very violent exercise, according to the exaggerated idea
cf muscular Christianity, you will very soon use up all the vitality of
your system in the bone-and-muscle development, and it will leave
you, not better, but less fitted for intellectual exertion. Yet there must
be enough care given to bone and muscle to furnish a good plat-

[7] *Lectures on Preaching,* p. 197.

form, on which your artillery is to stand."[8] Perhaps the most important thing to remember in taking exercise is regularity. Irregular and spasmodic exercise is worse than no exercise. Five or ten minutes of calisthenics each morning upon arising will add much to the maintenance of bodily efficiency. But if this is not done regularly each day it will be only a waste of time and energy. Besides this, every preacher ought to give a few hours each week to some other kind of outside exercise, not only for the exercise but also for the good wholesome fresh air which he will breathe into his lungs. Each preacher will choose an activity which fits his taste. Some find this exercise in golf, others in tennis, still others in gardening, etc. Any form of bodily exercise in the open is good, so long as it is not too strenuous. Then as age comes on it will need to be even less strenuous, but as long as a man lives he needs to have some time for bodily exercise.

Our fourth and last health hint concerns relaxation. There is a certain amount of relaxation in good wholesome exercise, but there is more to it than this. Happy and healthy is the man who has learned how to relax from the physical and mental strains of life. Many preachers have nervous breakdowns because they have not learned the art of relaxation. Mental and nervous relaxation is what the minister needs. To some degree the sincere preacher never clears his mind completely of mental and nervous anxiety concerning his people, and yet if the minister is to live and do well he must learn to relieve his mind of these mental and nervous anxieties at least for brief seasons. Constant pressure on the mental and nervous system will lead inevitably to physical collapse. The minister, therefore, ought to take at least one whole day a week away form his work. On this day he should occupy his mind with some diversion which will take his mind completely away from the nervous strains and responsibilities of his work. It is better, if possible, at least occasionally, to get away from the community of his labor. Some men can leave their jobs and stay at home, but not so with the minister. The activities of this day may vary in a thousand different ways, but whatever is done, it should be light, requiring no serious mental strain.

The day of the week for this mental diversion will be determined by the individual minister. Some may prefer one day, others another. Many preachers choose Monday for this rest day, recuperating from the nervous exhaustion of Sunday. In my own experience I have found that Saturday is much better. Unless some emergency arises, I do nothing on Saturday in connection with my ministerial respon-

[8] *Ibid.*, p. 194.

sibilities. I sleep a little later, sometimes do a little work in the yard, play tennis, go to a ball game, visit relatives or engage in some other light diversion. For the preacher who waits until Saturday to get up his sermon for the following day this would be impossible. But even if he took some other day for rest, any preacher is either foolish or lazy who waits until Saturday to work up his sermons. I agree with Dr. Charles Jefferson that "a man should come to his pulpit fresh, with nerves full of life and all his blood leaping through his veins. He should do but little mental work on Saturday, spending Saturday afternoon in the open air. His Saturday evening meal should be the best and most elaborate meal of all the week."[9] It seems to me that the mental relaxation should be taken before the strenuous day rather than after it.

But one day a week is not sufficient relaxation for the most efficient operation of the body and mind. Every minister ought to have one vacation a year of two or three weeks duration. Vacation time is not a waste of time or money, nor is it for idlers or sluggards. It will pay dividends throughout the year in the more efficient operation of the whole man. Jesus taught His disciples to "come aside and rest for a while." Vacation days are happy rest periods for people who have been living under the strain of intense and strenuous work. "Vacations should not encourage vacuities. Rest means a change of attitude toward things in general, and complete release for the time from the duties of one's special calling. There is a vast relief in such change."[10]

Not only is it important that the minister have a vacation, but it is even more important that he spend his vacation time wisely and profitably. In this connection let us offer several words of advice. First, do not try to take a vacation at home. Some men can do this, but the preacher cannot. He must get completely away from the environment of his field of labor. I have found that the only way that I can clear my mind of the responsibilities and problems of my field of labor is to get completely away from it. New scenery and new environment will add much to the mental relaxation which the minister needs. Second, if possible, do not spend vacation time visiting relatives. It is good to visit relatives, but what the preacher needs in a vacation is a new and fresh environment which will invigorate his mind and attitude. Third, do not make your vacation time a time of lazy existence and inactivity. Of course, there ought to be some physical rest, but what he needs most of all is mental diversion. There should be no real strenuous activity of any kind,

9 *The Minister As Prophet*, p. 52.
10 DeBlois, A. K., *Some Problems of the Modern Minister*, p. 207.

and yet there should be some light activity of both mind and body which will rehabilitate the minister for a more efficient ministry. Fourth, do not use your vacation time holding revival meetings. Preaching in another field will give some diversion from one's own field of responsibility, but the mental strain of preaching itself is not lessened but intensified. The minister should do little or no preaching at all during his vacation period. The custom of preaching or holding meetings during a vacation is unfair to the minister's own pulpit. It violates the whole idea and purpose of a vacation. A good, wholesome vacation will bring the minister back to his pulpit surcharged with eagerness and life, ready to put himself wholeheartedly into the work of his own field. The practice of mental and physical relaxation in whatever form is no sign of weakness or laziness, but a wise practice for the greatest usefulness of the whole man. No minister can stand the stresses and strains of modern-day ministerial living without some means or method of relaxation. Other things being equal, the minister who eats right, sleeps right, has regular habits of exercise, and knows how to relax his body and mind will have a long and effective ministry.

25 | THE MINISTER AND HIS FAMILY

THE GRAVITY OF THE MINISTER'S FAMILY RESPONSIBILITY

There is no profession in which a man's success is so largely determined by his family as that of the ministry. Unhappy and unwholesome family relationships are always a detriment to any man in any profession, but there are many professions in which a man may be successful in spite of unhappy or disrupted family relationships. This is not true in the ministry. If his family relationships are not happy and in order, his ministry will be doomed. The whole family is most vitally bound up with the minister in the effectiveness of his ministry. It behooves every preacher, therefore, to give extra care and consideration to the family ties. We cannot, and we must not, ignore or minimize the seriousness of the minister's relation to his own family. It is with this in mind that we give some consideration to the minister and his family.

THE MINISTER'S RESPONSIBILITY TO HIS WIFE

In thinking of a man's family we most naturally think first of his wife. There are usually three questions asked by a church seeking a pastor: Can he preach well? Is he a good pastor? How about his wife? This last question always comes out before the inquiry has gone very far. Ministers' wives have done more, humanly speaking, than any other group in developing great preachers. And some few preachers, who might have been great preachers, have been ruined and their usefulness nullified by their wives. The fact that a man has been called of God into the ministry does not guarantee that his matrimonial relationships will be always happy and pleasant. Ministers are just men and they have the same family problems that other men have. If their family relationships are wholesome, it is because they have given much time, effort, and prayer to the realization of that which contributes to matrimonial blessedness and consequently a more effective ministry. In considering the relationship of the minister to his wife there are two angles from which we wish to look at it. The first involves the choice of a wife.

Perhaps most of those who read these lines will be men who have already made the choice of a wife. But there will be some young men, no doubt, who have yet to make this choice. These are the ones about whom we are concerned just now. To the young minister may we offer several down-to-earth words of advice with reference to his choice of a wife. Every Christian young man ought to take these same precautions, and yet, because of the complications and implications involving his whole life and work, the minister must give special attention to these considerations.

First, remember that you are not hunting for a woman to fill a position professionally as a minister's wife. You are hunting for a companion, a life partner. Of course, you will give some consideration to the qualities which are ordinarily desirable for the wife of a minister, but remember that you do not want, nor do you need, "another preacher" for a wife. You want a wife, companion, and home maker first of all. Other things must be secondary.

Second, be sure that she is vitally interested in the work you feel called of God to do. She does not need to be an outstanding public leader, but she does need to have a deep and abiding interest in the thing to which you plan to give your life. Do not presume that she will develop this interest if she does not now have it. Most likely if she is not genuinely interested in your work before she marries you, she will not be after she marries you.

Third, remember that the secret of real love and matrimonial bliss is a common interest. Wherever there is a common interest between two people love will grow and thrive. Be sure that you have many things in common with the girl you expect to marry, that is, from the standpoint of your interests in life.

And fourth, be sure to make your choice of a wife an object of sincere and continuous prayer. There are many other things that might be said about the choice of a wife, but these few suggestions we have made are more or less peculiar to ministers, at least they have an unusual significance for ministers.

It is one thing to make the right choice of a wife, but it is another thing to maintain proper relations with the wife chosen. Successful marriage depends not only upon the right choice of a wife, but also upon the continuation of proper relationships after the choice has been made. Many marriages are failures or partial failures which do not end in divorce courts. It is not enough just to avoid a divorce; we must maintain the very highest possible state of happiness and contentment. And this is more imperious for the minister than for any other man. But how can we maintain this highest state of matrimonial happiness and blessedness? Of course, both parties must co-operate. One party cannot make a success of matrimony by himself. But right now we are thinking more particularly of the preacher in this relationship. He is more often in error in this relationship than is his wife. At least this is true in my case. May we, therefore, call attention to several words of admonition growing out of experience and observation.

First, in the early days of matrimony and ministerial training see that your wife has a chance to grow and develop along with you. If it is at all possible, the wife ought to be given the privilege of going to school with her preacher husband. As a minister's wife she also needs to receive special training and development. If the minister is finished with his school training, he ought to see to it that his wife has the advantage of special courses and conferences which will help her to grow along with him and to have a better understanding of his work. She does not need to know every thing that he knows, but a general understanding of his work will contribute greatly to the success of the marriage and the success of the minister's work.

Second, do not become so involved in your work that you neglect to give the attention that every husband ought to give to his wife. There is the grave danger that the minister will become so engrossed in his work that he will neglect his wife. Not that he will be mean to her or abuse her, but he may simply neglect to give the attention to her that she has a right to as a wife. And this is often more disastrous to marriage security and happiness than bodily cruelty. Ministers' wives are human like other women and they require and expect at least a reasonable amount of love and expressions of love from their husbands. The normal minister's wife finds her major interest in the life and work of her husband. When she receives only a little or no response from that husband in the form of attention and companionship, it will sooner or later result in serious reactions, sometimes in nervous breakdowns. Some might think that a preacher would never be guilty of neglecting his wife, and yet it has been done many times. No genuine preacher would intentionally neglect his wife, and yet it is easy for the minister to become so involved in his work that he will unconsciously neglect his wife. In order to avoid such a temptation every minister ought to set aside at least one evening or half a day a week to spend with his wife in some diversion activity. It will not only help him but will also strengthen and sweeten the matrimonial relationship. This date with his wife should involve some outside activity, nothing connected with the work of the church. It is not enough to ride to the church with his wife for some church meeting. At least once a week he ought to "go out" with his wife. Such practices will satisfy the normal human desire for companionship and love and will add much to the lives of both parties.

Third, do not allow your wife to be burdened down with an overload of church responsibilities. Immediately upon arrival in a new field the sisters will want to pile upon the preacher's wife every kind of responsibility. And if some precaution is not taken she will soon be sagging under the weight of responsibilities which are too much for any human being. It is the minister's responsibility to protect his wife from those who would take undue advantage of her in this way. Of course, the minister's wife, like any other Christian woman, will want to take her share of the responsibility in the work of her church. But just because she is the minister's wife, she is no super-human being capable of carrying loads beyond human strength.

A number of years ago I ran across these "Rules for a Happy Marriage" by Dr. Frank Crane, published in the American Magazine in 1920. They are worthy of serious consideration. "A common sense idea of the sex question; learn how to keep love; love is loyalty; use common sense; maintain your mutual reserves; express your affection; don't express your disapproval; don't regulate; avoid the 'intimate friend'; manage to play together; be equals; have faith; live by yourselves; don't take things too seriously; have an understanding about money matters; and don't both get angry at the same time." There is much wisdom in these rules and the preacher will do well to give some serious thought to their application.

We pause to pay tribute to all the noble-hearted women who have taken their places along side their preacher husbands and have held their hands up. Many of us as preachers would utterly fail if we were called upon to take the places of our wives. Only heaven can reveal the contribution which the unseen and unheralded wife makes to the effective ministry of her preacher husband. James M. Campbell has described her most vividly in these words:

> Ye gods! What wives these parsons have! Many of them make living sacrifices of themselves from day to day, never dreaming that they are doing more than their simple duty. It is pathetic to witness their self-effacement, as they seek to live through their husbands; shielding them from the petty cares of the home, that their minds may be undisturbed in their sacred studies; bravely taking up public duties, when they are already struggling under a load too heavy for their weak shoulders; endeavoring, with diplomatic skill, to conciliate some disaffected sister; and above all, fighting down their own troubles, and trying to charm away, with a sunny face, the demons of despondency and despair, that so often invade

the pastor's sanctum. In that day, when the first shall be last, and the last first, the pastor's wife will have a front seat; and the pastor, himself will have reason to be thankful if he gets within sight of her.[1]

THE MINISTER'S RESPONSIBILITY TO HIS CHILDREN

Let us turn now to another aspect of the minister's relation to his family — that of his relation to his children. If physically possible, every man and wife ought to have children, and the preacher is no exception. Most preachers do have children, and this, in itself, entails a tremendous responsibility which must be shared by both. Preachers' children have been the objects of much discussion. It has been commonly reported that preachers' children are usually bad. This is an erroneous and libelous report. The fact is that according to statistics the average minister's son is above the average. If you will examine a copy of "Who's Who in America," you will find that there are two preachers' children to the children of others in proportion to the number. Many facts could be piled up to disprove the popular but erroneous proverb that the minister's child always turns out bad. The popular acceptance of this erroneous proverb is encouraged by several facts:

First, most people expect more out of preachers' children than they do out of the children of others. An ordinary boy, the son of a minister, would be considered bad by the average person, while an ordinary boy, the son of another, would be considered good. There is absolutely no reason for this distinction and yet it is often made.

Second, when a minister's child goes wrong it is publicized out of all proportion. Thousands of men go wrong and conduct themselves disgracefully and perhaps only a passing comment is made, but when the son of a minister goes wrong it is played up and made a spectacle before all. People talk about it for weeks and months. It is true that a few ministers' children turn out to be failures. We do not deny this and we do not try to deny it. But it should not be surprising when now and then one turns out bad, seeing that they are human beings the same as other children and are subject to the same temptations. Someone has suggested that the reason a minister's child is bad sometimes is that he associates with the deacons' children! And it may be that in some cases the minister himself is so busy trying to help solve the problems of other people's children that he has neglected his own. But all in all the children of ministers have made an enviable record for themselves.

[1] *Clerical Types*, p. 34.

We are not intimating that the children of ministers are so much above other children. Indeed, they are just children and create problems for their parents just as other children do. And we are keenly conscious of the fact that there is room for much improvement in the relationship of the minister and his children. Much of the credit for the training of the minister's children must be given to the mother, but if the children are trained and guided properly the minister also must have a hand in it. In this connection we want to offer a few practical suggestions:

First, do not single out your child as an illustration from the pulpit, especially if he is present in the congregation. Some ministers have made their own children overly self-conscious by repeatedly using them as illustrations in their sermons. Such a practice, we believe, not only embarrasses the child but also leads to complexes of personality which may not be overcome.

Second, always give good sound logical reason for any inhibitions placed upon your children. Do not expect your children to follow rules or commands for which you cannot or do not give sufficient reason. And never try to make your children do a thing or not do a thing simply because their father is a preacher. If it is right, it is right and if it is wrong, it is wrong, whether or not their father is a preacher. The child should not be dogged with an idea that there are certain things which he cannot do just because he is the preacher's child.

Third, take time to have companionship with your children. Many times children suffer from lack of companionship with their father. And it is possible for the minister to become so engrossed in his church work that he will neglect this paternal companionship which every child needs. We agree with Dr. A. K. DeBlois that "the minister who is 'too busy' with parish duties to take time for frequent and affectionate conferences with his children is not worthy to be a father."[2]

Fourth, always keep the promises you make to your children. If promises are constantly made and not kept, children will soon lose confidence in their parents. And when this happens proper child training is impossible. Even in the matter of chastisement, this principle must be followed. The parent who repeatedly threatens his children with whippings which never materialize will soon discover that his program of child training will be impotent if not reactionary. As parents we must be as honest and as dependable in keeping promises made to our children as we are in paying our debts. Perhaps every parent has been guilty of making some promises to his

[2] *Some Problems of the Modern Minister*, p. 223.

children which he has not kept, but frequent repetitions of this can not be allowed without greatly jeopardizing the effectiveness of parental training.

And fifth, as ministers we must use great care and discretion in telling our people how to raise their children. The minister who assumes the know-it-all attitude in preaching on child training will not only embarrass his own family but will also hinder the effectiveness of his own ministry. The author is not trying to leave any such impression in this discussion. As I stand in the face of my responsibility as a father I am conscious of failures I have already made and look with great anxiety into the future with the realization of my limitation of wisdom in the art of child training.

Whatever the policy or plan no minister can maintain happy and effective family relationships without giving time and thought. And no minister can do well in his work who does not maintain these happy relationships. It behooves us, therefore, as ministers to make a place in our program for the necessary time and effort to build the kind of a home which will be an asset to us and a blessing to all.

26 | THE MINISTER AND HIS OWN CHARACTER

THE RELATION OF CHARACTER TO PROFESSION

It is possible for a minister to become so absorbed in his profession that he will neglect the qualities of personal life and character which make it possible for him to have a successful profession. A minister's personal life and professional duty are inseparably bound together. In this chapter we are not thinking of the professional side of the minister's life at all, and yet we are conscious of the fact that the proper cultivation of personality traits and character will have as much to do with his ministerial success as anything else. If the minister is to succeed he must throw his whole self into his work, but this "self" must be of the right caliber if it is to contribute to that success. Dr. Jowett appropriately points out that "we may become mere guide-posts when we were intended to be guides. We may indicate the way, and yet not be found in it. We may be professors but not be pilgrims."[1] And in his lectures to Yale students Dr. R. F. Horton has reminded us that "the preacher's sermons are but fragments of himself."[2] Let us, therefore, give our attention in this closing chapter to the qualities of personal life which ought to be discovered and cultivated in the life of every minister.

THE STANDARD FOR MINISTERIAL CHARACTER

In speaking of personality and character traits we realize that the same traits of character and personality ought to be found in the life of every Christian. There are not two standards for personal and moral conduct as some people seem to think — one for the minister and one for other Christians. In fact, there is only one standard of personal conduct for all men whether Christian layman, non-Christian, or preacher. This standard is the standard which God has revealed in His Word. From the standpoint of his personal relationship with the Lord no more is expected of the preacher than is expected of any other Christian. God expects the best of all of us. Therefore, in God's eyes, what is right for the layman to do is also right for the

[1] *The Preacher: His Life and Work,* p. 45.
[2] *Verbum Dei,* p. 87.

minister to do, and what is wrong for the minister is also wrong for the layman.

While all of this is true, society itself expects a little more out of the preacher and because of this it is imperative for the sake of his usefulness that his personal life and character be above par. His success, therefore, as a minister will depend largely upon a super-excellence of his moral and personal character. He must give unusual attention to his own personal life and soul. He must balance his personality before he can become truly effective as a minister. But what are the ingredients of a balanced ministerial personality? Many items might be included, but as we ponder all of our experiences and observations in ministerial living we are impressed with the necessity of the nine qualities of moral character and personality which every minister ought to inculcate into every fiber of his whole being.

OUTSTANDING QUALITIES OF A BALANCED MINISTERIAL CHARACTER

First, there is the idea of moral purity. The minister's personal moral character must be above reproach. It may seem unnecessary to remind the minister that his moral standards ought to be high, and yet some ministerial careers have been stopped short of their possibilities because of loose moral living on the part of the minister. God expects all men to be good morally, and yet how vital it is that the minister's moral life be kept on the very highest plane for the sake of his influence upon society! The tendency toward looseness and liberalism in moral conduct among ministers is becoming more and more alarming. If the ministry is to make its proper contribution to the life of the world, it must be made up of men who breathe the wholesome atmosphere of a pure life, free from the little worldly habits and customs which so often decrease the stamina of moral character. We are not saying that the preacher should hold himself aloof from others in society. This would be as harmful as the other. But a minister can have associations with society without surrendering any moral integrity.

Another ingredient of a balanced ministerial character is fidelity, the quality of doing one's very best in whatever responsibility may be assigned to him. We are not held responsible for accomplishing certain definite things, but we will be held responsible for being faithful and diligent in the task to which we have been called. The Apostle Paul reminds us that in our stewardship as ministers of God "it is required in stewards that a man be found faithful" (I Corinthians 4:1). It is easy for a minister to drift into lethargy and indolence since he has no time clock to punch. But the lazy and unfaithful minister will soon fall from the ranks and drift into uselessness.

Happy is the minister who takes his work seriously and goes at it with the zest and fervor of a bee. Fidelity and dependability are requisite to success in any realm, but how much more so with the minister!

Honesty and truthfulness are also vital elements of a balanced ministerial personality. Some might suppose that ministers are always honest and truthful, but this is not always true. Most ministers are honest and truthful in paying debts from a monetary standpoint, but there is a strong tendency among ministers toward ministerial and moral dishonesty and untruthfulness. The popular use of the term, "ministerially speaking," is a reproach upon ministerial honesty and truthfulness. In their desire to either magnify the work or exalt themselves, ministers have become guilty many times of "stretching the facts." Some may look upon it as an innocent exaggeration of facts growing out of the excitement of enthusiasm. But it is nothing short of lying. And the continuation of such practices will only add to the reproach and disgrace. There is some ground for the statement of Dr. W. J. Tucker that "the two besetting sins of the ministry are laziness and lying."[3] Plagiarism is nothing short of lying. When we take another man's idea in total and imply to our people that this idea is of our own concoction we are lying. Sometimes preachers are even guilty of using illustrations of experiences which never really happened. No matter how apt the illustration, if the minister is honest and truthful, he will not use it as if it actually happened when he knows that it did not. Neither will he "doctor up" the experience so that it becomes something entirely different from the original experience. A little boy once asked his minister father this question: "Daddy, was that story you told in the pulpit this morning really true, or were you just preaching?" So common has been the practice of ministerial lying in these things that many people wonder about the truthfulness of all stories told by ministers. And this is tragic. God deliver us from lying preachers! Some preachers might be prone to excuse such practice on the grounds that the deliberate purpose is not that of deception but in order to make a deeper impression upon the people with the message. But nothing really justifies a misrepresentation of facts, whatever the motive, and in the end such practices will do more harm than good. It is just a matter of applying the principles of honesty and truthfulness in every realm of life.

There is no more important quality of character for the minister than that of humility, and none more difficult to attain. Phillips

[3] *The Making and Unmaking of the Preacher*, p. 70.

Brooks correctly lists "self-conceit" as the first danger of the minister.[4] A spirit of pride has ruined more preachers and dwarfed more preachers than any other one thing. The honor of his calling and his place of leadership before people make him vulnerable to the darts of pride and self-elevation. These are the very things which ought to humble him, and yet so often they have the opposite reaction.

> The temptation of the minister is to play the role of the "star." He is the pitcher on the team, the player who carries the ball, the flying "ace," the general who plans the strategy and gives the commands. Before he realizes it, the minister is liable to violate Paul's injunction "not to think of himself more highly than he ought to think; but so to think as to think soberly, according as God hath dealt to each man a measure of faith" (Romans 12:3). It would not be difficult to call to mind ministers who have more or less deliberately put themselves in the spotlight, forgetting that they are members of a team and that while spectacular plays may be made by "stars," the season's victories and the campaign's final triumph depend upon the team.[5]

A self-conceited man is disgusting in any realm, but a self-conceited preacher is an abomination standing where it ought not. He is like the little steamer on the Mississippi which blew its own whistle so long and so loud that it had no more steam with which to run the machinery. Great preachers are made out of humble men. When we lift up ourselves we hide our Lord. Some preachers blow their own trumpets so loudly that they cannot hear "the still small voice of God." The daily prayer of every preacher's heart ought to be: "Oh Lord, deliver me from selfishness and pride!" And if we are humble, we do not need to remind people that we are humble or to put on appearances which are intended to impress people with our humility. The ugliest form of pride is expressed in that man who seems to be proud of his humility. In the words of James M. Campbell, "There is no form of pride so subtle as the pride of being humble. To see ourselves as others see us would bring some startling revelations."[6] The kingdom of Christ is built upon humility. Christ "humbled himself" and taught His disciples to be humble. Of all men, His ministers ought to be living expressions of His humble spirit if they are to serve Him effectively.

Another character trait which every minister ought to cultivate is a sense of humor. Of course, he ought to take his responsibility as a minister seriously, but at the same time he can and should cul-

---

[4] *Lectures on Preaching*, pp. 64-69.
[5] Dobbins, G. S., *Building Better Churches*, p. 147.
[6] *Clerical Types*, p. 85.

tivate and use a sense of humor to great advantage. There is nothing incongruous between a keen feeling of responsibility and a good sense of humor. Many nervous tensions can be released by a good sense of humor. Usually a preacher with a good sense of humor will get along well with his people. It often breaks down social barriers which arise between preacher and people. This does not mean that he must have a whole series of stereotyped jokes to tell before each sermon. In fact, I have never thought that the pulpit was the proper place for any preacher to unload a lot of jokes which he has heard or read. If there is something humorous which is relevant to the situation and the hour and it comes naturally, then the preacher may use it with profit. But there is a vast difference between the ability to relate a joke and a genuine sense of humor. Some preachers who never run out of stereotyped jokes have a very poor sense of humor. Some preachers enjoy a joke involving someone else as the "goat," but the preacher with a good sense of humor will also enjoy a joke in which he is the "goat." In fact the preacher who is willing to be made the "goat" without resentment is manifesting a token of humility which will find a ready response in the hearts of his people. One of the best ways for a preacher to win the affections of his people is to tell embarrassing experiences involving himself and let the people laugh with him about them. They will sense a spirit of humility in it and will love him the more for it. The following comment from the pen of Dr. A. K. DeBlois is appropriate at this point:

> Humor is hardly less valuable than common sense. The two usually go hand in hand. The distinction has often been drawn between wit and humor, and it is clearly understood by most people. Wit is a native endowment, a golden gift. It is a keen and lively play of fancy, a glancing ray of sunshine. It cannot be cultivated. Humor is less brilliant, quieter and more human, and it can be wooed and won by patient endeavor. It may be coaxed, as a shy bird, and held in the hand and hidden in the bosom. It is a precious benediction to the hard-ridden minister. It carries him over many a rough experience. It may become a habit of the soul.[7]

A kindred quality of character is optimism and every minister must have it if he is to succeed. There is no place in the ranks for a pessimistic and whimpering preacher. In spite of difficulties and trials he must always keep his spirit high. Nor does he have to close his eyes to reality to do this. We do not need the "whistling in the dark" kind of optimism. We need an optimism which is based upon the reality of a living triumphant Christ. The trials and problems

[7] *Some Problems of the Modern Minister*, p. 237.

of life are real and often distressing, and yet for the true minister of God the promises and assurances of God are more real. Because of these we have a right to be optimistic. "A preacher with a whine in his soul is a preacher whose usefulness is gone. Men who are ever-lastingly whimpering because of their misfortunes and trials can never lift men into the joy of the Gospel; for, if one is to keep his people on the sunny side of the street, he must walk on the sunny side of the street himself."[8]

Along with optimism comes patience. Of this the preacher needs a double dose. The minister cannot lose head nor heart. Patience is the art of knowing how to wait graciously. There will be many times when the minister will be tempted to "blow his top," but happy is the minister who has learned how to keep the lid on. Some men are born with a more patient disposition than others, but all men can, if they will, cultivate a spirit of patience and longsuffering without which no minister's life can be successful. This spirit of patience will grow with experience. The Apostle Paul was right in saying that "tribulation worketh patience," and the genuine preacher will have ample opportunity to learn the art of patience.

Few things will inspire patience like a sympathetic attitude to-ward people. Sympathy breeds patience. The minister who does not love people and have a sympathetic attitude toward people might as well give up the ministry today. His life will be a miserable failure. Sympathy puts meaning and soul into the ministry. It keeps the minister from becoming cold, formal, and lifeless. It gives breath and feeling to what might otherwise be drab duty. The genuine minister is one who feels the heart beat of his people, whose ear is never deaf to their cries. The spirit of sympathetic understanding must saturate and permeate his whole life.

And, last but not least, in a well-balanced ministerial person-ality there must be genuine consecration to God. It is possible for a man to answer the call to ministerial service without being wholly submissive to the will of God and fully dedicated to God. The minister cannot lift his people any closer to God than he is himself. God pity the people who do not find their best example of conse-crated, spirit-filled living in the life of their pastor. He cannot lift his people toward God by his preaching if he does not inspire them toward God by his living. Every minister ought to feel and express what Paul, the prince of preachers, felt and expressed to the Ga-latians: "I am crucified with Christ, nevertheless, I live, yet not I, but Christ liveth in me; and the life that I now live in the flesh I

[8] Jefferson, C. E., *The Minster As Prophet,* p. 67.

live by the faith of the son of God, who loved me, and gave himself for me." (Galatians 2:20).

We realize that no minister can attain the full measure of all of these qualities of personality, but these are ideals toward which every minister should constantly strive. And in every genuine minister these qualities will be found with varying degrees of fullness. The ideal ministerial personality is aptly described by the great teacher of preachers, Dr. Jeff D. Ray, in these words:

> An unselfish, sacrificial spirit-filled ministry; not a self-seeking, ease-loving, worldly-minded ministry; a pure, holy, spiritual ministry; not a gross, carnal, sensual ministry; a liberal, broad, bountiful ministry; not a niggardly, parsimonious, sordid ministry; a vigorous, forceful, efficient ministry; not a flabby, feeble, flat-minded ministry; a strong, valiant, sturdy ministry; not a weak, flaccid, limp ministry; a firm, dignified, stalwart ministry; not a stale, languid, insipid ministry; a fertile, fruitful, prolific ministry; not a lean, barren, sterile ministry; a keen, effective, diversified ministry; not a spiritless, pointless, monotonous ministry; a resilient, buoyant, fervent ministry; not a heavy, prosy, frigid ministry.[9]

THE CHALLENGE AND CHARM OF MINISTERIAL LIFE

As we glance back over this study we are impressed with the vast scope of the minister's life and work and with the tremendous challenge which is his. Ministerial life at its best is no child's play. It demands every quality of real manhood. It involves hardship, heartache, energy, sweat, anxiety, thought, tribulation, and persecution. But in and through all of these things we see the blessedness of a life of service and devotion the fruit of which only eternity can tell. The trials are many, but the compensations are more. The thrill of having some little part in pointing the way to eternal life for some wayward and hopeless soul and the thrill of helping new-born souls grow in the graces of Christ — these thrills far outweigh any trials we encounter along the way. And then the joy of that "well done" at the end of the way will transform all trials into beautiful rainbows of blessed memory. May we, therefore, as ministers of God give ourselves with renewed fervor and devotion to the task which is ours to the end that God's name may be glorified and His Kingdom come on earth as it is in heaven. Amen.

[9] *The Highest Office,* p. 237.

BIBLIOGRAPHY

This is not intended as an exhaustive bibliography in the field of ministerial ethics. It is simply a list of a few of the outstanding works in this field, both old and new, which will prove helpful in further study on this subject. Some excellent works have come from the press recently. We have included some of these.

Abbott, Lyman, *The Christian Ministry*, Boston: Houghton Mifflin Co., 1905.
Anderson, William K. (ed.), *Pastor and Church*, New York: Geo. H. Doran, 1920.
Barrett, Robert N., *Ethics of the Ministry*, Cleona, Pa.: G. Holzapfel, 1901.
Beecher, Henry Ward, *Yale Lectures on Preaching*, Boston: Pilgrim Press, 1902.
Blackwood, Andrew Watterson, *Pastoral Leadership*, New York: Abingdon-Cokesbury, 1949.
Bonnell, J. S., *No Escape from Life*, New York: Harper and Bros., 1958.
Broadus, John A., *On the Preparation and Delivery of Sermons*, New York: Harper and Bros., 1944.
Brooks, Phillips, *Lectures on Preaching*, London: H. R. Allenson, 1877.
Brown, Charles R., *The Making of a Minister*, New York: The Century Co. 1927.
Brown, W. A., *The Minister*, Nashville: Cokesbury Press, 1937.
Calkins, Raymond, *The Romance of the Ministry*, Boston: Pilgrim Press, 1944.
Campbell, James M., *Clerical Types*, New York: Funk and Wagnalls Co., 1902.
Clark, W. C., *The Minister Looks at Himself*, Philadelphia: Judson Press, 1957.
DeBlois, Austin K., *Some Problems of the Modern Minister*, Nashville, Tenn.: Sunday School Board of the Southern Baptist Convention, 1928.
Dobbins, Gaines S., *Building Better Churches*, Nashville, Tenn., Broadman Press, 1948.
Fairbairn, Patrick, *Pastoral Theology*.
Forsyth, N. F., *The Minister and Christian Nurture*, New York: Abingdon Press, 1957.
Garvie, A. E., *The Christian Preacher*, New York: Hodder and Stoughton, 1921.
Garvie, A. E., *A Guide to Preachers*, New York: Hodder and Stoughton, 1906.
Gladden, Washington, *The Christian Pastor and the Working Church*, New York: Charles Scribners, 1903.
Gladden, Washington, *Tools and the Man*, Boston: Houghton Mifflin Co., 1893.

Harmon, Nolan B., *Ministerial Ethics and Etiquette*, Nashville, Tenn.: The Abingdon-Cokesbury Press, 1950.

Hiltner, Seward, *The Christian Shepherd*, New York: Abingdon Press, 1959.

Hiltner, Seward, *Preface to Pastoral Theology*, New York: Abingdon Press, 1958.

Hiltner, Seward, *Pastoral Counseling*, New York: Abingdon Press, 1949.

Horton, Robert Foreman, *Verbum Dei*, New York: Macmillan Co., 1893.

Hutton, John A., *That the Ministry Be Not Blamed*, New York: Geo. H. Doran, 1921.

Jefferson, Charles E., *Quiet Hints to Growing Preachers*, New York: Thomas Y. Crowell, 1908.

Jefferson, Charles E., *The Minister as Prophet*, New York: Thomas Y. Crowell, 1905.

Jefferson, Charles E., *The Minister as Shepherd*, New York: Thomas Y. Crowell, 1912.

Jowett, J. H., *The Preacher: His Life and Work*, New York: Harper and Bros., 1912.

Lee, Mark W., *The Minister and His Ministry*, Grand Rapids: Zondervan Publishing House, 1960.

Lewis, Thomas H., *The Minister and His Own Soul*, New York: Geo. H. Doran, 1926.

McAfee, Cleland B., *Ministerial Practices*, New York: Harper and Bros., 1929.

MacClaren, Ian, *The Cure of Souls*, New York: Dodd and Mead, 1896.

Moyer, E. S., *The Pastor and His Library*, Chicago: Moody Press, 1953.

Nanney, T. Grady, *Dear Gene*, Shawnee, Okla.: Oklahoma Baptist University, 1950.

Narramore, Clyde M., *The Psychology of Counseling*, Grand Rapids: Zondervan Publishing House, 1960.

Newton, Joseph Fort, *Some Living Masters of the Pulpit*, New York: Geo. H. Doran, 1923.

Niebuhr, H. R., *The Ministry in Historical Perspectives*, New York: Harper's, 1956.

Oates, Wayne E., *Premarital Pastoral Care and Counselling*, Nashville: Broadman Press, 1958.

Oates, W. E., *An Introduction to Pastoral Counselling*, Nashville: Broadman Press, 1959.

Palmer, Albert W., *The Minister's Job*, New York: Harper and Bros., 1949.

Prater, Arnold, *Seven Keys to a More Fruitful Ministry*, Grand Rapids: Zondervan Publishing House, 1960.

Prichard, H. A., *The Minister, the Method, and the Message*, New York: Charles Scribners' Sons, 1932.

Ray, Jeff D., *The Highest Office*, New York: Fleming H. Revell, 1923.

Riley, W. B., *The Preacher and His Preaching*, Wheaton, Ill.: Sword of the Lord Publishers, 1948.

Riley, W. B., *Pastoral Problems*, New York: Fleming H. Revell Co., 1936.

Robertson, Archibald T., *The Glory of the Ministry*, New York: Fleming H. Revell, 1911.

Schuette, W. E., *The Minister's Personal Guide,* New York: Harper and Bros., 1953.

Shedd, W. G. T., *Homiletics and Pastoral Theology,* New York: Chas. Scribner, 1867.

Shoemaker, Samuel, *How You Can Help Others,* New York: E. P. Dutton and Co., 1946.

Sockman, Ralph W., *The Highway of God,* New York: The Macmillan Co., 1942.

Spann, J. Richard, *The Ministry,* New York: Abingdon-Cokesbury Press, 1949.

Spann, J. R., *Pastoral Care,* New York: Abingdon-Cokesbury Press, 1951.

Stewart, James S., *Heralds of God,* New York: Charles Scribner's Sons, 1946.

Tidwell, J. B., *Concerning Preachers,* New York: Fleming H. Revell Co., 1937.

Tucker, William Jewett, *The Making and the Unmaking of the Preacher,* Boston: Houghton Mifflin and Co., 1898.

Wallace, O. C. S., *Pastor and People,* Nashville: Broadman Press, 1936.

Westberg, Granger, *Premarital Counselling,* National Council of the Churches of Christ in U. S. A., 1958.

Wood, L. F., *Pastoral Counseling in Family Relationships,* New York: Federal Council of Churches, 1948.

Wynn, J. C., *Pastoral Ministry to Families,* Philadelphia: Westminster Press, 1957.